Once Known: A History of Slavery in Westford, Massachusetts

Leslie Gwen Howard

Published by Forge Pond Publishing
Westford, MA

Cover Design by Elani Coetzer
Author Photograph by Farmhouse Photography

First published 2024

Printed in the United States of America

ISBN 979-8-218-84801-9

CONTENTS

Part I: General History of Slavery in Massachusetts 1
The Slave Census 4
Religion and Slavery 7
Prominence in Town 11
Probate Records 11
Tax Records 12
Life of the Enslaved in Town 15
The Revolution 18
Emancipation 19
Life After Enslavement 20
The 1790 Federal Census 21
The Map 24

Part II: The Enslaved of Westford 26

Conclusion 93

Appendix A:
Taxation of Slave Owners in Colonial Westford 95
Appendix B:
Westford's Early Tax Records 125
Appendix C:
Westford's 1790 Census 144
Bibliography 147

Foreword and Acknowledgements

A journey of a thousand miles begins with a single step. When I first stepped into the Westford Museum in about 2013, I saw the Westford Women Doll Collection and was startled to see one dressed in colonial clothing with dark fabric for skin. I knew there had been enslaved people on the Royall Estate in Medford, so why was it so hard for me to believe that there were enslaved people in Westford? I learned this doll represented Peggy, an enslaved woman in the Joseph Hildreth, Jr. household. Throughout my time learning about Westford's history, I heard there were others enslaved in town and some free men and women after the Revolution.

The lack of information on Peggy bothered me. There were so many questions and the answers had to be there somewhere. Information like birth names, birthdates, birth location, parents, country of origin, their journey, their struggles, and their joys unknown to us now was all *once known*. Their stories are lost to us except for bits and pieces in the historical record. I hope to honor their lives by bringing together what information I could find and including images of the historical records that bear their names, even if they are not the birth names. The difficulty lies in telling their story through the story of the enslaver.

Thank you to Freedom's Way Partnership Grant Program for funding the original research as part of their Inclusive Storytelling program. Thank you to all of the other historians and archivists I've emailed and called seeking information. Thank you to Ginny Moore and the JV Fletcher Library for access to their materials, the Lawrence Library in Pepperell, Jean Downey, Judy Cataldo, Dan Lacroix, William "Bill" Prescott, Marilyn Day, Ellen Harde, Bob Oliphant, Massachusetts Historical Society, Massachusetts State Archives, American Antiquarian Society, Harvard University, National Archives online and in Waltham, Erika Slocumb and the New

England Museum Association's Community of Practice. Thank you to Stacey Fraser for reading a copy and whose comments were invaluable. At the First Parish Church United in Westford Lanea Tripp, Reverend Rebecca Lockwood, and June Kennedy for access to their archives, the Westford Town Clerk's office for access to early town records, and to Linda Greene, Director of the Westford Museum, and the Westford Historical Society Board for their support of this project.

An incredible thank you to Elani Coetzer for her design, vision, and especially, encouragement.

Most of all, thank you to my husband, family, and friends for their support and encouragement during this journey. I could not have done it without them.

This book is dedicated to the woman we know as Peggy, my constant inspiration to dig deeper. Your story deserves to be told. I am not done.

Part I
General History of Slavery in Massachusetts

In the earliest days of the Massachusetts Bay Colony, there was no difference between slavery and indentured servitude. It was a custom and legally ambiguous, neither legal nor illegal.[1] While there were enslaved people in the Colony, slavery became *legal* in the colony in 1641 with the passage of the Massachusetts Body of Liberties. The clause reads: "There shall never be any bond slaverie, villinage or Captivitie amongst us unles it be lawfull Captives taken in just warres, and such strangers as willingly selle themselves or are sold to us. And these shall have all the liberties and Christian usages which the law of god established in Israell concerning such persons doeth morally require. This exempts none from servitude who shall be Judged thereto by Authoritie."[2] Massachusetts was the first colony to do this.

Also from the earliest days, men from Massachusetts were involved in the slave trade. From 1725-1729, The *Boston Gazette,* the leading newspaper at the time, announced thirty-two parcels for sale. A "parcel" was the name given to a group of captives brought to the new land on a merchant ship for enslavement. From 1730-1734, there were twenty-seven parcels and from 1735-1739 there were ten, a marked decrease. After 1739, there were only twelve parcels marketed in the Gazette.[3] After 1739, the majority of enslaved individuals within the Commonwealth were likely being resold.

The African trade from Newport and Boston was conducted in sloops, brigantines, and schooners generally carrying forty or fifty tons. One brigantine was described as,

---

[1] Lorenzo Johnston Greene, *The Negro in Colonial New England,* Atheneum: New York, 1969, 125

[2] "Massachusetts Bodies of Liberty (1641)," accessed August 1, 2023, https://history.hanover.edu/texts/masslib.html

[3] Desrochers, Robert E. "Slave-for-Sale Advertisements and Slavery in Massachusetts, 1704-1781." *The William and Mary Quarterly* 59, no. 3 (2002): 623–64. https://doi.org/10.2307/3491467

"sixty feet length by the keel, straight rabbet, and length of the rake forward to be fourteen feet, three foot and one half of which to be put into the keel, so that she will then be sixty-three feet keel and eleven feet rake forward. Twenty-three feet by the beam, ten feet in the hold, and three feet ten inches between decks and twenty inches waste." The three feet ten inches between the decks was the space allotted to the captives.[4] That is hardly high enough for a small child to stand up.

According to "The Early African Slave Trade in New England" many of the ships from New England made voyages to Guinea.[5] The Guinea voyagers were known as "rum-vessels." There was no article of merchandise comparable to rum on the African coast. Historian William B. Weeden, author of "The Early African Slave Trade in New England," argues that the traders' intent was not immoral, but economic, in that they had tried to trade other dry goods and those were all rejected in Africa, except for the rum.[6]

Boston Merchant Peter Faneuil owned the ship *The Jolly Bachelor* which made an ill-fated voyage to Sierra Leone in 1742. When the *Jolly Bachelor*'s accounts were balanced on June 14, 1743, it revealed that a pound sterling was equal to twelve bars of iron in Sierra Leone. A captive was worth sixty bars, or £5. In other places at about the same time, a captive was worth £12 in "goods," or, rum. Weeden wrote, "We see the frightful scale by which merchandise ascends through rate after rate—paper priced rum, coast valued iron [and] sterling gold—while human flesh, sense, mind and spirit goes down in corresponding degradation."[7] About 1718, some would pay £30-50--up to £80--for a captive to enslave.[8]

---

4 Weeden, "The Early African Slave Trade in New England," American Antiquarian Society, 1887, issue 5, 115.

5 Weeden, 111.

6 Weeden, 117

7 Weeden, 128

8 Weeden, 113-114

Many ships arriving in New England had first stopped in the West Indies to either trade there or "season" the captives for future enslavement. This meant acclimating the captives to the new environment and helping them gain some immunity to new diseases. This seasoning process often included "achieving some fluency" in English.[9]

Given connections between Boston merchants like Hugh Hall and David Jeffries with Barbados, New Englanders also enslaved natives of that island. Robert E. Desrochers, in his study of Slave for Sale advertisements, suggests that, "Slaves of Barbadian provenance may have constituted a third or more of Massachusetts imports in the 1720s and 1730s."[10] In Westford, it is likely then, that the enslaved people came from Guinea and Barbados.

When the captives came to Boston, they were typically sold on Long Wharf and the King Street/Dock Square area, though evidence can be found for sales happening all over the city, including private sales in the enslavers' homes.[11]

Enslaved people had an interesting legal status. They were considered *property* of another person, but they also had certain legal rights as a *person*. Sometimes slaves were treated as persons. In New England, enslaved people had a right to life. It was a capital crime if an enslaver killed his enslaved, whereas in the South, death was considered punishment for the enslaved.[12] For a time, the enslaved were also taxed as polls and *not* personal property. Lorenzo Johnston Greene wrote, "It was as personal property that Negros were bought and sold, and transferred informal bills of sale were generally executed to affect transfer of title to the slave."[13] The record conflicts on this because Greene found that, in Massachusetts, that no bill of sale was needed to acquire a slave, but records show that bills of sale

---

[9] Desrochers, 645.

[10] Desrochers, 645.

[11] Desrochers, 623–64.

[12] Greene, 177.

[13] Greene, 172.

were produced and accepted.[14] In Massachusetts, a 1703 law required enslavers to post a bond of no less than £50 when manumitting an enslaved person.[15] The law states, "That no molatto or negro slave shall hereafter be manumitted, discharged or set free, until sufficient security be given to the treasurer of the town or place where such person dwells, not less than fifty pounds, to secure and indemnify the town or place from all charge for or about such molato [sic] or negro…in case he or she by sickness, lameness, or otherwise, be rendred [sic] uncapable [sic] to support him- or herself." If this security was not given, then the person was still considered enslaved.[16] So far, no bills of sale or bonds have been located for the people enslaved in Westford. *See the section on Tax Records and Appendix A for more on taxes.*

The Slave Census

Prior to the Federal Censuses starting in 1790, there were few censuses in colonial Massachusetts, and it is questionable if the information is reliable. In 1754, Massachusetts Bay Governor William Shirley ordered that an enumeration of all enslaved people, both male and female, over the age of sixteen

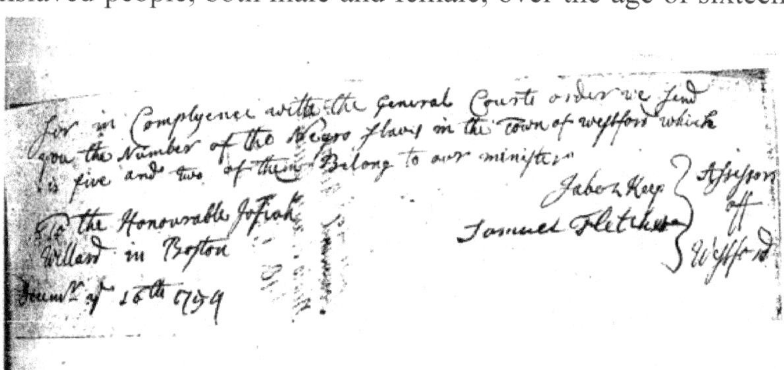
for in Complyence with the General Courts order we send you the Number of the Negro slaves in the town of westford which is five and two of them Belong to our minister

Jabez Keep
Samuel Fletcher
Assessors of Westford

To the Honourable Josiah Willard in Boston

Decemr ye 16th 1754

primaryresearch.org/1754slavecensus/64.jpg

[14] Greene, 172.

[15] *Acts and Resolves of the Province of Massachusetts Bay: Volume 1 1692-1714*, Wright and Potter: Boston, 1869, 519.

[16] *Acts and Resolves*, 519.

be completed by each town. According to this 1754 census, Westford reported that there were 5 enslaved people over the age of 16. Westford's Reverend Willard Hall is mentioned as enslaving two of them.[17]

There are ten potential enslaved people who could have been included as the five in the 1754 census. These are Jack, Peggy, Dinah, Jenny, Prince, George, Ishmael, Prince, Dinah, and Caesar. Ishmael and one of the Dinahs were enslaved by Reverend Willard Hall. The census results were not always reliable as people sometimes were not truthful about enslaved individuals. In an attempt to determine who was included in the census, this author created a spreadsheet. With certain data from taxes and other sources, the information could be discerned to a moderate degree of confidence. One bit of information is that Nathaniel Boynton had removed to Pepperell in 1754 and so Moses Sawyer is not included as a potential candidate for the census. The enslaved included in the census were probably: Peggy Hildreth, Ishmael, Dinah Hall, George, and Caesar. Prince Read was a child in 1754. Reflecting typically inaccurate results, data shows a likely miscount as Jenny Prescott and Prince Pollard were also likely in town and would have been included.[18] The data makes sense if it was actually five enslaved PLUS the two enslaved by Reverend Hall.

There was another colony wide census in 1764.[19] It was not a "slave census," but a general census. The *Boston Evening Gazette* posted a notice for a 1764 census of residents or else pay a fine. The census wanted to enumerate white males and females

---

17 PrimarySource.org, "1754 Slave Census," Accessed 24 April 2023, https://primaryresearch.org/1754slavecensus/64.jpg.

18 Leslie Howard, "Enslaved Persons in Westford," Excel Spreadsheet, Author files.

19 For more information on this census, see Samuel A. Green, "The First Census of Massachusetts," *Publications of the American Statistical Association*, Vol. 2, No. 13 (Mar., 1891), pp. 182-185 https://www.jstor.org/stable/2276526.

above 16, under 16, "negroes," "mulattoes," and "Indians."[20] Looking at the year 1764, one can assume that King George III wanted a better sense of his colonies and how to assess taxes after the end of the French and Indian War. It took a long time for results to be sent in, so the 1764 census was compiled in 1765. The census record was difficult to track down, but it identifies 5 Negro males and 7 Negro females living in Westford.

Again, to a moderate degree of confidence, it can be determined who was included in this Census: Jenny Prescott, Prince (Pollard), George (Chandler), Ishmael, Dinah Hall, Caesar, Dinah (Parker), Jethro Wilkens, Caesar Bason, once known woman enslaved by Samuel Fitch, Noble Comings, once known woman enslaved by Moses Burge, once known woman enslaved by Jonathan Keyes, and once known woman enslaved by John Robins. This count is 7 females and 7 males.[21] Again, there were likely inaccuracies in their count.

Westford's Results of the 1764 Census								
Houses	Families	White Males under 16	White Males over 16	White Females over 16	Whites Males under 16	Negro Males	Negro Females	Indians and French Nationals
143	169	231	233	217	269	5	7	0

The modern age of adulthood is eighteen, but these census records use sixteen. There are a few reasons for this. One reason is that sixteen was the age that the Puritans used as the *minimum* age for making a rational decision to enter into the church's covenant. Another reason is that at sixteen, white men had militia duties. Therefore, it was important information to know

[20] The Annotated Newspapers of Harbottle Dorr: The Boston Evening-Post, 6 May 1765. Massachusetts Historical Society Collection. https://www.masshist.org/dorr/volume/1/sequence/83

[21] Howard, "Enslaved Persons in Westford."

how many men were of this age and inform the government how many potential soldiers the government would have.[22]

Religion and Slavery

Slavery is mentioned in the Bible and some, like Boston's Reverend Cotton Mather, have used these mentions as justification. Mather wrote, "It is allowed in the Sciptures, to the Gentiles, that they may keep Slaves."[23] However, Judge Samuel Sewall (1652-1730), argued against it, calling it the most atrocious of crimes. He famously wrote, "And seeing GOD hath said, *He that Stealeth a Man and Selleth him, or if he be found in his hand, he shall surely be put to Death.* Exod. 12.16. This Law being of E-verlasting [sic] Equity, wherein Man Stealing is ranked amongst the most atrocious of Capital Crimes."[24] This 1700 commentary criticized Sewall's contemporaries for enslaving individuals and Sewall did not withhold his true feelings on the subject. He further wrote, "It is likewise most lamentable to think, how in taking Negros out of *Africa*, and Selling of them here, That which GOD ha's [sic] joyned [sic] together men do boldly rend asunder; Men from their Country, Husbands from their Wives, Parents from their Children."[25] He argued that the merchants were ripping families apart and tried to appeal to their faith to change their deeds. His arguments fell on deaf ears.

It's always a little jarring to learn that Ministers were also enslavers, as if they should be held to a higher moral standard. In fact, many ministers were also enslavers; like

---

[22] J.L. Bell, "Boston's Population in 1765," Accessed 24 April 2023, https://boston1775.blogspot.com/2006/05/bostons-population-in-1765.html

[23] National Humanities Center Toolbox, "What About Slavery is Unchristian?," Accessed 9 February 2025, https://nationalhumanitiescenter.org/pds/becomingamer/ideas/text3/slaveryunchristian.pdf

[24] Samuel Sewall, "The Selling of Joseph" https://www.masshist.org/database/53?mode=transcript

[25] Sewall, "The Selling of Joseph."

Reverend William Emerson in nearby Concord, Reverend John Hancock in Lexington, and Westford's Reverend Willard Hall.

How did Reverend Hall feel about enslaving individuals? We are not sure. Reverend Hall *was* an enslaver and performed nineteen documented baptisms on enslaved people and admitted one "to the table." One can then assume he was comfortable having them as Church members and probably preached in a similar manner as Cotton Mather. The Reverend Cotton Mather, the Boston theologian, clergyman, and enslaver, wrote in his diary, "I would always remember, that my servants are in some sence [sic] my children… I would make them as my children; and so far as the methods of instituting piety in the mind which I used with my children may be properly imprudently used with my servants they shall be partakers in them – nor will I leave them ignorant of anything wearing. I may instruct them to be useful to their generation."[26]

The Reverend Mather encouraged baptism of enslaved people on the grounds that enslavers were "the Elect of God," who must thus treat their enslaved people as "rational creatures whom God has made your servants." But the Reverend Mather had also thought that teaching the enslaved about Christianity was an avenue to elicit compliance by reminding them that their enslavement and commitment to Christianity would bring them spiritual rewards like "a mansion in Heaven" and "rest from their labors."[27]

We often see enslaved individuals referred to as servants, specifically in Reverend Hall's Church book. This stems from the Hebraic tradition and the status of a New England enslaved person being in the gray area between a plantation slave and an indentured servant. They were considered property, but also likely slept under the same roof and ate at the same table as the enslaver and his family.[28]

---

[26] Cotton Mather's Diary, Massachusetts Historical Society Collection, Seven Series, Volume Eight, Part Two, in Greene, 219.

[27] Elise Lemire, *Black Walden: Slavery and Its Aftermath in Concord, Massachusetts*, University of Pennsylvania: Philadelphia, 2009, 20.

[28] Greene, 324.

Much of what we know about names of the enslaved in Westford comes from Reverend Willard Hall's Church book (See "The Enslaved of Westford" below). It is also possible that there were other enslaved people living in town, but they were not baptized. Those not baptized might have appeared in tax records, but records are missing from many years in the 1700s (See Appendix A for *Taxation of Slave Owners in Colonial Westford*).

Some of the enslaved individuals who were baptized are listed as children. Typically, captives brought to the colonies prior to 1740 were often about 15 years old.[29] This begs the question if they were captured and brought to this country as children or if they were born here.

That some of the enslaved people in town were baptized shows that their enslavers likely allowed them to learn to read, and specifically *The Bible*. It also provided an opportunity to build a community with the other enslaved individuals in town and communicate. Church membership meant reading the Bible and learning to read, which in turn offered community, and certain rights, privileges, and language that allowed communication and ability to appeal to authority and the community if necessary.[30]

But what did reading the Bible mean to those who were enslaved? They may have read in the New Testament, "Let as many servants as are under the yoke count their own masters worthy of all honour [sic], that the name of God and his doctrine be not blasphemed. And they that have believing masters, let them not despise them…but rather do them service, because they are faithful and beloved, partakers of the benefit..."[31] For the enslavers reading this, they saw justification for their enslaving. In that sense, "the message of liberation contained in Exodus was meant only for God's chosen people, not for the enslaved

---

29 Desrochers, 623–64.

30 Jared Hardesty, *Black Lives, Native Lands, White World*, Bright Leaf/University of Massachusetts: Amherst, 2019, 106.

31 *The Holy Bible*, 1 Timothy 6:1-2

unable to partake in the communion."[32] Enslaved people learned that their enslavers were honorable; that liberation was not meant for the enslaved. Outside of the home, they received the message that they were subservient and their compliance would lead them to Heaven.

Perhaps the portions of the *Bible* enslaved people were allowed to read were carefully curated so they could not read about how being baptized could actually mean being "free" in one sense of the word, meaning emancipated. Therefore, some colonists disagreed about baptizing enslaved people, arguing that it gave the enslaved grounds to seek manumission or enfranchisement. Some feared that allowing enslaved or emancipated people into the Church membership would give them political equality and the right to vote in Massachusetts, which at some points in time that privilege was limited to church members.[33] In 1729, the Royal Attorney General assured English colonists that baptism did not enfranchise slaves.[34] Baptizing the enslaved seemed to be more of another act of domination than benevolence.

If enslaved people were baptized and allowed to attend services, where did they sit? In the first Meetinghouse (1725-1771), Town records mention separate staircases for men and women, so there was a second floor.[35] Westford's second Meetinghouse (1771-1793) had a large room with balconies around three sides and a high pulpit on the remaining side. There were long benches at the back of the room for those families who could not purchase a pew or had lesser social or religious status. Perhaps if the first Meetinghouse had a similar arrangement, the enslaved sat on the long benches at the back of the room, or maybe even on the floor.

---

[32] Hardesty, 4.

[33] Greene, 260-61.

[34] Lemire, 20.

[35] Town of Westford Records, Volume 1, 1726-1764.

Prominence in Town

In *Black Walden*, Elise Lemire described the circumstance through which Joseph Cuming acquired an enslaved person upon gaining some prominence in town. The story there is reminiscent of Joseph Hildreth Jr. 's. In 1731, Joseph Hildreth, Jr. inherited about 500 acres of land from his father's estate. About the same time, he was also named tax collector for the town on November 10, 1731. In Reverend Hall's Church Book, Jack, enslaved by Hildreth, was baptized on August 15, 1731. Peggy Hildreth was baptized on June 24, 1732.

Probate Records

Probate records are a listing of a deceased's property *at the time of their death*. If the deceased had been ill, then it was common to give some parts of the estate, like enslaved people or other property, to family members to reduce their estate or hide their enslaved person(s). Of the available probate records, none from Westford have shown evidence of enslaved people. This means that they did not enslave a person at their death, the enslaved individual was completely overlooked for the probate, or given away prior to the death. It's also important to note that after 1775, probate records from eastern Massachusetts lack explicit references to enslaved persons.[36] This indicates a shift in the documentation (or obfuscation) of enslaved labor, rather than a decrease in slavery.

[36] Gloria McCahon Whiting, "Belonging: An Intimate History of Slavery and Family in Early New England." YouTube video. Accessed 7 April 2025. 11:14. https://youtu.be/5QmNMdFF-iw?si=WJnN37xwet-lgloz

Tax Records

In 1675, enslaved people were rated as property as first seen in tax records of Newbury, MA. In Boston, they were in the same category as horses, sheep, and pigs.[37] In 1698, two acts specifically classified an enslaved person as personal property and their value was determined "according to the sound judgment and discretion of the assessors."[38]

In 1706, Judge Samuel Sewall and others were moved to protest the type of tax where humans were valued the same as animals. Their efforts were in vain and enslaved people continued to be included in this tax category until slavery was abolished in Massachusetts.[39]

In 1707, the tax law changed to distinguish between "slave" and "servant" but does not explain the distinction. The law stated that all "Indian, molatto and negro slaves" were to be taxed as other personal estate at one shilling in the pound. Each enslaved male over the age of 14 years would be valued at £20 and each enslaved female over 14 years at £15 but all "Indian, molatto, and negro male servants" were to be appraised as polls, not as personal estate.[40] The law does not mention female servants.

Starting in 1718, all enslaved for life over the age of 14 were assessed as "personal estate" and adjustments could be made for infirmity or disability. Males were typically £15 and females £10. But a servant for a certain length of time was assessed as a poll tax, NOT personal estate.[41]

William "Bill" Prescott, a former Westford resident, extensively analyzed Westford's tax records in 1987.[42] He found that tax records for the town were missing or incomplete for

---

[37] Greene, 169.
[38] See *Acts and Resolves*, pgs. 337, 359, 387.
[39] Greene, 171.
[40] *Acts and Resolves*, 615.
[41] George H. Moore, *Notes on the History of Slavery in Massachusetts*, D. Appleton and Co.: New York, 1866, 64-65
[42] See Appendix A.

some years. He was curious when he found taxpayers assessed for an extra poll tax and determined it must be on account of an enslaved person in the house.

In Westford, a slave was assessed the same rate as a horse. On the actual forms, the word "negro" appears next to the Taxpayer's line. The record exists on the "Single Rate" tax list, as opposed to the Provincial or Minister Rates that the town used.

This is an example from the 1770 tax record and Pelatiah Fletcher's entry.

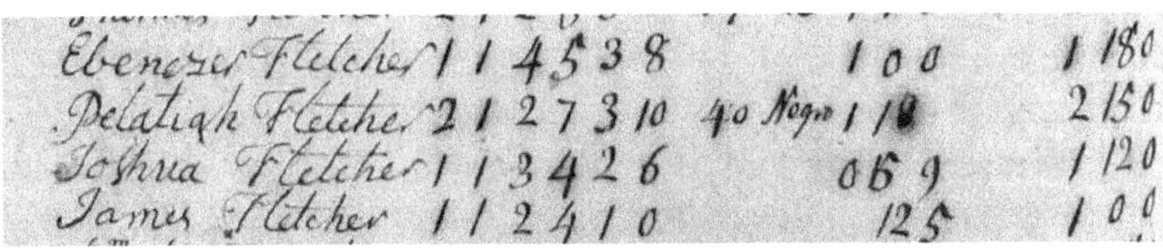

Ebenezer Fletcher	1 1 4 5 3 8	1 0 0	1 18 0
Pelatiah Fletcher	2 1 2 7 3 10	40 Negro 1 18	2 15 0
Joshua Fletcher	1 1 3 4 2 6	0 6 9	1 12 0
James Fletcher	1 1 2 4 1 0	12 5	1 0 0

According to Prescott's work on the tax valuations in Westford, 1757-58 shows a high point of people enslaved in town, followed by a decline reaching a low point in 1768, then another high in 1773.[43] When combined with other inferential data, the year with the most enslaved in Westford is 1764, with 15 enslaved.[44] Around 1760 in Massachusetts, it became increasingly harder to know whether people of color were free or not, so there was a decline in the slave trade. However, that advertisements continued in newspapers meant that slave traders were not deterred from continuing their activities.[45] Instead of hiring out the enslaved with no work, New England enslavers often offered them for sale instead. This practice increased during the unsettled economic depression that followed the French and Indian War (1754-1763).[46] In Westford, this shift is reflected in the tax records and in the decline of baptisms for the

[43] William B. Prescott, "Taxation of Slave Owners in Colonial Westford." Private Printing. December 1987. Collection of the Westford Historical Society W.2003.23).

[44] Howard, "Enslaved Persons in Westford."

[45] Desrochers, 623–64.

[46] Greene, 122.

enslaved. Does this data align with what was broadly happening in New England or is it due to the lack of surviving tax records? Without all the data, nothing is certain.

The 1771 Massachusetts Tax Inventory is notable because it was when the provincial governments required a special valuation be made for personal and real property. Of the columns for the list, "Servant for life" meant: "All Indian, Negro, or Molatto servants for life from fourteen to 45 years of age"[47]

On the 1771 Inventory, Westford residents William Read, Pelatiah Fletcher, Ephraim Comings, and John Robins are marked as having a "servant for life." Though it is difficult to determine the names of these enslaved, we know that they were here because the enslaver was taxed accordingly.[48]

Prescott also analyzed Westford's 1774 tax records and created a listing of the top 200 wealthiest men in town. If the enslavers were alive in 1774, all except William Read who was absent from this tax list, were ranked among the top 200 wealthiest men in town.[49]

In 1776, black polls were the same as white polls, not personal property.[50]

Among other missing tax records, the 1773 Single Rate has the North List but not the South List. Therefore, the 1773 tax year is incomplete. The 1774 "Single Rate" list is also missing, so there is no information for that year.

---

[47] Prescott, "Taxation of Slave Owners in Colonial Westford."

[48] For a full town listing, see https://legacy.sites.fas.harvard.edu/~hsb41/masstax/masstax.cgi

[49] See William B. Prescott, *Patriots and Taxpayers of Colonial Westford, Massachusetts in 1774*, Private Printing. Westford Museum files.

[50] Moore, 65.

Life of the Enslaved in Town

Names for the enslaved in New England were place names, classical names, Biblical slave names, or common English names. Names from these categories were "intended to advertise a slave owner's values, and characteristics whether his classical education, his religiosity, or his cosmopolitanism."[51] Popular place names used for first names were usually major ports in England or its colonies, showing off an enslaver's knowledge of the world.[52] In Westford, we see the names: Dinah, Jethro, Prince, Ishmael, Cesar, Moses, York, and Noble (See "The Enslaved of Westford" below).

Enslaved people in New England were allowed some semblance of a life outside of their labors. There's no indication that Westford made laws separate from the Colonial laws. The Massachusetts Bay Colony passed curfews for Indian and African slaves and free blacks to prevent "disorders, insolencies, and burglaries" that were allegedly perpetrated by these people at night.[53] Therefore, many towns had a curfew of nine o'clock PM. Sometimes enslaved people were also hired out to others when there wasn't sufficient work for the enslaver. This allowed them to earn a wage or have some property of their own.

Once enslaved people married, they were expected to maintain proper relationships with their spouse and were liable for arrest and punishment, as were white people.[54] In December 1705-06, the legislature enacted a law to outlaw interracial marriages.[55] Massachusetts Bay Colony was the only New England colony to do this. There were punishments for breaking this law, even for the person performing the ceremony. However, the law didn't prevent as much as it intended. The interracial marriage wouldn't always be annulled and economic considerations by the enslaver took priority- he didn't want to

---

[51] Lemire, 17.
[52] Lemire, 17.
[53] *Acts and Resolves*, 535. See also Hardesty, 67.
[54] Greene, 202-203.
[55] *Acts and Resolves*, 579.

lose his "property!" As such, some enslavers helped enslaved with their secret relationship.[56]

The enslaved seem to be well fed and they were probably given the same food as the family, and in many cases they ate at the same table with their enslavers. They also generally slept under the same roof as their enslavers, maybe on the same floor, but more frequently in the extra story above the main floor.[57] There isn't evidence of slave quarters in Westford, so we can assume they slept in the same house and likely ate at the same table. The enslaved in some cases seemed to be a part of the family. There are stories of enslavers in other towns shedding tears over the graves of their enslaved. This family structure, however generous in its accommodations, like baptizing the enslaved people, was a constant reminder of their position and held them in a state of constant surveillance.[58]

Because the enslaved in Westford would have performed a variety of jobs, from farming to mending fences, to sewing and childcare, it would behoove an enslaver to provide some rudimentary education. That would also make the enslaved person more valuable. Greene argues this, "was not the result of a general movement, but was fostered by kindly disposed masters, members of the clergy, and by religious organizations."[59] The enslaved were taught the trades because that is what the industry of the region demanded. Greene noted, "there was no color line in colonial industry."[60] Barring the enslaved from learning the trades was subsequently ignored as it was necessary for the enslavers' livelihood and the economy. Jared Hardesty argued there was some backlash in the colony about using enslaved people for trade work as some thought it undermined the trade.

Even though the enslaved were baptized, they were likely segregated in the Church. If they were buried in a

---

[56] Greene, 208-210.
[57] Greene, 222-223.
[58] Hardesty, 57.
[59] Greene, 237.
[60] Greene, 111-112.

cemetery, then it was likely in back corners and along rock walls.[61] We don't have confirmed burials (as in, Church or Town records) of enslaved people in Westford (see Peggy's story below).

Warning Out

The process of warning out was common in New England. A town would "warn out" people who could not support themselves and the town did not want them on their poor lists. Essentially, warning out meant the people could not establish a legal residency in that town. If they owned land, sometimes the land would be sold or reclaimed by the town. The pressure of being warned out often meant that the people had to leave the town. If they remained in town and on their land, then they would not be eligible for benefits and support from the town.[62]

Lemire notes that self-emancipated people sometimes were warned out of the towns in which they tried to settle. There was concern that not only might they appear on the town's poor list, but also because white residents did not want free blacks in the vicinity of their enslaved people.[63] Westford town records mention Brister and Anne, a Black couple from Chelmsford, who were warned out in 1781.[64] See below the story of Sarah and Frances Tony.

---

[61] Greene, 284.
[62] See Josiah Hart Benton, *Warning Out in New England*, W.B. Clarke Company, Boston, 1911.
[63] Lemire, 45.
[64] Town of Westford Records, Volume 2, 1765-1790, 157.

The Revolution

The 1652 Act of the General Court of Massachusetts, allowing "negroes and Indians" to serve in the Militia was repealed in May 1656. It stated, "...henceforth no negroes or Indians although servants to the English, shall be armed or permitted to train…" for the Militia.[65]

In 1660, Massachusetts Bay Colony Governor Simon Bradstreet reiterated, "We account all generally from sixteen to sixty that are healthfull [sic] and strong bodys [sic], both Householders and Servants fit to bear Armes [sic], *except Negros and slaves, whom wee [sic] arme [sic] not*" (emphasis in source).[66] These laws accentuated the subordinate status of emancipated men who were not allowed to bear arms. Yet, in 1707, on the call of an alarm, *all* able-bodied men, regardless of race, were expected to report to the training ground for assignment. If they failed to do this, it was punishable by a fine of 20 shillings or by 80 days labor.[67] Even up to the eve of the American Revolution, enslaved and free blacks were prohibited from bearing arms. Slowly the restrictions eased, especially as the army needed more soldiers and some enslaved men were self-emancipating to join the British.

In June 1775, the Continental Congress created the Continental Army. At the Battle of Bunker Hill on June 17, 1775, there were many Patriots of Color on the battlefield, including one from Westford. Despite their patriotism, in November 1775, General George Washington prohibited enlistment of free and enslaved Black men. There was some fear about arming the enslaved men for fear they would rise up against their enslavers, which was the case in Concord. In January 1776, Black men were allowed to enlist *if* they previously served in the Revolution. By 1777, any free man was eligible to enlist. By 1778, states began to enlist free and enslaved Black men (See the stories of

65 Moore, 243.
66 Moore, 243-4.
67 Greene, 303.

Cesar Bason, Jethro Wilkens, Noble Comings, and York Hambleton in "The Enslaved of Westford" below).

There is no Massachusetts law providing manumission for an enslaved man in exchange for his service in the war. Any such conversations happened privately and any historical record likely does not exist.

Emancipation

There is no evidence that an enslaved person in Westford was ever emancipated. In Massachusetts, it was required of enslavers to post a bond of £50 upon emancipation so that person could support themselves.[68] There are no court records of any suing for their freedom. Except when noted below, there is no record of a death or marriage.

68 "Massachusetts Bodies of Liberty (1641)"

Life after Enslavement

Massachusetts abolished slavery with their Constitution in 1780 and confirmed it in 1781 by the Supreme Judicial Court decision on the Quock Walker case.[69] Presumably, all servants by that time and after were paid for their labor. What was to come of the formerly enslaved?

The records in Westford are not clear who may have remained in town and what their living situation may have been. The Massachusetts Constitution did not discriminate against Blacks, but custom and tradition apparently prohibited them from exercising the right to vote.[70]

Enslavers sometimes kept unusual arrangements for their former enslaved people. They demanded loyalty and sometimes the formerly enslaved needed permission from their former enslaver to marry. A marriage would mean the former enslaver would no longer support the person. Permission was also sometimes required to move in with emancipated's own family.[71]

Barred from purchasing property in order to start a farm, competing with white people for jobs, and because of their inferior status, many emancipated people remained with their former enslaver as a hired servant. Greene notes they were, "frequently denied the opportunity of earning a living and forced into idleness. As a consequence, free Negros were to be later stigmatized as an idol lazy, and dissolute class."[72] The white workmen "manifested a sullen antagonism" to the competition, which, as John Adams remarked, in 1795, might have resulted

[69] See "Massachusetts Constitution and the Abolition of Slavery," Accessed 9 February 2025, https://www.mass.gov/guides/massachusetts-constitution-and-the-abolition-of-slavery#-the-quock-walker-case-

[70] Greene, 302.

[71] Lemire, 110-111

[72] Greene, 304.

in the white tradesmen destroying slavery had it not already been abolished.[73]

Emancipated women in particular accepted food and shelter from their former enslaver in return for their continued labor. [74] They continued life as it was, only now they were choosing it. What choice did some have? Many stayed close to the town because people knew them and knew their emancipated status. They were also familiar with the terrain. Should they venture out and settle in another town and be warned out from there, they would be forced to return on the basis that the town should accept responsibility for them.[75]

The 1790 Federal Census

The 1790 Census was the first official one for the new country. As slavery was abolished, there were no enslaved people listed in the Westford 1790 Census. Knowing that some emancipated people remained with their former enslaver, or were living somewhere in town but not in a traditional house, the results from the 1790 census are curious. Lemire called this a "sleight of hand."[76] Perhaps they were not enslaved, but were they still living there? Like the 1754 census that indicated zero Native Americans lived in town, it is hard to believe that these numbers are accurate. Or perhaps they were not counted in the census at all, the census taker turning a blind eye towards the situation?

Cato Grey lived in Westford by 1790 and is listed in a household of 3 "non white" individuals. He was from Boston, served in the Revolution and made his way to Westford afterwards.

---

73 Greene, 322.

74 Greene, 305.

75 Lemire, 109, 116-117.

76 Lemire, 111.

Perhaps the enslaved individuals in town were emancipated in 1780 and all decided to live together in one house. This is not unheard of.

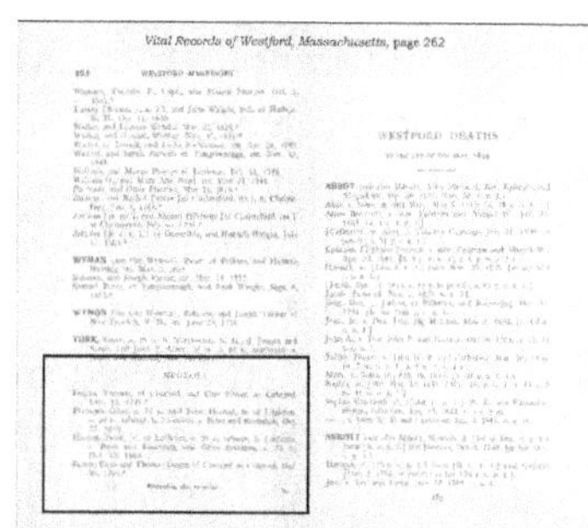

There is also a woman, Cate Porter, who married Thomas Dugan of Concord. Thomas Dugan's story is detailed in the book *Black Walden* by Elise Lemire. Dugan was a self-emancipated slave from Virginia. He was the third formerly enslaved man to purchase land in Concord. His land was near Old Marlborough Road. [77] This marriage is recorded in Westford Vital Records, but they were married in Concord on December 29, 1791. The only other marriage listed under "NEGROES" was in 1849. Now, was Cate Porter formerly enslaved in Westford? How did she come to live

77 See Lemire, 11 and 157.

here? How did she come to know Dugan? More research is needed there as well.

The 1800 Federal Census for Westford lists "4 Blacks" and 3 of them lived with Phillip Jackson. The other lived with Reverend Caleb Blake, the third Minister in Westford.

The Map

Using information compiled from tax records, Hodgman's *History of Westford*, the 1730 Map of Westford, and Bill Prescott's research on the 1730 Map of Westford,[78] it was possible to create a map of where the Enslavers lived in Westford. Locations are approximate as the "white oaks" and "large stone" are no longer adequate to determine property lines. Another caveat being that what is considered the 1730 Map of Westford has been debunked by Bill Prescott. It is actually an 1880s illustration of what the town *might have* looked like in 1730. For example, there are roads on the 1730 map that did not exist in 1730.

From this map, we can determine that slavery was widespread through the town, but clustered in the center of town, where there was less agriculture and more commerce and business, like Reverend Hall, Abel Boynton, and James Pollard.

---

78 See William B. Prescott, *Map of Westford in 1730,* Private Printing, Westford Historical Society files.

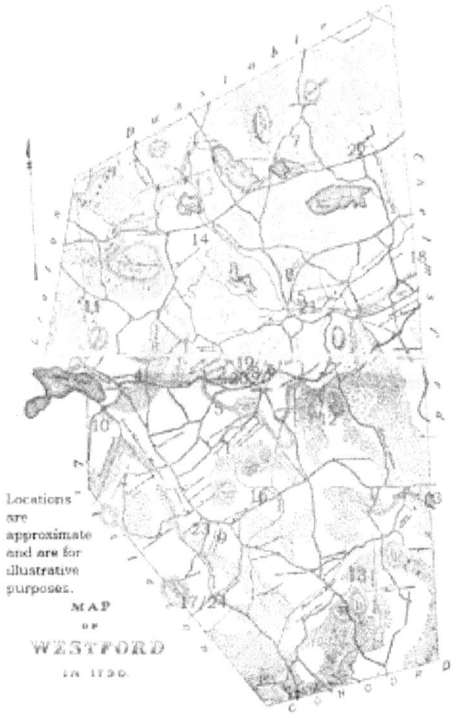

Locations are approximate and are for illustrative purposes.
MAP
OF
WESTFORD

Enslavers in Westford, MA

1. Joseph Hildreth, Jr.
2. Nathaniel Boynton
3. Jonathan Proctor
4. Jonas Prescott
5. Joseph Dutton
6. James Pollard
7. Ephraim Chandler
8. Rev. Willard Hall
9. John Read
10. Samuel Lawrence
11. Gershom Fletcher
12. Enoch Cleveland
13. Moses Parker
14. Abner Wilkins
15. Ephraim Comings
16. James Burn
17. Samuel Fitch
18. Peletiah Fletcher
19. Abel Boynton
20. William Read
21. Moses Burge
22. Jonathan Keyes
23. Francis Leighton

Part II
The Enslaved of Westford

Alice

Alice was baptized on March 15, 1730.[79] The Church book lists her name with "Boston" in brackets. She was also listed as Incognitis Parentis, meaning her parents were unknown. Unlike the others, there is no note indicating she was a servant in a household. Enslaved men were sometimes given the name Boston, as that is the port at which they likely arrived. Perhaps Alice also traveled through Boston and was given that surname. No other records could be found at this time.

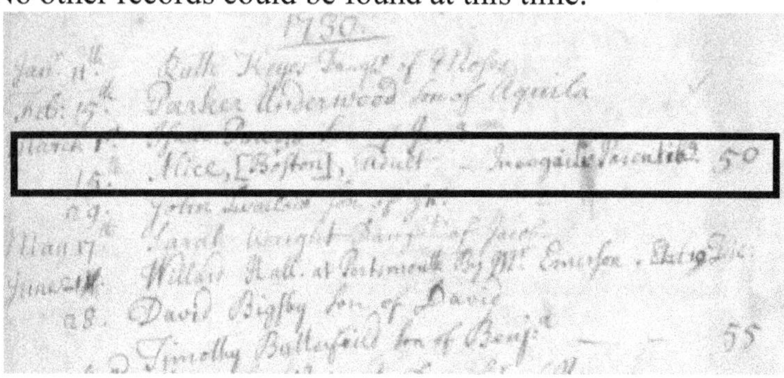
1730
Parker Underwood son of Aquila
Alice, [Boston], Adult
David Bigsby son of David
Timothy Butterfield son of Benj.ª 55

Jack

Jack was baptized by Reverend Hall on August 15, 1731, just two weeks after Joseph Hildreth Jr.'s son, Wilson.[80] Jack was enslaved by Joseph Hildreth, Jr. He was not listed as a child, so was likely over 16 years old. Due to the extensive size of Hildreth's property, Jack likely farmed this land. No other records could be found at this time.

---

[79] Reverend Willard Hall et al, *The Church Book Belonging to the Second Church in Chelmsford 1727,* 3.
[80] Hall, 5.

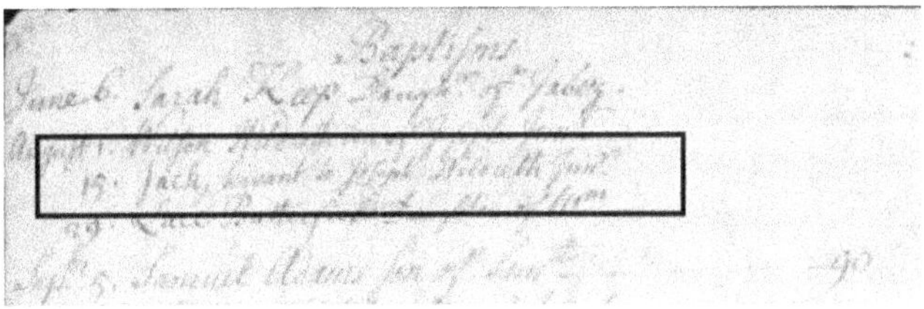

Peggy Hildreth

Peggy was baptized by Reverend Hall on June 24, 1732.[81] She was also enslaved by Joseph Hildreth, Jr. Joseph lived with his wife, Deliverance, and their children. In Reverend Hall's book, Peggy is not listed as a child, so we can assume she was over the age of 16.

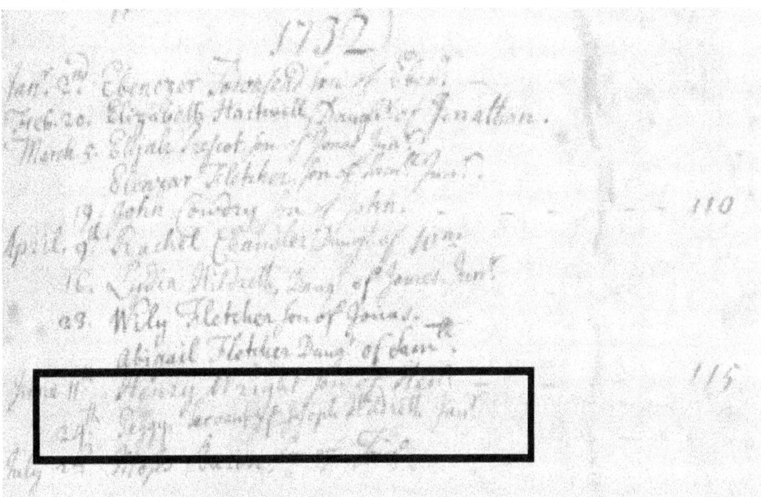

Joseph Hildreth, Jr. was assessed for slaves in 1752, and then again from 1757 to 1762, just one year before his death.

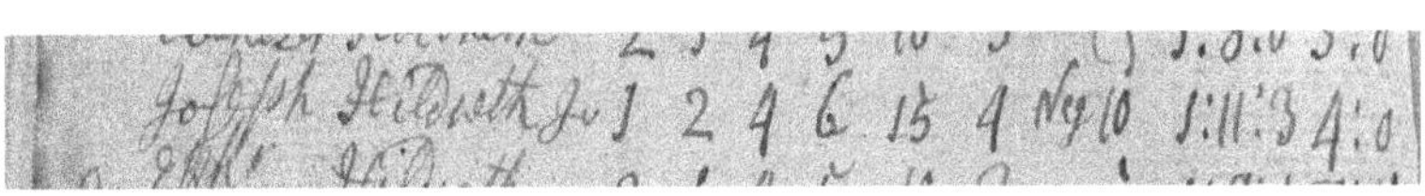

81 Hall, 5.

The tax records could mean that Peggy was in the house from at least 1732 to about 1763. If Peggy was at least 16 in 1732, then she was at least 47 in 1763 when Joseph died. There is no mention of her in Joseph's probate. His wife, Deliverance, lived another 10 or so years. There is no probate for her.

Joseph Hildreth had died by the census in 1764. So the twelve total enslaved reported in town (5 males and 7 females) might *not* include Peggy and Jack, unless they were not reported upon his death. There is no indication that Peggy was ever emancipated.

In the 1980s, women from the First Parish Church United got together and created The Westford Women Doll Collection as a fundraiser for the Church. They handmade dolls that represented important women in Westford's history. One of the women chosen was Peggy. Jean Downey, wife of First Parish Church Reverend George Downey wrote some articles on Peggy and slavery in Westford. Peggy's doll, and the other dolls are on view at the Westford Museum.

On the land between what is now Hildreth Street and Boston Road, the land that once belonged to Joseph Hildreth, Jr, there lies a marker, likely a footstone. It is marked: "P. Hildreth." According to Historian Judy Cataldo, footstones were placed at the foot of a burial place, opposite a headstone. Joseph Hildreth's house was most likely about a mile north of where Flagg Road meets Hildreth Street (58 Hildreth Street). That land abuts the property on which this stone is, so in theory, this could have been a grave for Peggy. Footstones were often moved. The photo below is courtesy of Marilyn Day.

But was it moved? The original theory was that this stone was once placed at a grave. Charles L Hildreth, who owned extensive property on the land between Boston and Hildreth Streets, built extensive rock walls on his property.

Rock walls being built on Charles Hildreth's land. Photo from Westford Museum S-25.

As a result, this footstone may have been moved from closer to Hildreth Street to its current location closer to Boston Road to accommodate these rock walls. Resident Angela Harkness, who used to reside at 25 Boston Road, remembers finding the stone and resting it next to a tree on the property.

However, in June 2024 after the initial publication of this research, Thomas Crawford, a former resident of Hildreth Street, explained how Arthur Hildreth used to drive him on his tractor throughout the Hildreth property. He would drive up the hill to the land where Hildreth Hills development is and Arthur would stop at a place where there was a square rock wall jutting out from the main rock wall. There was a stone in the middle of this square. Crawford remembers Arthur saying, "this is where they buried the slave."[82]

This author maintains that this stone once marked where Peggy was laid to rest. That she was beloved as Historian Jean Downey once claimed and was given a burial and stone.

Moses Sawyer

Moses Sawyer was admitted to the table on February 6, 1732.[83] He was a servant of Nathanial Boynton, the father of the Westford Town Clerk of the same name, and grandfather to Abel Boynton. It is unclear if Moses was enslaved or not from Reverend Hall's entry.

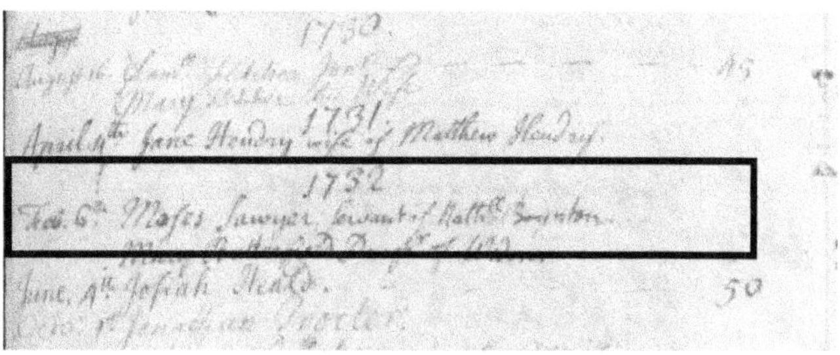
1730
1731
1732
Feb. 6th Moses Sawyer
June 4th
50

82 Phone interview with author, June 26, 2024.

83 Hall, 21.

We don't have a record of a baptism, just that he was allowed Communion. We know from the Boynton genealogy, that Nathaniel Boynton lived on his father's homestead (near where Patten Road meets Forge Village Road) and "like him" was a house carpenter. As Moses was male, we can assume that Moses helped Nathaniel with his carpentry work, as opposed to working inside the house. Boynton was dismissed from First Parish Church, Westford to the Church in Pepperell on March 17, 1754. Groton West Parish had just formed into Pepperell on April 12, 1753. Nathaniel Boynton died on August 5, 1757 in Pepperell and is buried in Walton Cemetery there. He was 62 years old. Pepperell Vital Records states the cause of death was a fever. There is no mention of Moses in his probate. No other records could be found at this time.

Dinah

Dinah was baptized on July 1, 1733.[84] She was enslaved by Jonathan Proctor. Jonathan Proctor was born on July 8, 1693 in Chelmsford.[85] He married Elizabeth Robbins of Stow after Feb 7, 1719, when they published their intention in Chelmsford.[86] Hodgman places his property near Pond Brook. William Prescott does not list where his property might have been.

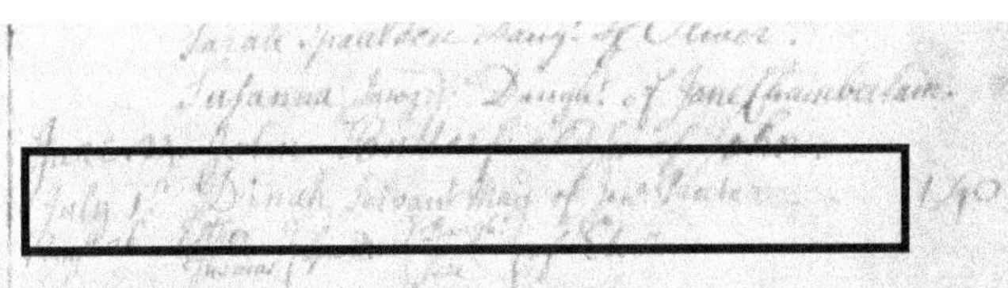

In 1745, the Proctors were dismissed from the Church to go to Harvard. In Harvard, he was a farmer, or husbandman. It's not clear if Dinah also went to Harvard. He died on October 2,

---

[84] Hall, 6.

[85] Essex Institute, *Vital Records of Chelmsford, Massachusetts to the End of the Year 1849*, Salem, MA, Newcomb & Gauss, 1914, 125.

[86] *Vital Records of Chelmsford*, 299.

1755 in Harvard.[87] There is no mention of Dinah in his probate.[88] No other records could be found at this time.

Jenny Prescott

Jenny was baptized by Reverend Willard Hall on September 23, 1733.[89] She was enslaved by Captain Jonas Prescott. She was not listed as a child, so she was likely over 16. She likely worked in the household.

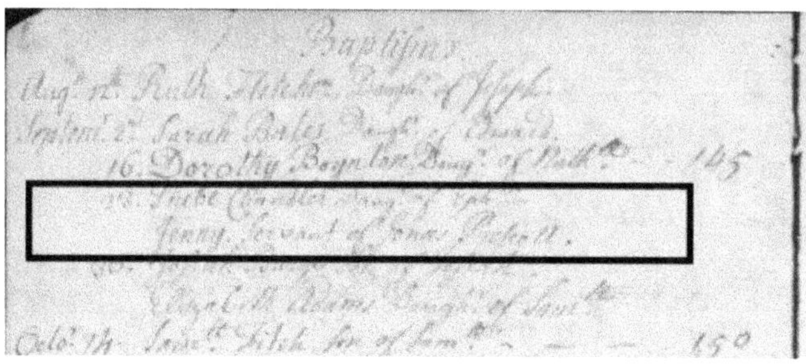

Jonas Prescott was a farmer in Westford. William Prescott places his property on the North side of the railroad tracks in Forge Village near the intersection of East and West Prescott streets.[90] Hodgman calls it "near the promontory formed by the brook and margin of the pond."[91] Jenny likely worked in the house.

---

87 Mr. and Mrs. William Lawrence Proctor, *Genealogy of Descendants of Robert Proctor of Concord and Chelmsford, Mass.*, Republican & Journal Print: Ogdensburg, NY, 1898, 9.

88 Worcester County, MA: Probate File Papers, 1731-1881. Online database. AmericanAncestors.org. New England Historic Genealogical Society, 2015. (From records supplied by the Massachusetts Supreme Judicial Court Archives.)

89 Hall, 7.

90 Prescott, *Map of Westford in 1730.*

91 Reverend Edwin R. Hodgman, *History of the Town of Westford in the County of Middlesex, Massachusetts, 1659-1883*, Morning Mail Company: Lowell, 1883, 31.

Jonas Prescott is not listed as a "servant owner" in the 1771 Tax Inventory.[92] Jonas Prescott died September 9, 1784 in Westford, Massachusetts. He is buried in Westlawn Cemetery in Westford. There is no mention of Jenny in Prescott's probate. From this, we can assume Jenny was emancipated prior to 1771.

Records show there is a Jenny Prescutt that married a York Ruggles on February 13, 1785.[93] If she were 16 in 1733, she would have been 68 years old. There is a York Ruggles living in Cambridge, born in Africa, who served in the Revolution. He was 31 in 1781 and 5' 6."[94] This places his birth year in 1750. Undeniably, there is a significant age difference between York and Jenny. That is not to say their marriage could not have happened. If this Jenny is the Jenny from Westford, she could have traveled to Cambridge, met and fallen in love with York. Or perhaps it was a marriage for financial security.

York, and presumably Jenny, are on the 1790 Federal Census as "all other free persons."[95] York is head of the family and there are a total of 7 people living together in Boston. No other Federal Census records could be found for them.

---

92 "Interactive Massachusetts Tax Inventory, 1771," https://legacy.sites.fas.harvard.edu/~hsb41/masstax/masstax.cgi?state=person&person=03490535

93 Stephen Sharples, "Early Records of the First Church in Cambridge," in *The Genealogical Magazine* Vol. 1 No. 1, Eben Putnam: Boston. April 1905, 216.

94 Muster/payrolls, and various papers (1763-1808) of the Revolutionary War [Massachusetts and Rhode Island] Vol. 62, Mass. muster and payrolls, Drake Collection 1775-1797 Vol. 63, Miscellaneous rolls 1777-1783 Vol. 64, Warrants and receipts 1775-1783

95 1790 United States Federal Census

However, in 1800, York appeared on a tax list. He was living in Boston on "Newberry" Street at the back of Widow Merrett's house, which was in Ward 12. He was assessed 1 Poll.[96]

As York is from Cambridge, perhaps he was enslaved by George Ruggles of Cambridge and also a known enslaver. George was a Tory and fled to England around 1774. It is after this time that York's military records appear.

No other records could be found at this time.

---

[96] *Boston, MA: Taking Records, 1800.* (Original Online Database: *AmericanAncestors.org*, New England Historic Genealogical Society, 2014. (Transcribed by David Allen Lambert, NEHGS Chief Genealogist, from original volumes held by the Boston Public Library.) https://www.americanancestors.org/DB528/rd/14154/12-54/258997074

Phillis

Phillis was baptized October 24, 1736.[97] Joseph Dutton was born in 1711. He married Rebecca Adams of Chelmsford November 6, 1735. Hodgman's genealogy notes the Duttons lived near the Flagg place (31 Flagg Road) and Colburn's place.[98] She is not listed as a "negro" servant. She is assumed to

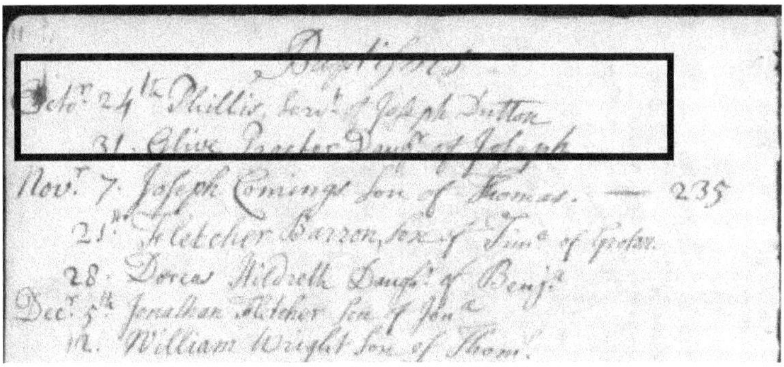
Baptisms
Octo. 24th Phillis, serv.t of Joseph Dutton
31. Olive Procter Daug.r of Joseph
Nov.r 7. Joseph Comings son of Thomas. — 235
21. Fletcher Barron, son of Tim.o of Groton.
28. Dorcas Hildreth Daug.r of Benj.
Dec.r 5th Jonathan Fletcher son of Jon.
12. William Wright son of Thom.

be over 16 as she is not listed as a "child."

In 1751, Joseph Dutton was Westford's treasurer and Selectman in 1756. In the 1771 tax list, Joseph Dutton is listed as owning an ironworks. His real estate was valued at 12 pounds. He had 8 acres of pastures, enough for 7 cows. He produced about 25 barrels of cider per year and 8 tons of hay per year. He owned one horse, two oxen, 4 cows, and 1 swine. He is *not* listed as owning any servants nor servants for life. In the tax records, Joseph Dutton was *never* taxed for enslaving a person.

Joseph Dutton died 1775 at 63 years old. He's buried in Fairview Cemetery. On his gravestone is written, "Memento Mori" which in Latin means remember that you have to die. He seems to have died intestate, a probate record could not be located in the index.

On April 5, 1799, Dutton's house caught fire. It once stood opposite Amos Day's house, which was occupied by Jonathan T. Colburn when Hodgman wrote his history in 1883.

---

[97] Hall, 11.

[98] Hodgman, 155.

The town voted to raise $150 for "Mr. Dutton" and his family.[99] Joseph and Rebeka had 4 sons and 2 daughters. Hodgman does not indicate to which "Mr. Dutton" he is referring, although it is most likely his eldest son, Joseph.

In *Old Houses of Westford*, the authors surmise that the house may not have burned fully to the ground but may have still existed until another fire burned it down in 1906. Here is a picture of that house.[100] If correct, Phillis could have lived in this house. No other records could be found at this time.

OLD DUTTON PLACE
APPROXIMATELY 27 FLAGG ROAD
north of Robinson Road

Prince

Prince was baptized on July 10, 1737 and listed as a Negro.[101] He was enslaved by James Pollard. Pollard was born

---

99 Hodgman, 155.

100 Colonel John Robinson Chapter of the Daughters of the American Revolution (DAR), *Old Houses of Westford*, 1957, compiled by Gertrude Fletcher and Julia Fletcher; revised by Marilyn Day and Ellen Harde with permission of the DAR, 2004.

101 Hall, 12.

October 5, 1708 to Thomas and Sarah, likely in Billerica.[102] For the first tax list for the town, James Pollard is in the North List but is without homestead.[103] James married Abigill Chimberlim [Abigail Chamberlain] of Chelmsford on December 17, 1734.[104]

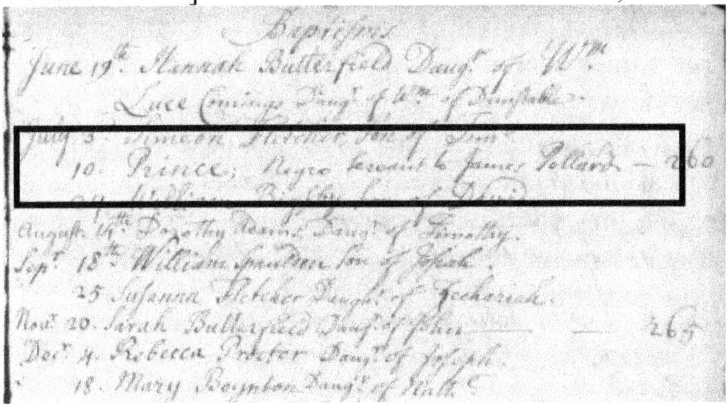

Baptisms
June 19th Hannah Butterfield Daug.r of W.m
Luce Cemings Daug.r of W.m of Dunstable
July 3 Simeon Fletcher Son of Tim.
10. Prince; Negro servant to James Pollard — 260
August 14th Dorothy Adams Daug.r of Timothy.
Sept 18th William Spaulding Son of Joseph.
25 Susanna Fletcher Daught. of Zechariah.
Nov.r 20. Sarah Butterfield Daug.r of John — 265
Dec.r 4. Rebecca Proctor Daug.r of Joseph.
18. Mary Boynton Daug.r of

Early Town records also indicate that Pollard was paid to regularly clean the Meetinghouse.[105] These records date to the late 1730s and through the 1740s. This record is from 1741.

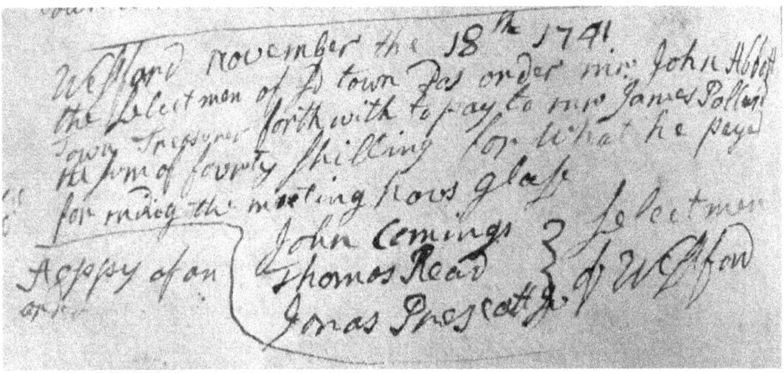

Westford november the 18th 1741
the Selectmen of sd town Doe order mr John Abbot Town Treasurer forthwith to pay to mr James Pollard the sum of fourty shilling for what he payd for mending the meeting house glass
John Cemings
Thomas Read
Jonas Prescott Jr
Selectmen of Westford
A coppy of an order

102 F. Apthorp Foster (ed.). *Vital Records of Billerica, Massachusetts, to the Year 1850*. (Boston, MA: New England Historic Genealogical Society, 1908), 150.

103 Hodgman, 32.

104 *Vital Records of Westford, Massachusetts, to the end of the year 1849*, The Essex Institute: Salem, 1915, 215.

105 Town of Westford Records, Volume 1, 1726-1764, 167.

It is hard to believe that an enslaver would do the work of cleaning the Meetinghouse glass and other maintenance activities. There is a high probability that Prince actually did this work. This begs the question: who kept the money?

James Pollard eventually owned land that is now 33 Main Street. Hodgman notes that it is the Sherman D. Fletcher place, however, that house was built in 1849.[106] This map below shows that during the years 1762-1781 (when Pollard died), he lived at one point where 33 Main Street is and also across the street at the end of what is now Connell Drive.[107] This map lists Isaac Patten as the owner in 1782 after Pollard's death (see below regarding Pollard's estate).

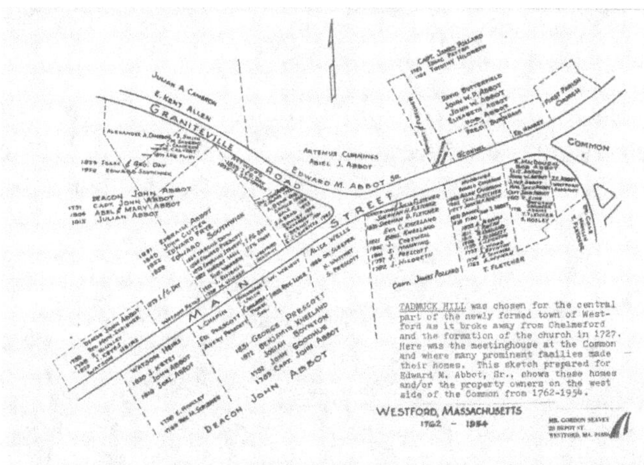

Westford records of 1750 indicate he was a tavern keeper. Prince may have also worked in the tavern. James Pollard was a Captain in the French and Indian War. In January 1760, he was commissioned as a Captain of the First Company.

---

[106] Hodgman, 249.

[107] Found in the Archive of the First Parish Church, United in Westford. Its author is unclear, perhaps Bill Prescott and printed by Gordon Seavey in one of his articles.

Pollard is on the 1771 tax inventory.[108] However, he is not listed as a servant owner so we can assume Prince was ignored, had died, or was emancipated by 1771.

James' first wife, Abigail, died April 19, 1774 at 63 years old.[109] Possibly in 1775, he remarried Elizabeth Abbot.[110] He refers to his "beloved wife" Elizabeth in his will.[111] Elizabeth's death is not listed in Westford Vital Records, perhaps because she remarried again after James' death. It does not appear that they had any children.

James Pollard died on March 7, 1781 in his 73rd year and is buried in Fairview Cemetery, which he helped to establish.[112] Probate indicates he was of sound mind but a failing body in 1781. He left half of his land, dwelling, and entire barn to his wife Elizabeth so that she could live there and not pay rent. She also received some livestock to do with what she wanted. The other parts of the estate went to an Isaac Patten (born 1761), under the direction of his Executors, until he reached 21 years old. From this probate record, it can be deduced that Pollard took on Isaac Patten to work on his farm, probably around 1770, and having no children of his own, left half of his estate to him in return.

Isaac married Lydia Keyes and their first son was born in 1783. They named him James Pollard Patten. Clearly, there was a close relationship.

No other records could be found at this time.

---

108 https://legacy.sites.fas.harvard.edu/~hsb41/masstax/masstax.cgi?state=person&person=03490406

109 Westford Vital Records, 302.

110 "James Pollard (abt. 1708-1781)," WikiTree, Accessed 9 February 2025, https://www.wikitree.com/wiki/Pollard-104#_note-residence

111 Middlesex County, MA: Probate File Papers, 1648-1871.Online database. AmericanAncestors.org. New England Historic Genealogical Society, 2014. https://www.americanancestors.org/DB536/i/14465/17684-co2/38360412

112 Westford Vital Records, 302.

Phillis

Phillis was baptized in Westford on August 5, 1739.[113] Job Spauden/Spaulding was born October 19, 1714 in Chelmsford. He married Lydia Barrett. Job served in Captain Daniel Fletcher's regiment for the Reduction of Canada alongside Cesar Negro (see Cesar Negro's story). Job died sometime after 1810, also in Chelmsford. In Phillis' baptism record, Job is noted as being "of Chelmsford." It does not seem that he had a home in Westford. Given that their son, Joseph, was baptized in Chelmsford on October 22, 1739 (just a few weeks after Phillis), it is a possibility that the church in Chelmsford would not baptize enslaved people so he had her baptized in Westford. No other records could be found at this time.

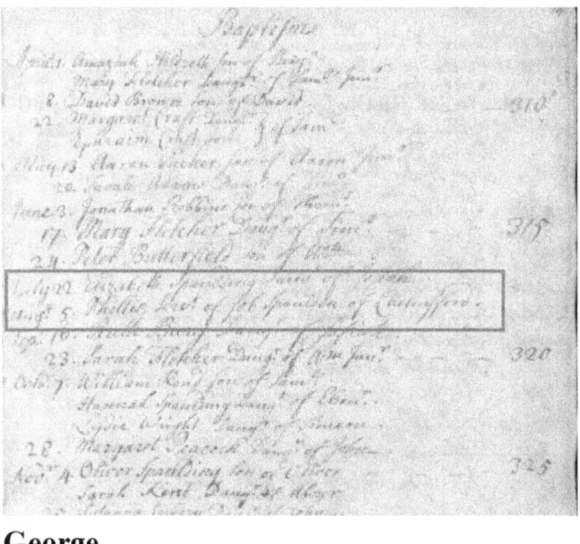

George

George was baptized on July 9, 1741. He was listed as mulatto in the Church Book.[114] He was enslaved by Ephraim Chandler. Chandler was born October 2, 1696, in Andover, the

---

[113] Hall, 19.

[114] Hall, 16.

son of Thomas and Mary (Peters) of Andover. Ephraim married Sarah Adams (Adames) of Chelmsford. Sarah was born April 2, 1697 in Ipswich, MA to Thomas and Bettiah Adams.[115] Their intentions were recorded on June 15, 1724.[116] They had two children, Sarah (b. October 20, 1724) and Phoebe (b. 1733).

In 1728, Ephraim was admitted to the table at Church, by a letter of dismission from Reading.[117] A letter of dismissal releases membership from one church so the person is able to join another.

According to Bill Prescott, Ephraim Chandler lived on the east side of Tyngsboro Road just north of the intersection of Flushing Pond Road.[118] The family genealogy states that Chandler lived on a farm about two miles north of the Westford Depot, where William Chandler lived. He's listed on Hodgman's "1730" map on the northeast side of Long Sought For Pond, where Summer Village now is. Hodgman places his property northwest of Flushing Pond. According to a family genealogy, Ephraim was a tanner.

The family genealogy also states Ephraim enlisted in Captain John Shepley's company against the Spaniards in the West Indies. The date given is June 26, 1724 and also states Ephraim was 24 years old. In 1724, he would have been 28 years old, so the enlistment record is incorrect. This would also have been 11 days after he filed marriage intentions with Sarah and a few months before his first daughter was born. Men from Massachusetts participated in the Cartagena expedition in the Spanish West Indies of 1740 during the War of Jenkins Ear (1739-1742).[119] Shepley's company may have been one of these.

---

[115]Ipswich *Town Records*, Book 1 1664-1734, 24. https://www.familysearch.org/ark:/61903/3:1:3QS7-8979-M96T-4?view=index&personArk=%2Fark%3A%2F61903%2F1%3A1%3AQG1V-R3C9&action=view Accessed 5 May 2024.

[116] *Chelmsford Vital Records*, 204

[117] Hall, 20.

[118] Prescott, *Map of Westford in 1730.*

[119] George Chandler, *The Chandler Family. The Descendents of William and Annis Chandler who settled in Roxbury, Mass 1637,* Press of C.

Soon thereafter, Ephraim enslaved a man named George, as evidenced by the 1741 baptism record. Could Ephraim have brought George back from the West Indies?

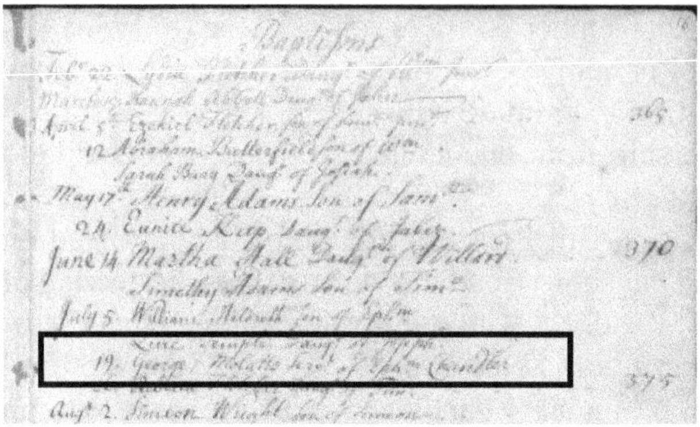

Ephraim died intestate in May 1767. His wife, Abigail, made her mark on the document, naming Mr. Thomas Lund as administrator as she was of old age. Lund is listed as, "heir at law." Among Ephraim's inventory was flax and a loom, wooden measures, troughs, cider casks, grindstone, cider mill, iron, oxen, cows, heifers, and sheep. His personal estate totaled £ 44 14 pence. His real estate (lands and buildings) totaled £ 123.[120] The list of Ephraim's possessions provides an idea of what George may have done for labor, like cider pressing, animal care, and preparing flax for linen.

No other records for George could be found at this time.

Hamilton: Worcester, MA, 1883. Accessed 3 Mar 2024. https://archive.org/details/chandlerfamilyde00chan/page/72/mode/2up?q=ephraim

120 *Middlesex County, MA: Probate File Papers, 1648-1871.*Online database. *AmericanAncestors.org.* New England Historic Genealogical Society, 2014. (From records supplied by the Massachusetts Supreme Judicial Court Archives. Digitized images provided by FamilySearch.org) https://www.americanancestors.org/DB536/rd/14461/4248-co1/263806861

Ishmael

Ishmael was baptized June 5, 1743.[121] He was enslaved by Reverend Willard Hall. He is listed as a negro and is included in the 1754 Slave Census. There are no tax records for Willard Hall to verify dates.

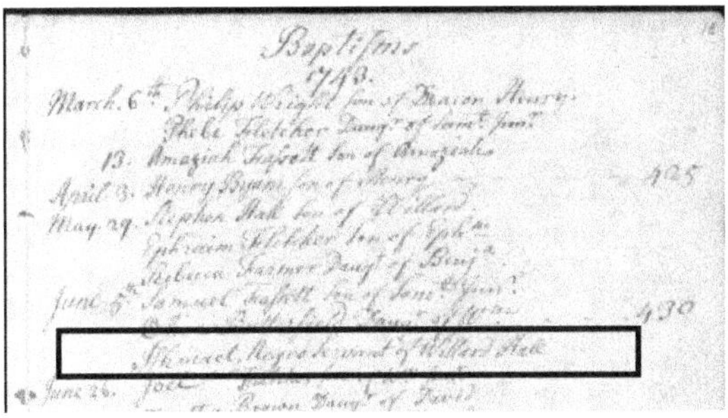

Baptisms
1743.

However, there is mention of Ishmael once in the Town Records. This is the only *official* mention of slavery in our Town Records. Dated February 12, 1753, the town Selectmen ordered the town treasurer, Ephraim Hildreth, to "...pay to Mr. Craft, the sum of eight shillings and eight pence for corn he bought of Mr. Hall's Negro man servant."[122]

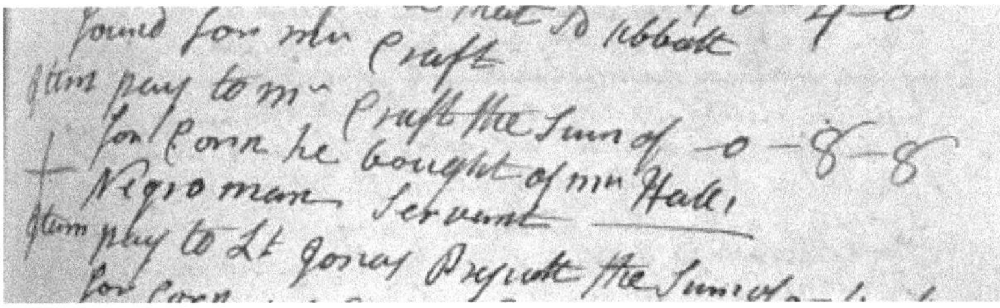

Item pay to mr Craft the Sum of 0-8-8
for Corn he bought of mr Hall,
Negro man Servant

As Reverend Hall likely would have baptized any enslaved people in his house, we can confirm Ishmael as one of the enslaved in the 1754 census. No other records could be found at this time.

[121] Hall, 18.

[122] Westford Town Records, Volume 1, 285.

Prince Read

Prince, a child, was baptized September 4, 1743.[123] In the Church book, he is listed as, "negro child of John Read," as well as in Westford Vital Records which refers back to the Church Book (C.R. 1).

John Read was born in 1685 in Chelmsford. He married Jane Chamberlain. They wed in Charlestown, MA, on January 10, 1706-7. Their children were Samuel (b. 1711), Thomas (b. 1713), William (b. 1715), Jane (b. 1717), Sarah (b. 1719), Betsy (b. 1721), Hannah (b. 1723), Lucy (b. 1727), and Jacob (b. ?).[124]

Hodgman places his property in Westford near E.J. Whitney. The 1730 map shows John Read near present day Robbins Road. Prescott's research places Read on the Southwest side of Concord Road and Littleton Road about 500 feet east of where Concord Road splits southerly from Littleton Road.[125] This is near present day Powers Road, the Olde Boston Square, and Sugar Maple Lane.

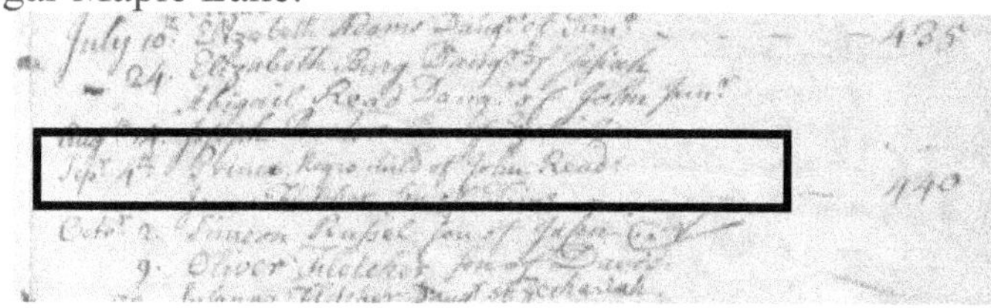

123 Hall, 18.

124 Hodgman, 470.

125 Prescott, *Map of Westford in 1730.*

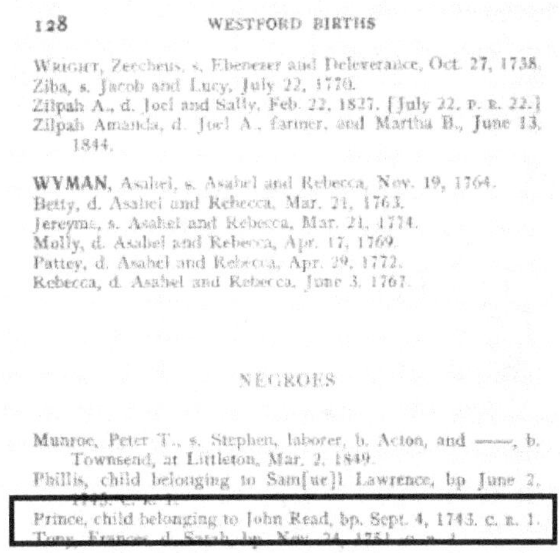
128 WESTFORD BIRTHS

WRIGHT, Zeccheus, s. Ebenezer and Deleverance, Oct. 27, 1738.
Ziba, s. Jacob and Lucy, July 22, 1770.
Zilpah A., d. Joel and Sally, Feb. 22, 1827. [July 22, P. R. 22.]
Zilpah Amanda, d. Joel A., farmer, and Martha B., June 13, 1844.

WYMAN, Asahel, s. Asahel and Rebecca, Nov. 19, 1764.
Betty, d. Asahel and Rebecca, Mar. 21, 1763.
Jereyms, s. Asahel and Rebecca, Mar. 21, 1774.
Molly, d. Asahel and Rebecca, Apr. 17, 1769.
Pattey, d. Asahel and Rebecca, Apr. 29, 1772.
Rebecca, d. Asahel and Rebecca, June 3, 1767.

NEGROES

Munroe, Peter T., s. Stephen, laborer, b. Acton, and ——, b. Townsend, at Littleton, Mar. 2, 1849.
Phillis, child belonging to Sam[ue]l Lawrence, bp June 2, [illegible]
Prince, child belonging to John Read, bp. Sept. 4, 1743. C. R. 1.
[illegible]

Vital Records of Westford, Massachusetts to 1849, 128

This wording on the baptism record leads one to believe Prince was a small child, perhaps a newborn. The words "child belonging to" can mean the Prince's father was John or Prince was born with slave status. Prince is not listed as a mulatto, so likely Prince was born with slave status. To whom was he born? Did John Read enslave a woman? Who could the father be? Did John Read actually enslave three people? John Read was assessed for a slave in 1757 and 1758.

John died intestate on January 17, 1767. Jane left her mark on the probate note, indicating she could not write. She said her old age prohibited her from administering his estate and named Samuel Read, the eldest son, as the administrator. Presumably a farmer, John had calves, heifers, block ox, and swine in his probate inventory. Among other things, there was a loom, woolen wheel, and a walking cane. The probate also mentioned his dwelling and about 3 acres of land on the north side of the highway. The probate appears to list 80 acres of land with a barn on the south side of the highway. These were valued at £356. The distribution of his estate was still in process when Jane died, causing them to redistribute the real estate that was promised to her. John and Jane are buried in Westlawn Cemetery in Westford.

Due to the difference of about ten years between the last tax assessment and John's death, one can assume Prince was still enslaved at the time of John's death.

There are few records for Prince Read and no burial information. This assumes he continued using that given name. However, a Prince Read appears in Boston records as a city resident.

On March 6, 1775[126], a Prince Read, Prince Hall, and twelve other emancipated Black men were made Masons as part of Lodge No. 441. Masons were still under the British Order of Masons, but when the British left Boston, Hall, Read, and the others were allowed to form a lodge with *limited* privileges. In 1775, Westford's Prince Read would have been about 32 years old and of a good age to move to Boston and join a lodge. By 1779, there were thirty-three Masons on the rolls. On September 29, 1784 the Lodge, then called African Lodge No. 459, was given a Charter with *all* of the rights and privileges.[127] In 1791, a Prince Rees was named Grand Tiler for the lodge.[128]

A record for a Prince Reed/Rees [sic] exists in the Thwing Collection at the Massachusetts Historical Society. In the index area, there is a Code A which means that this Prince was African American. The reference number is 47956.[129] Attempts were made to contact the Prince Hall Masonic Lodge with no response. In 1869, a fire at the Massachusetts Grand

---

126 The Thwing Collection records this date as 1778 (see note 127), but makes more sense to be 1775.

127 Yawu Miller, "Black Masons Owe Lineage to 18th Century Pioneer Prince Hall," *Bay State Banner*, February 8, 2017. https://baystatebanner.com/2017/02/08/black-masons-owe-lineage-to-18th-century-boston-pioneer-prince-hall/

128 William H. Grimshaw, *Official History of Freemasonry Among the Colored People in North America,* New York: Broadway Publishing Company, 1903, 84.

129 Boston, MA: Inhabitants and Estates of the Town of Boston, 1630-1822 (Thwing Collection). *Inhabitants and Estates of the Town of Boston, 1630–1800 and The Crooked and Narrow Streets of Boston, 1630–1822.* CD-ROM. Boston, Mass.: New England Historic Genealogical Society, 2001. (Online database. *AmericanAncestors.org*. New England Historic Genealogical Society, 2014.) https://www.americanancestors.org/DB530/i/14226/15279/260131498

Lodge Headquarters destroyed many records. No other records for Prince Reed could be found at this time.

Dinah Hall

Dinah was baptized on March 3, 1745.[130] She was the other enslaved person in Reverend Willard Hall's house. She is listed as a "maid servant." She is included on the 1754 Slave Census. There are no tax records for Willard Hall.

Littleton Town Records show that on March 13, 1788, Dinah Hall, a middle aged "Negro woman" was buried.[131] If Dinah was born in 1729 (16 in 1745), then in 1788 she would have been 59 years old, certainly "middle age." This Dinah, enslaved in Westford by Reverend Hall, likely moved to Littleton after Hall was dismissed from his duties as Minister in 1775 or after his death in 1779. No other records for Dinah could be found at this time.

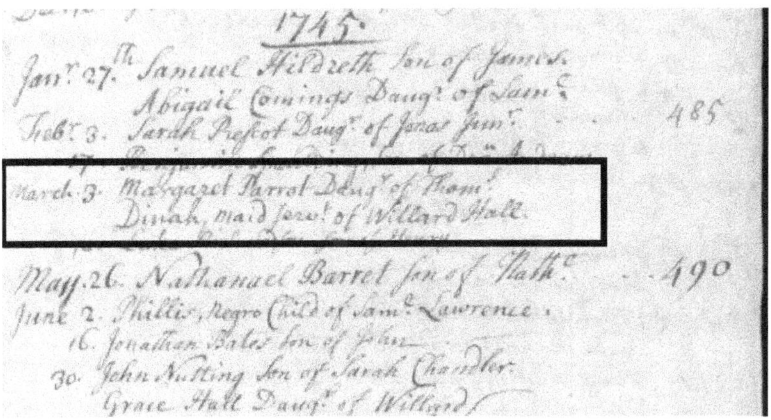
1745

Jan.^r 27.th Samuel Hildreth Son of James
Abigail Comings Daug.^r of Saml
Feb.^r 3. Sarah Prescot Daug.^r of Jonas Junr 485

March 3. Margaret Barrot Daug.^r of Thom.^s
Dinah, maid Servt of Willard Hall

May 26. Nathanael Barret Son of Nathl 490
June 2. Phillis, Negro Child of Saml Lawrence
16. Jonathan Bales Son of John
30. John Nutting Son of Sarah Chandler
Grace Hall Daug.^r of Willard

---

130 Hall, 110.

131 Littleton Town Records, 339.

Phillis Lawrence

Phillis was baptized on June 2, 1745.[132] She is listed as the "negro child" of Samuel Lawrence in Hall's Church Book as well as in Westford Vital Records which refers back to the Church Book (C.R. 1). It's unclear, but there is a possibility that she is Samuel's daughter. More likely, she was born to a woman enslaved in Samuel's house.

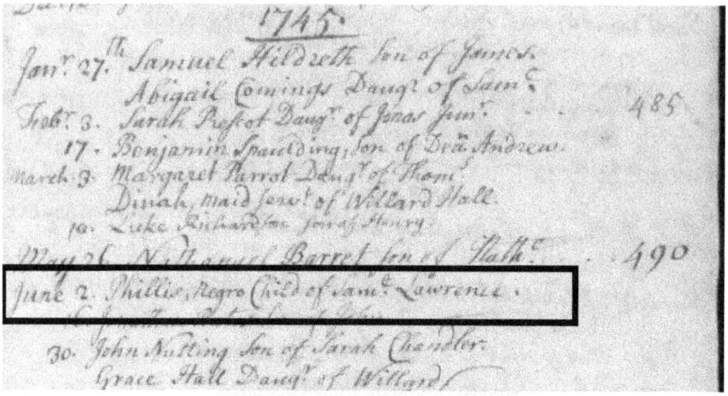

1745.

Jan.r 27.th Samuel Hildreth Son of James.
Abigail Comings Daug.t of Sam.l
Feb.r 3. Sarah Prescot Daug.r of Jonas jun.r 485
17. Benjamin Spaulding, Son of Dea. Andrew.
March 3. Margaret Parrot Daug.t of Thom.
Dinah, maid Serv.t of Willard Hall.
10. Luke Richardson Son of Henry.
May 26. Nathaniel Barret Son of Nath.l 490
June 2. Phillis, Negro Child of Sam.l Lawrence.
30. John Nutting Son of Sarah Chandler.
Grace Hall Daug.t of Willard

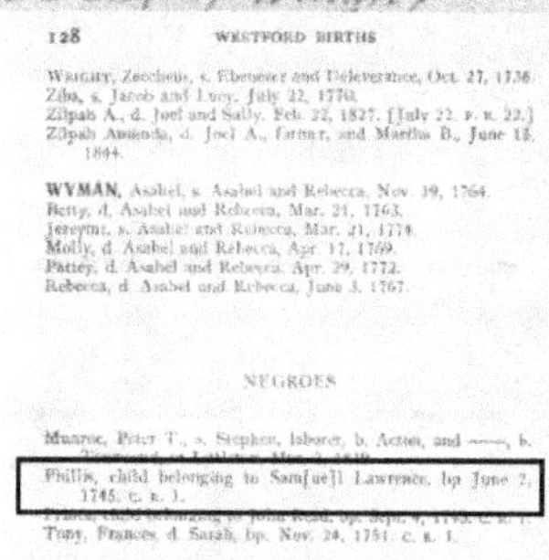

128 WESTFORD BIRTHS

WRIGHT, Zacheus, s. Ebenezer and Deliverance, Oct. 27, 1736.
Ziba, s. Jacob and Lucy, July 22, 1770.
Zilpah A., d. Joel and Sally, Feb. 22, 1827. [July 22. P. R. 22.]
Zilpah Amanda, d. Joel A., farmer, and Martha B., June 13, 1844.

WYMAN, Asahel, s. Asahel and Rebecca, Nov. 19, 1764.
Betty, d. Asahel and Rebecca, Mar. 21, 1763.
Jeremiah, s. Asahel and Rebecca, Mar. 21, 1774.
Molly, d. Asahel and Rebecca, Apr. 17, 1769.
Pattey, d. Asahel and Rebecca, Apr. 29, 1772.
Rebecca, d. Asahel and Rebecca, June 3, 1767.

NEGROES

Munroe, Peter T., s. Stephen, laborer, b. Acton, and ——, b.
Phillis, child belonging to Sam[ue]l Lawrence, bp. June 2, 1745. C. R. 1.
Tony, Frances, d. Sarah, bp. Nov. 24, 1751. C. R. 1.

Vital Records of Westford, Massachusetts to 1849, 128

Samuel Lawrence was the youngest son of Major Eleazar Lawrence and was born May 7, 1714 in Littleton. The land he grew up on in Littleton was purchased from Nashoba Praying Indian tribe by Peleg Lawrence and was on the land between Spectacle and Forge Ponds. Samuel Lawrence married Mary Hildreth on May 6, 1737 in Westford. He became a voter in

132 Hall, 110.

Littleton in 1738, then settled in Westford.[133] His name appears on the tax records for the "North List" in Westford, but never taxed for a slave. Mary's parents were Joseph and Deliverance Hildreth, the enslavers of Peggy. Mary, born in 1718, was a teenager when Peggy was in their household.

After the death of Mary in 1788, Samuel removed to Ashby where his sons Samuel Jr., and Charles were living."[134] Samuel died the following April. His Probate is dated April 25, 1789 in Ashby with Samuel and Charles listed as administrators. According to the probate papers, it appears Samuel was a farmer, with land in Boxborough as well as Ashby. He died intestate. It also appears that at the time of his death, he was unable to pay the debts that he owed. There is no mention of Phillis in his probate. Slavery was outlawed in the Commonwealth in 1780. There are some stories of formerly enslaved people suing their enslaver for past wages. Presumably, Phillis was still alive in 1789 and she did not claim to have any debts needing to be paid from Lawrence's estate. Instead of removing to Ashby with Samuel, Phillis likely stayed in the Westford area, where she was comfortable with the terrain and people.

On a death record from Groton dated 1879, Rosilla (Tuttle) Hazzard died at 98 years, 6 months, and 8 days old. It lists parents, Phillis, who was born in Littleton, and Titus Tuttle. It lists Littleton as Rosilla's birthplace. [135] Littleton Town Records show Phillis Lawrence marrying Titus Tuttle.[136] Their

---

133 Robert M. Lawrence, M.D., Historical Sketches of some members of the Lawrence Family. With An Appendix., Boston: Rand Avery Company. 1888, 29-35.
https://ia800501.us.archive.org/17/items/historicalsketch1888lawr/historicalsketch1888lawr.pdf

134 "Samuel Lawrence Sr 1714- bef. 1789," accessed August 10, 2023. https://www.wikitree.com/wiki/Lawrence-4624

135 "Massachusetts Deaths, 1841-1915, 1921-1924," images, *FamilySearch* (https://familysearch.org/ark:/61903/3:1:S3HY-XCZ7-SC2?cc=1463156&wc=MJZM-MNL%3A1043012301 : 13 December 2022), 0960216 (004221431) > image 495 of 743; State Archives, Boston.

136 "Massachusetts, Town Clerk, Vital and Town Records, 1626-2001," *FamilySearch* (https://www.familysearch.org/ark:/61903/1:1:QG1K-

intentions were filed December 18, 1794 and they were married on January 6, 1797. Rosilla's birthday, if correct, places her with a birth year of 1781. This means Phillis would have given birth in her late 30s and before she married Titus. No other records for Phillis could be found at this time.

Cesar Negro

Cesar was baptized on May 4, 1746.[137] This is our first record of him. He was enslaved by Gershom Fletcher.

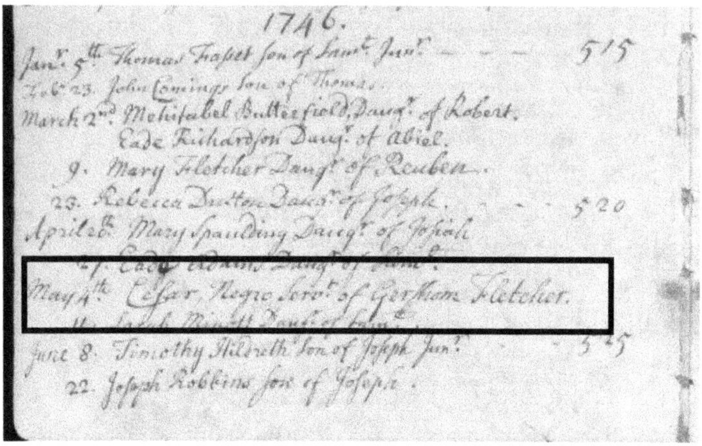
1746.
Janr. 5th Thomas Tarbell son of Saml. Junr. — 5/5
Feb. 23. John Cummings son of Thomas.
March 2nd. Mehitabel Butterfield Daugr. of Robert.
Eade Richardson Daugr. of Abiel.
9. Mary Fletcher Daugr. of Reuben.
23. Rebecca Dutton Daugr. of Joseph. 5/20
April 20th Mary Spaulding Daugr. of Josiah
27. [illegible]
May 4th. Cesar, Negro Servt. of Gershom Fletcher.
11. [illegible]
June 8. Timothy Hildreth son of Joseph Junr. 5/25
22. Joseph Robbins son of Joseph.

Gershom Fletcher was born in Chelmsford on July 27, 1712, the son of Joshua and Dorothy Fletcher. According to probate documents, upon his father Joshua's death in 1732, Captain Jonas Prescott was named Gershom's guardian.[138] Joshua's estate totaled over 300 acres. Gerhsom was 20 years

---

6KTQ : Sat Mar 09 13:31:58 UTC 2024), Entry for Titus Tuttle and Phillis Lawrence, 6 January 1797.

137 Hall, 111.

138 Middlesex County, MA: Probate File Papers, 1648-1871.Online database. AmericanAncestors.org. New England Historic Genealogical Society, 2014. (From records supplied by the Massachusetts Supreme Judicial Court Archives. Digitized images provided by FamilySearch.org) https://www.americanancestors.org/DB536/i/14471/7876-co2/38245472

old. Two daughters apparently stayed with Dorothy Fletcher. His sister Sarah went under the guardianship of Timothy Heald.

Joshua died intestate. Dorothy was given her widow's thirds. Gershom was given, besides many acres of land, "the West end of the dwelling hous and the westerly half part of the back Leanto with Liberty of door room and stair room." The land given to Gershom in his father's estate is tricky to pinpoint, but there are some mentions of land north of "the Groton Road."[139]

Gershom Fletcher married Lydia Townsend on May 28, 1733. Lydia was daughter of Ebenezer Townsend whose land was annexed to Westford from Groton in 1730. The connections to Captain Prescott and Ebenezer Townsend lend itself to Gershom and Lydia settling in the Forge Village area of town. Hodgman notes that they at one time did live in Groton, perhaps before the annexation.[140] Gershom was a farmer, with cows and horses.

Gershom was assessed for a slave 1757-1763. Cesar was one of the enslaved men counted on the 1754 census.

Hodgman noted that Cesar served in Captain Daniel Fletcher's company in 1759 for the reduction of Canada.[141] It is unclear if he enlisted or was sent in place of Gershom. Cesar's name appears as Cezar Negro on this Muster Roll for Daniel Fletcher's company.

---

139 Middlesex County, MA: Probate File Papers, 1648-1871.Online database. AmericanAncestors.org. New England Historic Genealogical Society, 2014. (From records supplied by the Massachusetts Supreme Judicial Court Archives. Digitized images provided by FamilySearch.org) https://www.americanancestors.org/DB536/i/14471/7875-co42/38245465

140 Hodgman, 446.

141 Hodgman, 64.

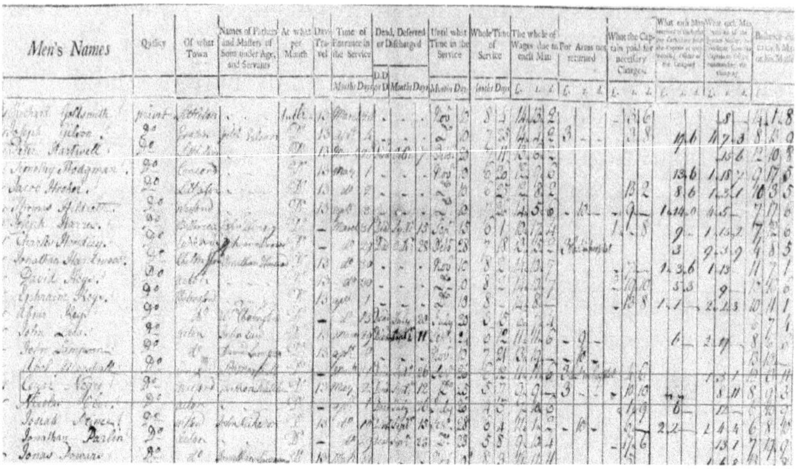

He is listed as a Private. Under "Names of Fathers and Masters of Sons under Age, and servants," Gershom Fletcher's name is given.

Cesar entered the company on May 2, 1759. He had 13 days of travel. He was discharged in September after 5 months and 7 days of service. His wages were £9, 9 shilling. For Arms not returned, he has £3. The Captain paid 10 shilling 10 d. for "necessary charges." Cesar did not receive anything from the Commanding Officer, but received 8 shillings 11 d. For "Balance due to each Man or his Master," Cesar was owed £8 9 shilling and 3d. It's unclear if Cesar received this money or if it went to Gershom. This is where the historical record for Cesar ends.

According to some genealogies of Plymouth, New Hampshire, Gershom moved there in 1770 and was continually taxed until his death. He was a farmer there, and bought and sold many tracts of land. He was apparently a wealthy man there. There is no mention of enslaving anyone.[142]

---

142 Ezra S. Stearns, History of Plymouth NH, Vol. II Genealogies, University Press, Cambridge, MA 1906, 270. https://books.google.com/books?id=KTETAAAAYAAJ&pg=PA296&lpg=PA296&dq=john+haselton+history+of+plymouth+nh&source=bl&ots=1B4

Gershom still was a landowner in Westford in the 1770s and was involved in settling his mother's estate for her third of Joshua's land.

In emails to the Plymouth Historical Society, President Stacey Yap wrote that there was no indication that Gershom Fletcher had an enslaved man there as there was only one confirmed enslaver, Colonel David Webster.[143]

Gershom Fletcher died on June 28, 1779, while visiting Westford. We can assume then, that Cesar was no longer enslaved by Gershom Fletcher by 1770. Perhaps he self-emancipated, perhaps Gershom emancipated him, perhaps he died. No other records can be found at this time.

Sarah and Frances Tony

On November 24, 1751, Sarah Tony was written in Reverend Hall's book for "Penitents Reformed." She was admitted to the Covenant.[144] Her baptism, and Frances Tony's were also recorded by Reverend Hall on this date.[145]

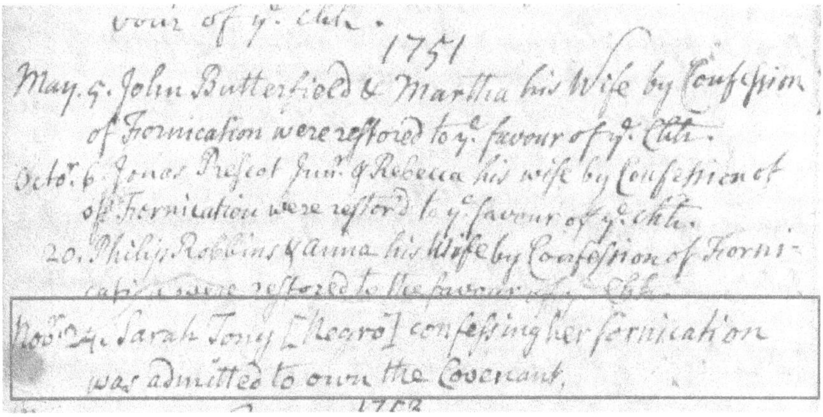
vour of ye Chh.
1751
May. 5. John Butterfield & Martha his Wife by Confession of Fornication were restored to ye favour of ye Chh.
Octor. 6. Jonas Prescot Junr. & Rebecca his wife by Confession of Fornication were restor'd to ye favour of ye Chh.
20. Philip Robbins & Anna his Wife by Confession of Fornication were restored to the favour of ye Chh.
Novr. 24. Sarah Tony [Negro] confessing her fornication was admitted to own the Covenant.
1752

wbpaon1&sig=ACfU3U0900M-r5jQpL6CKS1wRTivINrhaA&hl=en&sa=X&ved=2ahUKEwiCmMu-6_LxAhV_F1kFHZYACZgQ6AEwB3oECAkQAw#v=onepage&q=john%20haselton%20history%20of%20plymouth%20nh&f=false

143 Stacey Yap Email to Author. 3 November 2023.

144 Hall, 73.

145 Hall, 118.

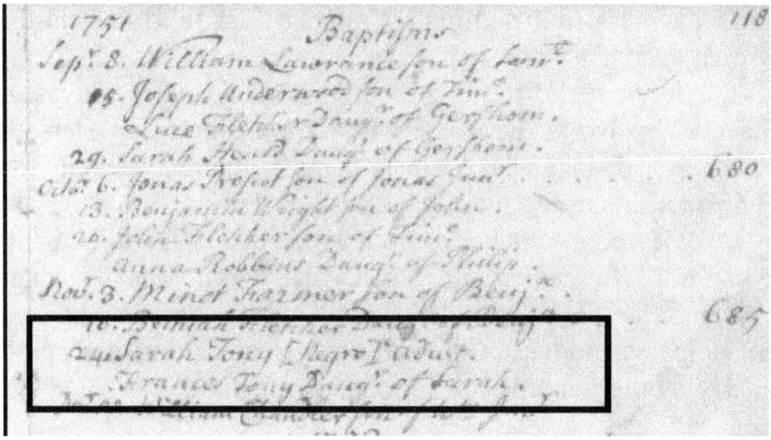

1751 Baptisms 118
Sepr. 8. William Laurance son of Saml.
15. Joseph Underwood son of Timo.
Luce Fletcher Daugr. of Gershom.
29. Sarah Heald Daugr. of Gershom.
Octr. 6. Jonas Prescot son of Jonas Junr. 680
13. Benjamin Wright son of John.
20. John Fletcher son of Timo.
Anna Robbins Daugr. of Philip.
Novr. 3. Minot Farmer son of Benjn.
10. [illegible] Fletcher Daugr. of [illegible] 685
24. Sarah Tony [Negro] Adult.
Frances Tony Daugr. of Sarah.
Decr. 22. William Chandler son of [illegible]

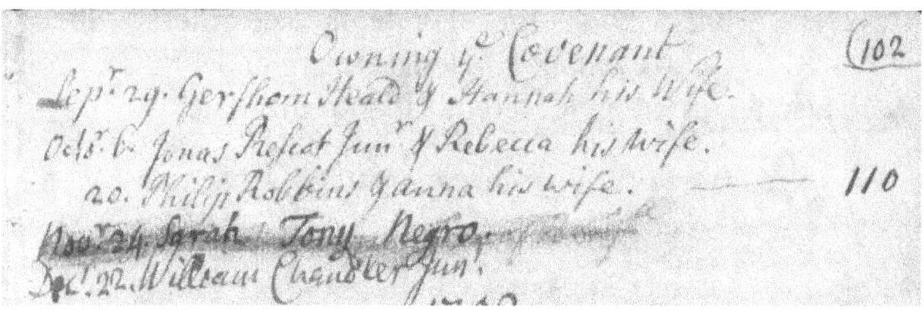

Owning ye Covenant 102
Sepr. 29. Gershom Heald & Hannah his Wife.
Octr. 6. Jonas Prescot Junr. & Rebecca his wife.
20. Philip Robbins & Anna his wife. 110
Novr. 24. Sarah Tony Negro.
Decr. 22. William Chandler Junr.

Hodgman surmises that Sarah and Frances were servants in Enoch Cleveland's household.[146] There is no written evidence to indicate that Enoch was an enslaver. Sarah's baptism is not listed as "servant of…" That does not mean that there wasn't a relationship, working or otherwise, especially considering her confession of fornication and the land in Providence Meadow. Cleveland lived near an old mill site in Providence Meadow (west of the current Providence Road and south of Leland Road). There is an "island" rising 14 feet in the middle of the marsh that is known as "Tony's Island."[147] If Sarah and her daughter were warned out, perhaps they were emancipated and were squatting

146 Hodgman, 72-73.

147 Hodgman, 72-73. See also Oliphant, *The Westford Gazetteer*, 275.

on that land. A 2024 visit to that land showed evidence of rock walls.[148]

In 1751, Enoch Cleaveland's name appeared on a petition to the Commonwealth of Massachusetts for aid.[149] His name is also listed for Jonathan Cleaveland who was deceased. Jonathan fought in Captain Gershom Davis's company in Louisburg. According to Hodgman, Jonathan Cleaveland may have been the son of Samuel Cleaveland who lived "near the old mill-site" in Providence Meadow.[150] It appears serving the country left Enoch without the ability to support himself.

Enoch Cleaveland was warned out of town in 1751, along with Sarah Tony and her child.[151] It's unclear if the warning out happened before or after the Baptism and Penitents Reformed. They were also warned out with Hannah Kibbery, another suspected enslaved woman in town.[152]

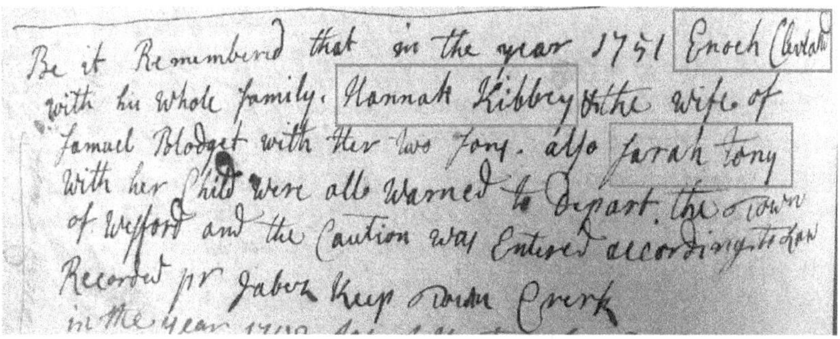
Be it Remembred that in the year 1751 Enoch Clevland
with his whole family. Hannah Kibbey & the wife of
Samuel Blodget with Her two Tony. also Sarah tony
with her Child were all Warned to Depart the town
of Westford and the Caution was Entered according to Law
Recorded pr Jabez Keep Town Clerk
in the year [illegible]

Cleaveland may not have been a Westford resident, but his marriage intentions to Martha Butterfield were filed in Westford on Jan 20, 1753. However, he was listed as a Chelmsford resident. Their son, Enoch Cleaveland Jr., was born at Westford on July 26, 1754. He is not on the 1774 Westford tax return. No other records could be found at this time.

---

148 Mike Presti, text message with author, July 20, 2024.

149 Hodgman, 56.

150 Hodgman, 33.

151 Westford Town Records, Volume 1, 272.

152 http://54lowellroad.com/index_files/Page583.htm

Dinah

Dinah was baptized on May 29, 1757.[153] She was enslaved by Moses Parker. Her skin color is not noted.

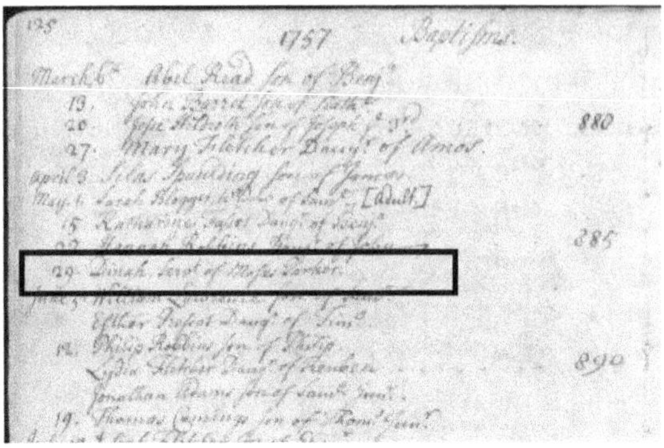
1757 Baptisms

29 Dinah Servt of Moses Parker.

Moses was born to Aaron and Abigail Parker on May 16, 1718. Abigail Hildreth was Moses's grandmother. He married Bridget Cummings (b. 1722) in 1744. Bridget's brother was Ephraim Cummings, another enslaver. Moses Parker of Westford served in the American Revolution. Moses Parker is not listed as an enslaver on the 1771 tax list. If accurate, Dinah was either emancipated or died. His real estate holdings are quite large (about 35 acres), with an ironworks, 1 horse, 4 oxen, 5 cows, and 3 swine. He produced 14 tons of fresh meadow hay, 150 barrels of grain, and 5 barrels of cider.

Bridget died on October 19, 1778. Moses filed intentions to marry widow Anna Barrett on August 20, 1779 in Westford. Moses died July 13, 1797. No probate could be found.

According to *The Hildreths of Westford*, Parker was at the Old North Bridge and also at the Battle of Bunker Hill. He was wounded and taken prisoner at Bunker Hill. He died in a military prison on July 4, 1775. *That* Moses Parker was born in Chelmsford and is *not the same* as this Moses Parker.[154] No other records could be found at this time.

---

153 Hall, 125.

154 See J.L. Bell's blog posts: https://boston1775.blogspot.com/2017/06/remembering-moses-parker.html, https://boston1775.blogspot.com/2017/06/moses-parker-and-his-comrades-in-redoubt.html, https://boston1775.blogspot.com/2017/06/moses-parker-most-prominent-military.html

Jethro Wilkins

Jethro was baptized on November 26, 1758.[155] He was enslaved by Abner Wilkins. He is not listed as a child, so we can assume he is at least 16 years old, born about 1742.

All that can be found so far as a location for Wilkins' property, is that in 1757, Abner was on Westford's North Tax list. Abner is not listed as an enslaver on the 1771 Tax Inventory. Taxpayers reported Servants for Life in 1771 if the enslaved was between the ages of 14 and 45. If Jethro was born in 1742, age 16 at baptism in 1758, then he was 29 in 1771 and *should* be listed. On the 1771 tax inventory, he is listed as Abner Wilking. Some men listed on the tax list are marked as non-residents. This distinction is absent from Wilking's list, so he was probably an actual resident. Wilkins was assessed for a slave in 1773 and 1775.

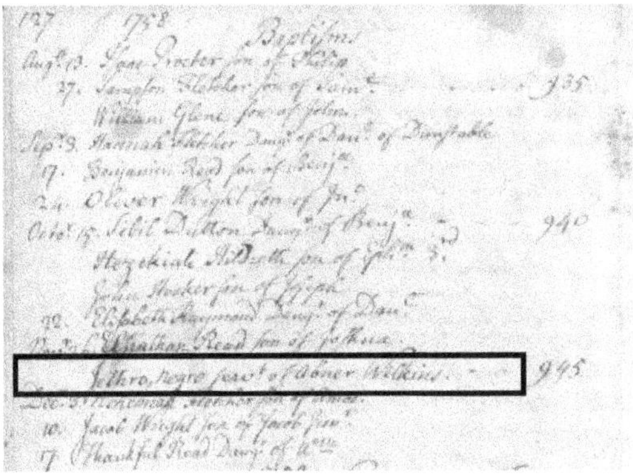

In 1774, Abner Wilkins was listed as the 131st out of 200 wealthiest men in Westford. Abner also signed the 1774 Solemn League and Covenant. Abner is not listed in the 1790 census for Westford. No death or burial information could be found.

155 Hall, 127.

There is a listing for Jethro Wilkins in *Massachusetts Soldiers and Sailors of the Revolutionary War.*

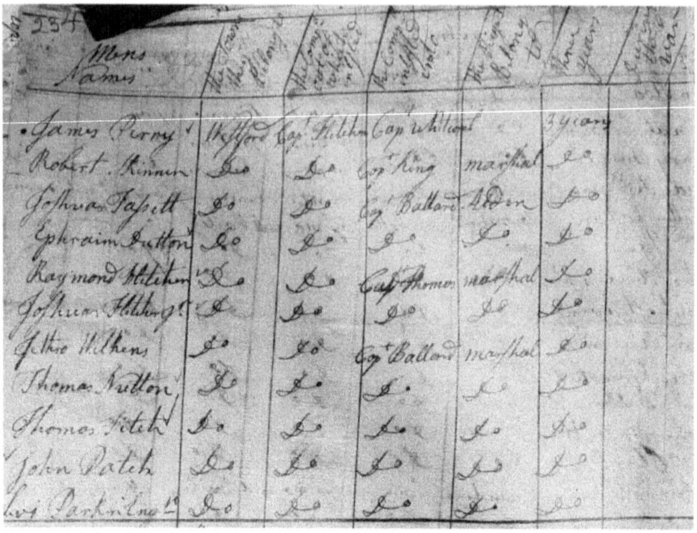

Mens Names						
James Perry	Westford	Capt Fletcher	Cap Whitney		3 years	
Robert Kinnen	Do	Do	Capt King	Marshal	Do	
Joshua Fassett	Do	Do	Capt Ballard	Alden	Do	
Ephraim Dutton	Do	Do	Do	Do	Do	
Raymond Fletcher	Do	Do	Capt Thomas	Marshal	Do	
Joshua Fletcher	Do	Do	Do	Do	Do	
Jethro Wilkins	Do	Do	Capt Ballard	Marshal	Do	
Thomas Nutton	Do	Do	Do	Do	Do	
Thomas Fitch	Do	Do	Do	Do	Do	
John Patch	Do	Do	Do	Do	Do	
Levi Parkhurst	Do	Do	Do	Do	Do	

This is a record for Jethro's three year "enlistment" on September 17, 1777.[156]

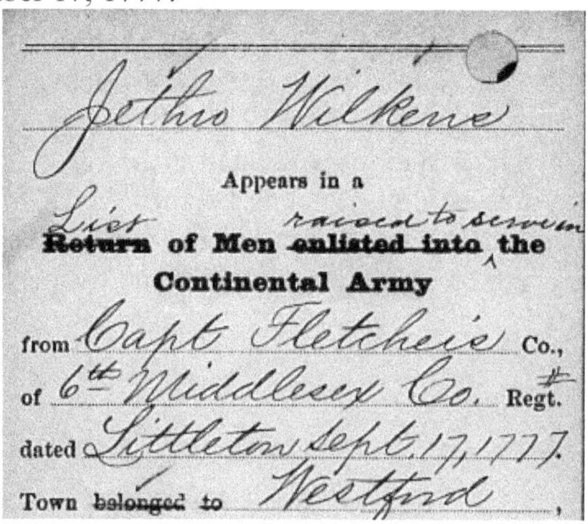

Jethro Wilkens

Appears in a

List of Men ~~enlisted into~~ raised to serve in the

Continental Army

from Capt Fletcher's Co.,

of 6th Middlesex Co. Regt.

dated Littleton Sept. 17, 1777.

Town ~~belonged~~ to Westford,

---

156 Muster/payrolls, and various papers (1763-1808) of the Revolutionary War [Massachusetts and Rhode Island]
Vol. 53, miscellaneous loose rolls, no. 2 1776-1783, 234, image number 591-592.

The index card to this record has "enlisted" crossed out and instead is written, "raised to serve."[157] As Abner's historical record trail ends in 1775 with the tax record, it is likely he died and Jethro likely became a ward of the town. Perhaps the town solved their problem by drafting Jethro to fill their quota of soldiers.

There is a record of him for wages for September 1776 in the late Capt. Butler's, received by Benjamin Heywood, Paymaster of the 4th regiment. The receipt is signed with "his mark."[158]

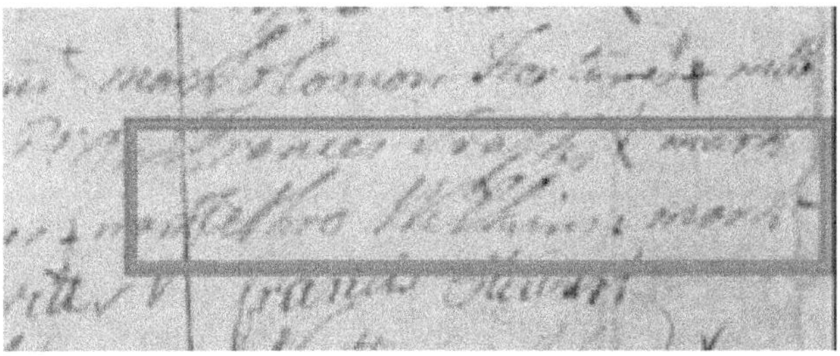

This is his Massachusetts Soldiers and Sailors of the Revolutionary War record:

> *Under Jethro Wilkens*: Westford. List of men raised to serve in the Continental Army from Capt. Fletcher's co., Col. Jonathan Reed's (6th Middlesex Co.) regt., as returned to Brig. Gen. Prescott, dated Littleton, Sept. 17, 1777; residence, Westford; enlisted for town of Westford; joined Capt. Ballard's co., Col. Marshal's (also given Col. Alden's) regt.; enlistment, 3 years.[159]

---

157 "Massachusetts, United States records," images, FamilySearch (https://www.familysearch.org/ark:/61903/3:1:3Q9M-CSQZ-KY5L?view=index : Dec 29, 2024), image 1965 of 2921; Massachusetts. State Archives.

158 Muster/payrolls, and various papers (1763-1808) of the Revolutionary War [Massachusetts and Rhode Island], Vol. 52 (part 2), misc. loose rolls, no. 1 1775-1783, 106-27, image 239.

159 Westford Entries Massachusetts Soldiers and Sailors of the Revolutionary War for https://www.westford.org/westford1775/MSSRW_V_Z.html

The one thing missing from these war records is Jethro's skin color. It can be hard to deny the strong coincidences around the name and timing of his entry into the War. There are instances where skin color was not listed on these records, or the skin was just light enough that the recorder did not write "negro" on the ledger. No Jethro Wilkins appears on tax records or other records in Westford. He was an anomaly for his military service with no other records for birth or death. No records of any kind could be found at this time.

Noble Comings

Noble was baptized on April 19, 1761.[160] He isn't listed as "negro" or "mulatto." However, because Ephraim is later identified as having a "servant for life" the assumption is made that Noble is Black.

Ephraim Comings was born November 13, 1720 in Chelmsford to Deacon John and Elizabeth Cummings. Deacon John Comings lived near Westford Depot at Stony Brook. John married Mary Hildreth October 12, 1742 in Westford. They had children, including a son. Ephraim, Jr. was born on September 6, 1747. His aunt, Bridget, married Moses Parker in 1744. Ephraim, Sr. was likely the enslaver, as Jr. was only 14 years old at the time of Noble's baptism.

Baptisms. 1761 130
Mar. 15. Eunice Prescot Daug.r of David of Groton.
22. Asa Bigsby son of Asa.
29. Andrew Fletcher son of David.
April 19. Noble, Serv.t of Eph.m Comings. 1020
10. Hannah Keyes Daug.r of Jon.a Jr
Anna Prescot Daug.r of Tim.o
June 7. Ephraim Wright son of Eph.m
July 5. Dolly Wright Daug.r of Joseph. 1025

160 Hall, 130.

In the 1771 Massachusetts Tax Inventory, there is only one Ephraim Cummings listed as a taxpayer. One Ephraim was 51 years old, the other was 24 years old. In 1771, Ephraim Comings was listed as having a servant for life. He had an ironworks and several acres of land in town, along with 1 horse, 2 oxen, 4 cows, 10 goats and sheep, and 3 swine. He produced 150 bushels of hay per year and 20 barrels of cider.

CUMINGS, EPH'M Town of Westford, Middlesex County			
Farm Animals/Livestock			
Horses 01	Oxen 02	Cows 4	Goats and Sheep 10
Owns Goats or Sheep Y	Swine 03		
Buildings and Boats			
Dwelling Houses and Shops Adjoining 1	Shops Adjoining 0	Tanhouses -- etc. 0	Stillhouses 0
Warehouses 0	Superficial Feet of Wharf 00000	Gristmills -- etc. 0	Ironworks -- etc. 1
Tons of Vessels			
Land and Agriculture			
Acres of Pasture 12	Number of Cows the Pasture will Keep 7	Acres of Tillage 14	Bushels of Grain Produced per Year 150
Barrels of Cider Produced per Year 020	Acres of Salt Marsh 0	Tons of Salt Marsh Hay per Year 0	Acres of English and Upland Mowing Land 4
Tons of English and Upland Hay Per Year 2	Acres of Fresh Meadow 15	Tons of Fresh Meadow Hay Per Year 15	
General Population Characteristics and Assessed Worth			
Servants for Life 1	Servant Owner Y	Annual worth of the Whole Real Estate (£) 010	Value of Trading Stock (£) 00000
Value of Factorage or Commissions (£) 0000	Value of Money Lent at Interest (£) 00000		

Assuming this was still Noble, then in 1771, Noble was between the ages of 14 and 45, and most likely at least 26 in 1771.

Ephraim, Jr. married Lydia Adams of Chelmsford in 1773. Ephraim signed the Solemn League and Covenant in 1774, it's unclear which Ephraim signed.

Ephraim, Sr. died in January 1775 at 54 years old.

Ephraim, Jr. is listed as a Private under Capt. Timothy Underwood's company in Col. William Prescott's regiment that "marched on the alarm" on April 19, 1775. He served 7 days.

Ephraim, Jr. enlisted in the Continental Army in April 1777. He served as a Private for Captain William Hudson Ballard's company, Colonel Brooks's regiment. He also served in Capt. Ballard's company, and Colonel Ichabod Alden's (6th) regiments. On a Return for Captain William Ballard's Company in 6th Battalion of the late Ichabod Alden, Ephraim is reported dead on August 10, 1777. This return was made on January 12,

1778 in Albany, New York. No further information on his death or burial was found. Records seem to indicate he was not killed in action, but died from another cause. You can see the difference in recording from James Emory at the top, to Ebenezer Porter to Ephraim Cummins.[161]

Ephraim died intestate. His probate is dated 1777 but wasn't complete until 1789. Lydia made her mark as the administrator. It says Ephraim was a yeoman. Among his

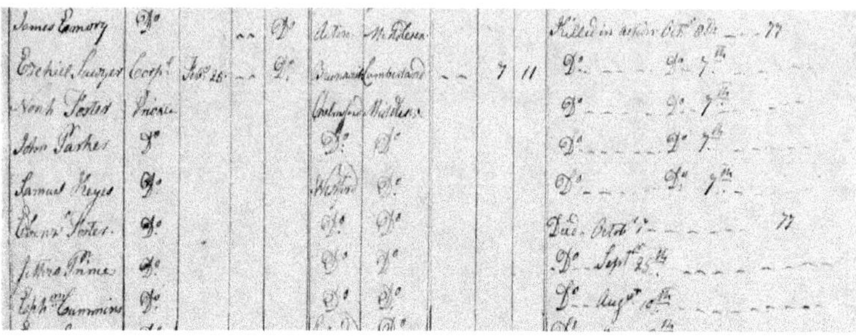

inventory were cider barrels, oxen yoke, and a dung fork. A corn barn is also listed. He owned about 50 acres of land, with a barn and dwelling valued at £250.[162] Moses Burge was compensated £97=14=0=0 for caring for the two small children for "243 weeks" (about 4 years 8 months). Lydia was given her "Widow's Thirds." There is no mention of Noble in the inventory or probate.

In one scenario, Noble from Westford could have been emancipated after Ephraim's death and sought a better life by

161 Muster/payrolls, and various papers (1763-1808) of the Revolutionary War [Massachusetts and Rhode Island]
Vol. 65, Various papers 1775-1783 Vol. 66, Miscellaneous rolls: muster rolls, U.S. Army pensioners 1776-1787 Vol. 67, Muster rolls, officer returns, payrolls 1777-1783 Vol. 68, Muster rolls, returns of companies and of the county militia 1776-1790, image 273.

162 *Middlesex County, MA: Probate File Papers, 1648-1871.*Online database. *AmericanAncestors.org.* New England Historic Genealogical Society, 2014. (From records supplied by the Massachusetts Supreme Judicial Court Archives. Digitized images provided by FamilySearch.org). Case number 5418.
https://www.americanancestors.org/DB536/i/14461/5418-co4/38217691

enlisting in the army. In another scenario, Noble may have seen Ephraim's death as his opportunity to self-emancipate. There are stories from Concord where men left the homes of their enslaver's when the enslaver was off at war, seizing an opportunity.[163] There are also stories from Concord where the enslaver's wife feared for her family's safety without her husband in the house, so they did not pursue the fleeing enslaved person. As Noble was a "servant for life," when Ephraim's life was over (1777), presumably Noble was emancipated.

It's *after* 1777 that records show up for Noble down in Somerset, Massachusetts. Some archival records list Somerset or Swanzey as a birthplace, but no birth record can be found (Somerset broke away from Swansea in 1790). The Somerset area of Massachusetts was known for its progressive views on slavery, perhaps this is what drew him to this area.

A Noble Comings/Cummings appears as enlisting in the Continental Army for a 9 month period of time on August 1, 1779.[164] This Noble does *not* have listed a town from which he enlisted.

---

163 See Lemire, *Black Walden.*

164 Muster/payrolls, and various papers (1763-1808) of the Revolutionary War [Massachusetts and Rhode Island] Vol. 42, Enlistment rolls, bounties, officers 1776-1789, 226. Image 614.

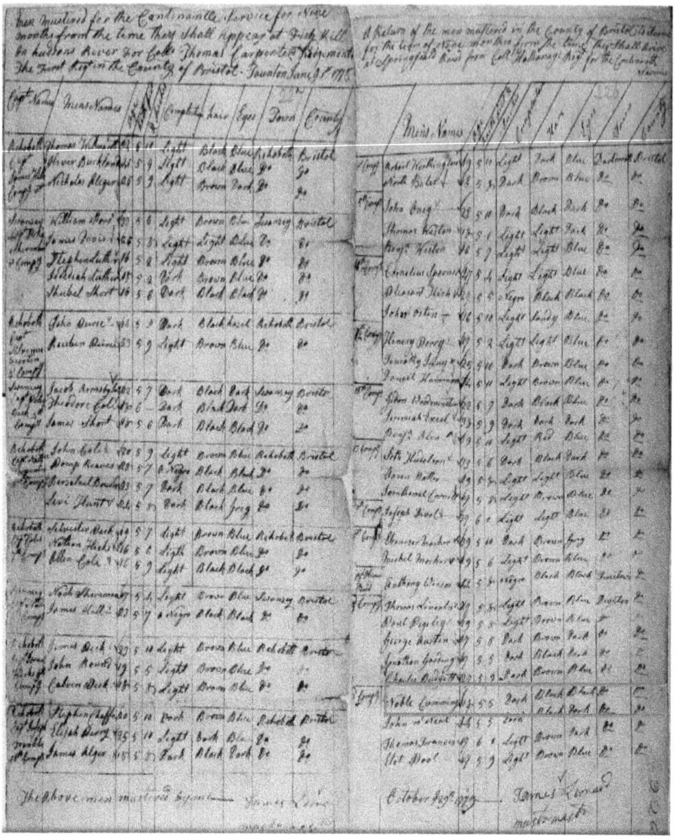

Noble continued to serve in the Army. He was included in the list of men raised from Dighton in Bristol County, Massachusetts for 9 months. He marched to Fishkill, arriving on June 17, 1778. He served as a Private in Captain Zebedee Redding's Company in Col. Gamaliel Bradford's Regiment. He also was part of the call for men in 1780. These records all describe him as dark skin, dark hair, and dark eyes. Finally, he was discharged in 1780.

Vital Records indicate that Noble settled in Somerset, Massachusetts and could have married a woman named Rhoda. The death record of Martha Cummings Davis in 1868, lists parents as Noble Cummings and Rhoda, both of Swansea. The listing says Martha was 82 years old, which makes her birth year 1786, and plausible to be Noble's daughter.[165]

Noble applied for a pension. This could have been around 1833. As part of the application, he dictated a testimony on his military record and his need for financial support.[166] This account is heartbreaking for a few reasons. One, he did not write it. He appears to have written his name, but it calls into question the extent of his literacy. He was baptized in Westford, but was he taught to read and write as the tradition of baptism suggests or just enough? He outlines his service and ends with: "I…testify and say that I am in misfortunes and reduced circumstances and am in absolute need of assistance from my country for support. I further testify that my discharge aforementioned is now lost and that it is not in my power at this time to produce it."

---

165 "Massachusetts Deaths, 1841-1915, 1921-1924," images, FamilySearch (https://familysearch.org/ark:/61903/3:1:S3HY-DZCS-HF9?cc=1463156&wc=MJCG-PTL%3A1043009201 : 13 December 2022), 0960192 (004221408) > image 151 of 666; State Archives, Boston.

166 Pension Number: S. 34270 . Case Files of Pension and Bounty-Land Warrant Applications Based on Revolutionary War Service, compiled ca. 1800 - ca. 1912, documenting the period ca. 1775 - ca. 1900. https://www.fold3.com/image/15213354/cummings-noble-page-8-us-revolutionary-war-pensions-1800-1900. Accessed 29 April 2024.

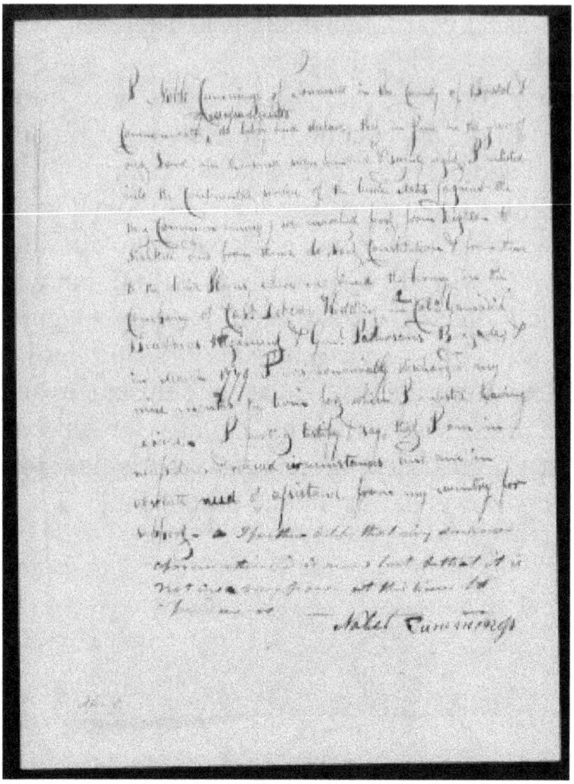

And here is his signature:

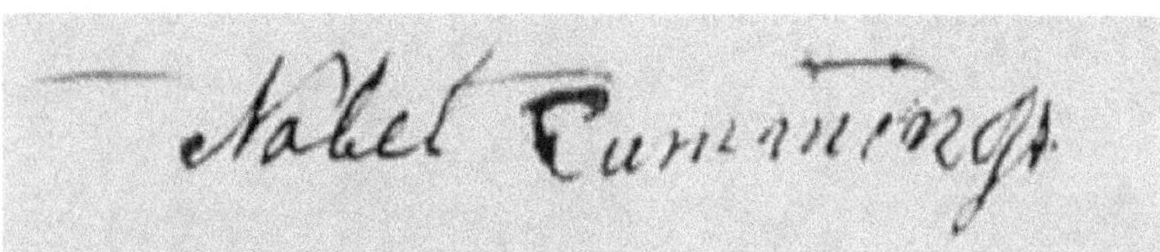

The handwriting is distinctly different three times on this page, so he had some assistance in writing down his testimony. The shakiness of the signature and not “his mark” leads me to believe that this is his actual signature. The second reason this account is heartbreaking is that he experienced further misfortunes in life, after being enslaved and was in absolute need of assistance. Thankfully, Noble was granted a pension.

The 1840 census lists Noble Cummings living with one 60 and one 70 year old woman, back in Somerset. In 1840, his daughter would have been 54 and Rhoda has been shown in census records to be younger than him. He is listed as being 80 years old. His entry includes mention of his Veteran status. Curiously, they are listed as *free white people*. His war records never explicitly state he was Black, or "negro," but they also never explicitly state he was white. In Reverend Hall's book, he is also not listed as "negro." There are stories of mistaken race due to lighter skin color or it depends on the person writing the description. Perhaps this is one of them.

A pension record filed upon Noble's death in 1849, states he was 88 years old placing his birth year in 1761. No parents are listed. The place of birth IS listed as Somerset, but perhaps he just didn't know and Somerset is where he ended up. Noble left the military with the rank of Private as shown by his pension records. He earned 8 dollars a month.[167]

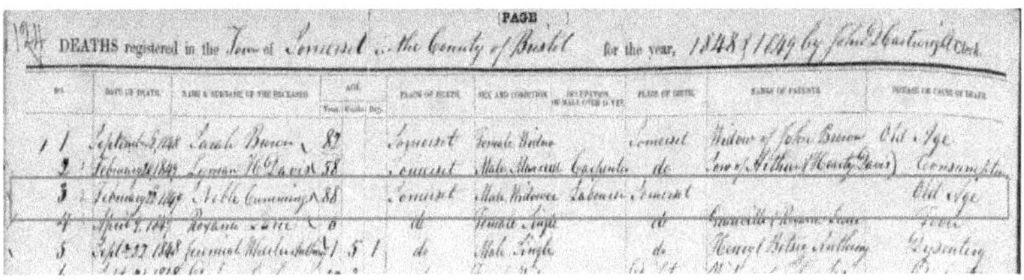
PAGE

DEATHS registered in the Town of Somerset in the County of Bristol for the year, 1848/1849

Noble was baptized in 1761 but was not listed as a child. So, he was either a child and Hall did not record it, or Noble used the 1761 date as his birthday because he had no other information, or these are two different men. He would have been 16 in 1777 when he entered the Revolution. No other records could be found at this time.

167 United States. Military Records, Government Pensions, Image 82. https://www.familysearch.org/ark:/61903/3:1:3QS7-89WB-HSNR?view=index&action=view

Cesar Bason

Cesar's beginnings are unclear. The first mention of him is in 1773 when he was paid 4 shillings for four crows that he killed in town.[168] The town receipt lists "Ceasor Burn" as the recipient.

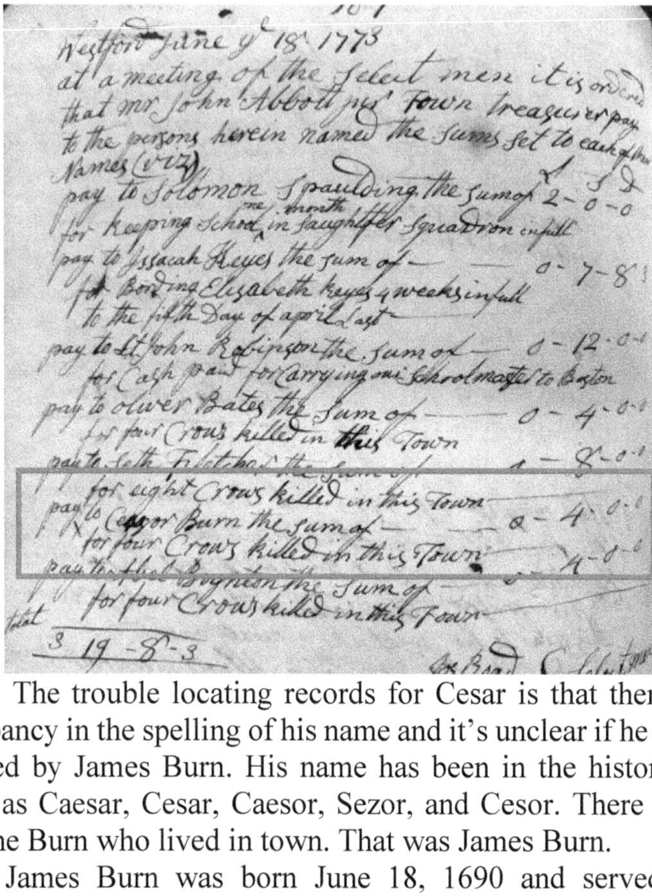
Westford June ye 18 1773
at a meeting of the select men it is ordered
that mr John Abbott now Town treasurer pay
to the persons herein named the sums set to each of their
Names (viz) £ s d
pay to Solomon Spaulding the sum of 2-0-0
for keeping School one month in [illegible] Squadron in full
pay to Issacah Keyes the sum of — 0-7-8
for Bording Elizabeth keyes 4 weeks in full
to the fifth Day of april last
pay to Lt John Robinson the sum of — 0-12-0
for Cash paid for carrying our Schoolmaster to Boston
pay to oliver Bates the sum of — 0-4-0
for four Crows killed in this Town
pay to Seth Fletcher the sum of — 0-8-0
for eight Crows killed in this Town
pay to Ceasor Burn the sum of — 0-4-0
for four Crows killed in this Town
pay to [illegible] the sum of — 0-4-0
for four Crows killed in this Town
total 3-19-8-3
[illegible] Selectmen

The trouble locating records for Cesar is that there is discrepancy in the spelling of his name and it's unclear if he was enslaved by James Burn. His name has been in the historical record as Caesar, Cesar, Caesor, Sezor, and Cesor. There was only one Burn who lived in town. That was James Burn.

James Burn was born June 18, 1690 and served in Lovewell's War in the snowshoe company in Chelmsford in 1724. He was the son of James and Mary (Proctor) Burn. Burn lived on land once owned by Samuel N. Burbeck. On the 1730 map of Westford, there is a "Jas Burns" who lived near Rattlesnake Hill. James Burn was a potter. According to Hodgman, there is a pasture near where he lived that in 1883 was

---

[168] Westford Town Records, Volume II, 1764-1790, 167.

still called "Burn's Pasture." According to Hodgman's history, shards of pottery were found on the land he formerly owned. Burn's land also abutted John W. Abbot's property in the town's center. Prospect Hill was once known as Clay Pit Hill.[169] William Prescott's research on taxation of enslavers in Westford, found that James Burn was assessed for a slave in 1752 and 1768.

James Burn died January 19, 1771 at the age of 80 and is buried in Fairview Cemetery. A probate could not be located. When an enslaver died intestate and without heirs, the enslaved individual became the charge of the town. By his first mention in 1773, Cesar's enslaver was no longer alive, however, we do not know if he was emancipated after 1768 (the last year James Burn was assessed for a slave). He is not included in the 1771 Tax list.

Cesar was a Private in the Second Foot Company of the Westford Militia. The Captain was Jonathan Minot. Enslaved and Free Blacks were prohibited from bearing arms and serving in the Militia. However, controls like this were partially removed or removed entirely in time of emergency, like during the impending Revolution. Along with the other members of the Westford Militia, Cesar answered the Lexington Alarm on the morning of April 19, 1775 and fought the British Regulars on the Battle Road in Lexington.

He officially enlisted in the Army on April 26, 1775 for an eight month period. This was in Captain Abijah Wyman's company in Colonel William Prescott's Regiment. Colonel Prescott's regiment constructed the redoubt the night prior to the battle of Bunker Hill. There is an account in Hodgman's *History of Westford*, where he recounts the story "on good authority" that in the battle, Cesar found that he was almost out of his powder and putting in his last charge said to himself, "Now, Cesar, give 'em one more." He fired his musket and was then shot and fell back into the trench and died. According to tradition, it was Leonard Proctor who was near Cesar and could have heard this. The surname Bason appears because a Mr. Francis Tinker,

---

169 Hodgman, 242.

of Ashby, said that Jacob Bascom of Westford was killed at Bunker Hill. However, no such person existed. Bason seems to be some combination of Bascom and Burn.

Cesar is most likely the only Patriot of Color from Westford to be present at Battle Road *and* Bunker Hill.[170] According to *Patriots of Color*, there were 13 men named Cesar who fought on Battle Road or Bunker Hill. The return of Prescott's Regiment dated October 3, 1775 from Cambridge lists Cesor Bason of Westford having died on June 17, 1775.[171]

Cesar was owed £3 11 shillings for the 26 miles he traveled in Prescott's regiment. In the August 1775 return, he isn't listed as owning a gun or a bayonet. His name is also written as Sezor.[172]

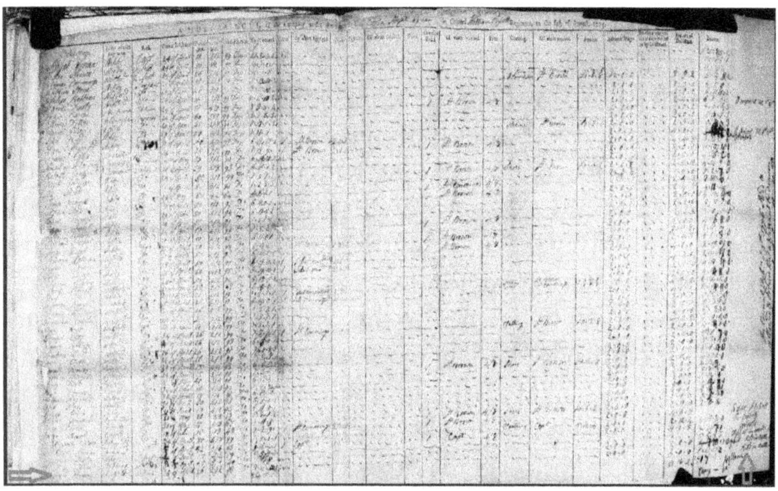

Muster/payrolls, and various papers (1763-1808) of the Revolutionary War [Massachusetts and Rhode Island] Vol. 16, Siege of Boston 1775

---

[170] George Quintal Jr., *Patriots of Color: "A Peculiar Beauty and Merit": African Americans and Native Americans at Battle Road & Bunker Hill,* Division of Cultural Resources- Boston National Historic Park: Boston, 2004. 247.

[171] Muster/payrolls, and various papers (1763-1808) of the Revolutionary War [Massachusetts and Rhode Island] Volume 16, Page 76

[172] Muster/payrolls, and various papers (1763-1808) of the Revolutionary War [Massachusetts and Rhode Island] Volume 16, Page 76

The report was made *after* Cesar's death. So, does he not own a weapon because he is dead or because he was prohibited from doing so? In the Westford Town Archives, there is a record of the town paying Joseph Prescott £2 and 9 shillings. The note states that Prescott lent a gun to someone and it was lost at the Battle of Bunker Hill so the town reimbursed him for his lost property.

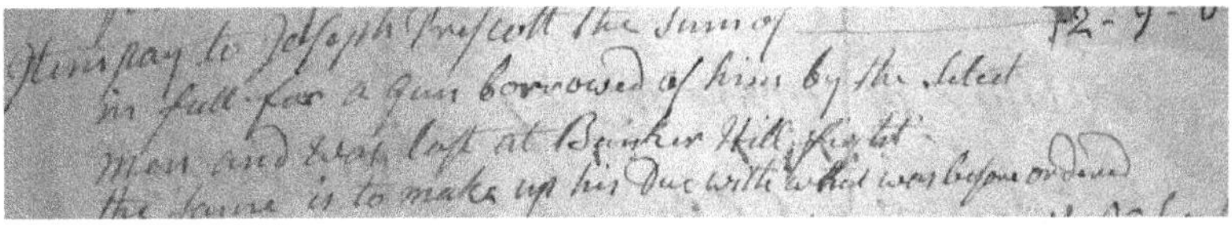
Item pay to Joseph Prescott the Sum of £2-9-0
in full for a Gun borrowed of him by the Select
men and was lost at Bunker Hill fight
the same is to make up his Due with what was before ordered

May 20, 1782, Westford Town Archives, Box 1, 1776-1738 some undated documents

It's curious that Cesar was not allowed to own a gun, but needed one in order to fight. Could he have borrowed it from Prescott and it was lost at Bunker Hill because it did not return to Westford as that was where Cesar died? Or was the gun lost by someone else in the chaos of battle? Cross checking the returns of both Westford's men at Bunker Hill show that Simeon Kemp and David Fish, both of whom fought with Cesar, borrowed guns from the Selectmen of Westford. Cesar most likely owned his own gun.

On February 16, 1776 Abijah Wyman certified that "Cesor Bason" was a soldier in Colonel Prescott's regiment and was slain at Bunker Hill and that he hadn't yet received his coat and blanket as a bounty granted him by Congress.[173] [174] On March 15, 1776, there was an order for a bounty coat or its equivalent in money. A bounty coat is a heavy coat offered as an enlistment bounty when men enlisted for a 8 month period as Cesar did. It is awarded (or its equivalent in money) at the end

---

173 https://archive.org/details/memorialofameric00bost/page/110/mode/2up?q=bason

174 Muster and pay rolls vol 57 page 62-63 file 7

of the enlistment period.[175] As Selectmen for the Westford, Joseph Read, Zaccheus Wright, Zechariah Hildreth, Francis Leighton, and Jonathan Keep requested a Bounty Coat and Blanket on behalf of Cesar to be paid to Zaccheus Wright for Cesar's family, as there was no estate to administer.[176]

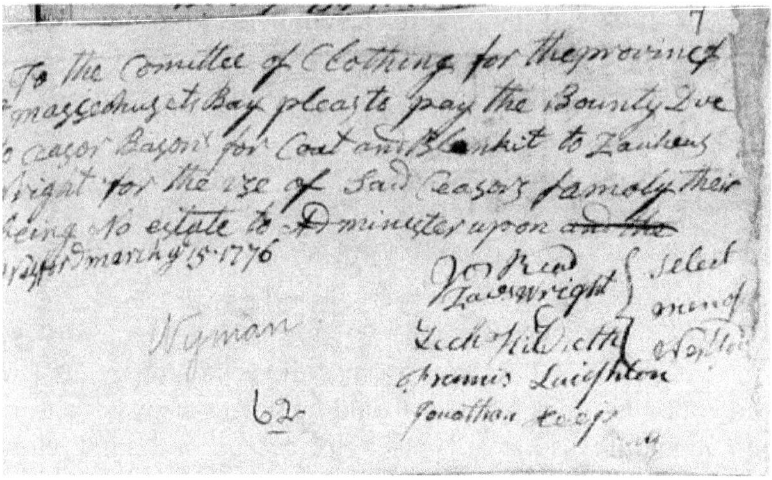

7

To the Comittee of Clothing for the province of Massachusetts Bay pleas to pay the Bounty Due to Ceasor Bason for Coat and Blankit to Zacheus Wright for the use of said Ceasors famoly their being No estate to Administer upon
Westford march ye 15 1776

Jos Read
Zacs Wright
Zech Hildreth
Francis Leighton
Jonathan Keep
Select men of Westford

Wyman

62

That the document cites a family, indicates that there was someone to receive this money.

A Francis Bason married Philip Smith of Westford. Their intentions were filed in Westford on December 17, 1775.[177] This is after Cesar's death. Could Francis have been his widow? Daughter? It's unclear if Francis and Philip are White or Black. Their marriage intention is <u>not</u> listed under "NEGROES" in Westford's vital records. Their deaths aren't recorded in Westford Vital Records. We know Cesar was Black and his surname became Bason and that the only other Bason is Francis. As interracial marriages were illegal (though still sometimes occurred), we have to wonder about Francis.

Philip Smith was not born in Westford, but he is indicated as from Westford on the Muster Rolls. He was not a

---

175 Quintal, 14.

176 Muster and pay rolls vol 57 page 62-63, file 7.

177 Westford Vital Records, 237.

taxpayer in Westford in 1771. On the coat roll dated June 26, 1775 in Charlestown, Philip Smith made his mark that he received his payment that was previously agreed upon. That he left his mark, means that he didn't know how to write and probably didn't know how to read either. Philip and Francis are not listed separately in the 1790 census but could possibly be the two "all free other persons" living with Cato Gray. They are not listed in the 1800 census.

Reflecting back on being paid for the killing of crows, this author wonders why Cesar did this. Simply, this was a way a formerly enslaved man could earn some money. No other records could be found at this time.

York Hambleton

York Hambleton was enslaved by Abel Boynton, son of Nathaniel Boynton, Westford's Town Clerk. Hambleton is a government district in the United Kingdom and it is located near York, England. York Hambleton's name follows the convention of naming enslaved people after cities or regions from the enslaver's ancestry. Indeed, the Boynton family arrived in 1638 from Yorkshire, England.

Abel Boynton was probably a member of this Middle Class and enslaved a man prior to him being married and having a family. His father hadn't even passed away yet, so he would not have gotten an inheritance allowing him to purchase a large tract of land or gain prominence in the community.

Abel was a Private in the First Foot Company of the Westford Militia and answered the Lexington Alarm on April 19, 1775. Abel was just a few months shy of his 20th birthday. He officially enlisted in the Continental Army on May 5, 1775 and fought in the Battle of Bunker Hill. After 1774 and prior to 1781, most likely by 1778, Abel enslaved the man he called York Hambleton. It is assumed after 1774, because Abel does not appear on the town's tax list as he was not a landowner yet at 18.

If Hodgman is right, and Abel Boynton owned a tannery on Heywood Street, then York likely worked there. He also may have lived in the center of town, near present day 39 Main Street.

At one point prior to that, Boynton lived in the house now known as the John W. Abbot House. It once stood where the Northern Bank and Trust is in Westford Center. In the 1870s, JW Abbot moved the house to its current location at 44 Boston Road. The house was built in 1713.

In December 1780, the town agreed to raise a certain number of men to supplement the Army. On February 12, 1781 the town met to divide into classes and procure their proportion of soldiers required to serve in the Continental Army. Captain Pelatiah Fletcher was one of the men on the committee. On February 16, 1781 the town voted to accept the several classes. There is no description of the classes in the town meeting notes.

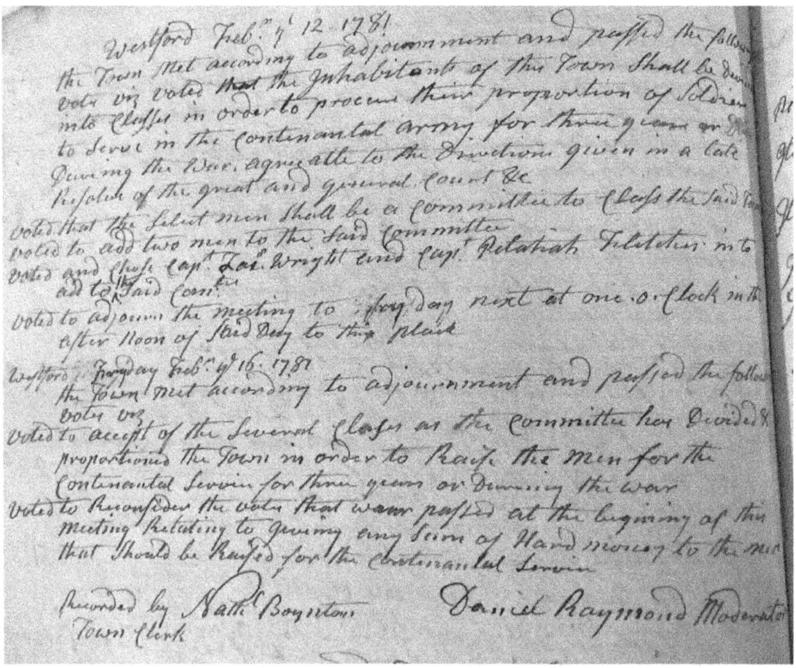
Westford Feb^ry 12 1781
the Town Met according to adjournment and passed the follow
vote viz voted that the Inhabitants of this Town Shall be Div
into Classes in order to procure their proportion of Soldiers
to serve in the Continental army for three years or
During the War agreeable to the Direction given in a late
Resolve of the great and general Court &c
voted that the Select men Shall be a Committee to Class the said Town
voted to add two men to the said Committee
voted and chose Capt Zac. Wright and Capt Pelatiah Fletcher in to
add to said Comtee
voted to adjourn the meeting to Friday next at one o'clock in the
after Noon of Said Day to this place
Westford Friday Feb^ry 16 1781
the Town met according to adjournment and passed the follow
vote viz
voted to accept of the several Classes as the Committee have Divided &
proportioned the Town in order to Raise the men for the
Continental Service for three years or During the war
voted to Reconsider the vote that was passed at the begining of this
meeting Relating to giving any Sum of Hard money to the men
that Should be Raised for the Continental Service
Recorded by Nathl Boynton Daniel Raymond Moderator
Town Clerk

There is a record of Abel Boynton being listed as a member of Class No. 12, in which he "engaged a negro."[178] York's enlistment is less than six months after this call. Does

178 Massachusetts Muster and PayRolls, Volume 32, Page 447.

"engaged a negro" mean that Abel engaged York to fight as his substitute?

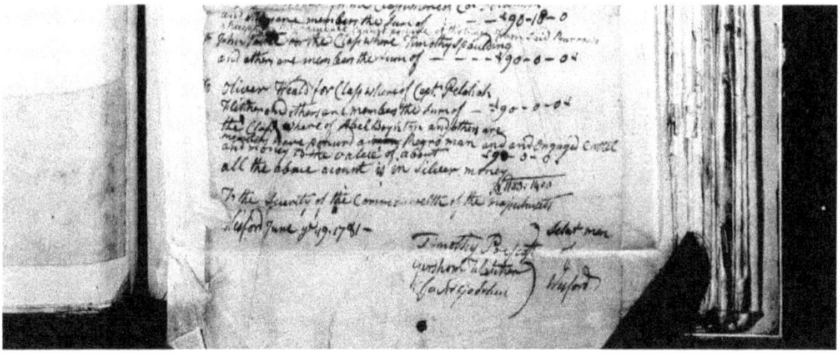

Our first record of York Hambleton is his enlistment in the Continental Army on May 7, 1781. He was listed as 31 years old and 5' 7" in height. His trade was listed as "Laborer." His time for enlistment was 3 years.[179]

The document below is taken from Hosmer's list. The index card notes that York enlisted from Middlesex County under the resolve of December 2, 1780.[180] This resolve was in accordance with Congress's call for more soldiers. Each town was tasked with raising a proportional number of men for voluntary enlistment and creating a descriptive list. They were then to march on to Springfield. There, another descriptive list was to be made. The men were to be credited to the town in which they had spent the previous three months. Presumably York had resided in Westford for that time. In March 1781, the towns were supposed to make a return of all the bounties that

---

179 Muster/payrolls, and various papers (1763-1808) of the Revolutionary War [Massachusetts and Rhode Island] Vol. 54, Worcester rolls, parcels 2nd and mixed rolls, no. 1 1774-1783 Vol. 55, Worcester rolls, parcels 2nd and mixed rolls, no. 2 (incl. Cpt. Coburn's company, part N of Col. Sheldon's Dragoons (1777) 1775-1783, Image 258

180 "Massachusetts, Revolutionary War, Index Cards to Muster Rolls, 1775-1783," database with images, FamilySearch (https://familysearch.org/ark:/61903/3:1:3Q9M-CSQZ-ZRSV?cc=2548057&wc=QZZQ-M7P%3A1589088615 : 27 January 2017), Haley, William - Hancock, David > image 319 of 2457; Massachusetts State Archives, Boston.

were to be remitted to the town for the men who enlisted and the town would receive a tax credit based on the average cost for each man to serve in the Army. If the town did not send the designated quota, then the town would not receive the full tax credit. The town was to pay each man 6 shillings per mile marched to Springfield as well as a blanket. The act prohibited any prisoner or deserter from serving and receiving credit.

The resolve also stated that, "the several towns and plantations within this Commonwealth be, and hereby are authorized to agree (if they think fit) upon classing the inhabitants thereof at a legal town-meeting called for that purpose, in order to procure their proportion of soldiers to serve in the Continental army, for three years or during the war: and in all towns and plantations where the mode of classing shall be adopted, the selectmen of such towns...shall divide all the inhabitants thereof, with others who were assessed in the hard-money-tax, into as many classes as according to the annexed schedule, there are men required of such town or plantation, in proportion of their several taxes, intermixing the poor with the rich, so as to make the several classes as nearly equal in property and in number of polls as may be with convenience; and each of said classes shall, on or before the twentieth day of *January* (emphasis in original) next, procure a good able bodied effective soldier to serve in the Continental army three years or during the way, unless such town or plantation shall in some other way procure the whole number of soldiers to be by them raised"[181]

When the men arrived at Springfield, the towns received fifty DOLLARS "in the new emission of money." The Superintendent at Springfield was Colonel William Shepard.

---

181 Acts and Laws of the Commonwealth of Massachusetts 1780-81, pages 190-201,
https://archive.org/details/actsresolvespass178081mass/page/n39/mode/2up

Westford was to raise 15 men. There were 523 total from Middlesex County.

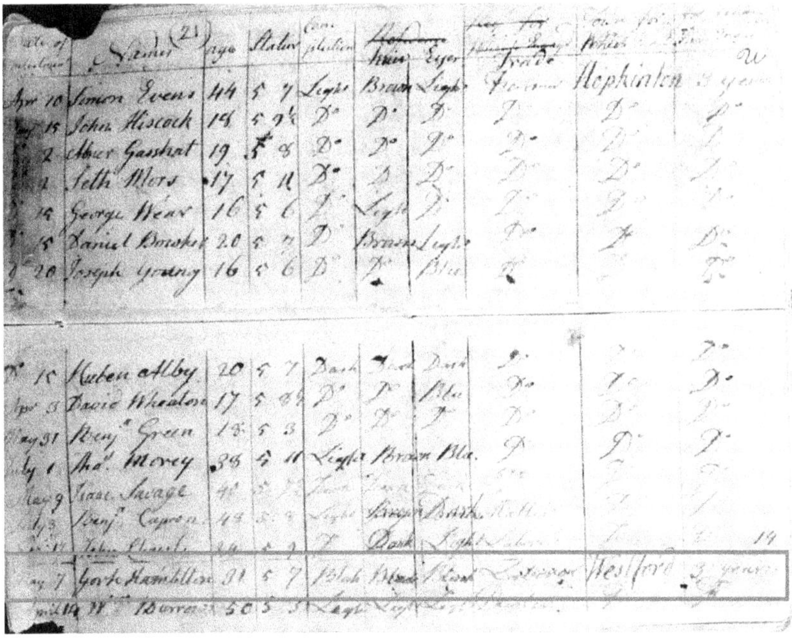

Date of Enlistment	Names	Age	Stature		Complexion	Hair	Eyes	Trade	Town	Time
Apr 10	Simon Evens	44	5	7	Light	Brown	Light	Farmer	Hopkinton	3 years
May 15	John Hiscock	18	5	7½	D°	D°	D°	D°	D°	D°
2	Abner Gasshat	19	5	8	D°	D°	D°	D°	D°	D°
[illegible]	Seth Mors	17	5	11	D°	D°	D°	D°	D°	D°
15	George Wear	16	5	6	D°	Light	D°	D°	D°	D°
5	Daniel Brooks	20	5	7	D°	Brown	Light	D°	D°	D°
20	Joseph Young	16	5	6	D°	D°	Blue	D°		D°
D° 15	Ruben Allby	20	5	7	Dark	Dark	Dark	D°		D°
Apr 8	David Wheaton	17	5	8½	D°	D°	Blue	D°	D°	D°
May 31	Benj^a Green	18	5	3	D°	D°	D°	D°	D°	D°
July 1	Thos Morey	38	5	11	Light	Brown	Blue	D°	D°	D°
May 9	Isaac Savage	40	[illegible]	[illegible]	[illegible]	[illegible]	[illegible]	[illegible]	[illegible]	[illegible]
July 3	Benjn Capron	48	5	8	Light	Brown	Dark	Hatter	[illegible]	[illegible]
[illegible] 17	John Chasel	24	5	9	D°	Dark	Light	Laborer	[illegible]	[illegible] 14
May 7	York Hamblton	31	5	7	Black	Black	Black	Laborer	Westford	3 years
[illegible] 14	Wm Burrows	50	5	3	Light	Light	Light	[illegible]	[illegible]	[illegible]

He enlisted with other men from town including John Nutting, Asa Patch, Oliver Heald, William Spaulding, and Thaddeus Read.

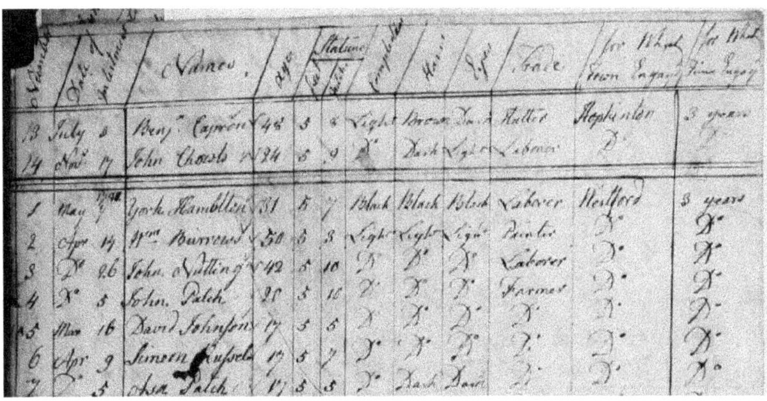

No.	Date of Enlistment		Names	Age	Stature Feet	Stature Inches	Complexion	Hair	Eyes	Trade	For What Town Engaged	For What Time Engaged
13	July	8	Benjn Capron	48	5	8	Light	Brown	Dark	Hatter	Hopkinton	3 years
14	Nov	17	John Chasel	24	5	9	D°	Dark	Light	Laborer	D°	D°
1	May	7	York Hamblton	31	5	7	Black	Black	Black	Laborer	Westford	3 years
2	Apr	14	Wm Burrows	50	5	3	Light	Light	Light	Painter	D°	D°
3	D°	26	John Nutting	42	5	10	D°	D°	D°	Laborer	D°	D°
4	D°	5	John Patch	25	5	10	D°	D°	D°	Farmer	D°	D°
5	Mar	16	David Johnson	17	5	5	D°	D°	D°	D°	D°	D°
6	Apr	9	Simeon Russel	17	5	7	D°	D°	D°	D°	D°	D°
7	D°	5	Asa Patch	17	5	5	D°	Dark	Dark	D°	D°	D°

York Hambleton's enlistment, Descriptive List, Vol. 29, Page 12

He was mustered as a Private into Captain Holbrook's regiment and was sent to West Point via Springfield. In a letter from Captain Holbrook to Colonel Shepard dated June 7, 1781, it took the regiment six days to march from Springfield to West Point, without losing any men.[182] The letter also includes a transcription of a General Orders from General Washington regarding successes from Nathaniel Greene and others in the southern campaign that ultimately led to Cornwallis' surrender.

York appears in a muster roll in January 1782 into Captain David Holbrook's Company of the 4th Regiment and commanded by William Shepard. This is presumably at West Point.

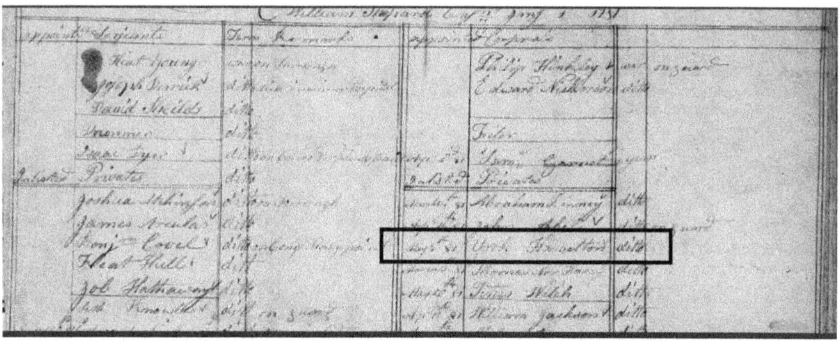

"Massachusetts, Revolutionary War, Index Cards to Muster Rolls, 1775-1783," database with images, FamilySearch (https://familysearch.org/ark:/61903/3:1:3Q9M-CSQZ-ZLH8?cc=2548057&wc=QZZQ-M7P%3A1589088615 : 27 January 2017), Haley, William - Hancock, David > image 500 of 2457; Massachusetts State Archives, Boston.

At some point between January and October 1782, it seems that York passed away. York was likely still enslaved at the time of his enlistment because Abel Boynton puts in a request to the state for money owed to him, as *lost property*. This gives weight to the assumption that York was sent in Abel's stead.

---

[182]7 June 1781 letter from Captain David Holbrook to Colonel William Shepard. https://www.icollector.com/1781-Important-Revolutionary-War-Content-ALS-David-Holbrook-to-William-Shepard_i27058005, accessed 1/13/2024.

On October 20, 1792, three men in town noted that they were informed that a "certain negro man by the name of York Hambleton who was the property of Colonel Abel Boynton" died at West Point towards the end of the Revolution. Oliver Prescott, Judge of Probate, appointed Abel Boynton as administrator of the probate. York died intestate, that is, without a will. They found no debts that he owed, except a sum of about £9 to Abel Boynton for clothes to go into the army. No further information has been found regarding his death. The probate record is dated 1792, eleven years AFTER York enlisted in the Army. No other records could be found at this time.

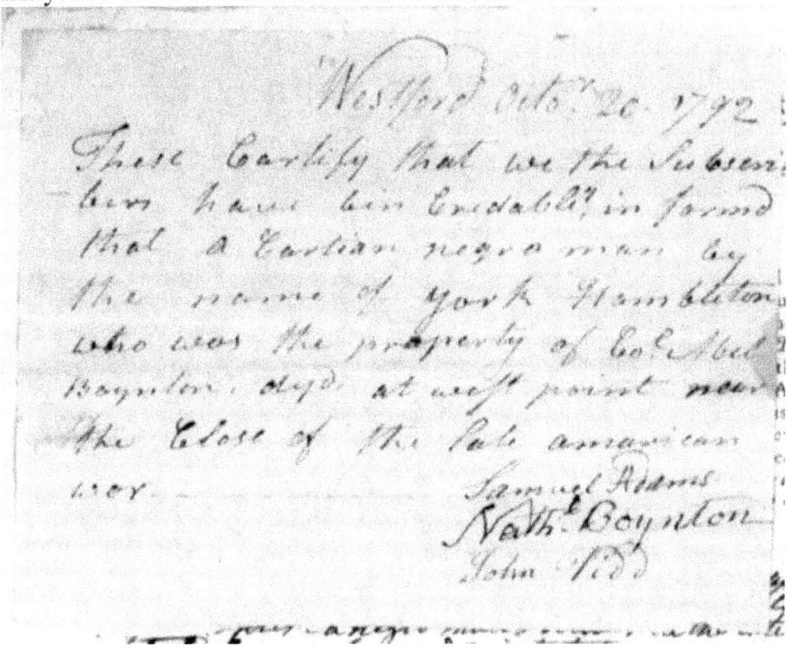

Westford Octr 20 1792
These Cartify that we the Subscri-
bers have bin Credabl? in formd
that a Cartian negro man by
the name of York Hambleton
who was the property of Col. Abel
Boynton. dyd at west point near
the Close of the late american
war.
Samuel Adams
Nath. Boynton
John [illegible]

Hannah Kibbery

She and her sons were "warned out" of Westford.[183] It's unclear if they were enslaved here. No other records could be found at this time.

---

183 "Slavery, " Accessed 10 June 2023, http://www.54lowellroad.com/index_files/Page583.htm

Once Known Enslaved People in Westford

For these people, we do not know their name. Their name however, was once known. The only record is the tax record or other record of the enslaver. For this reason, the enslaver's name is listed.

Once Known (enslaved by Peletiah Fletcher)

Pelatiah Fletcher was born May 3, 1727.[184] Pelatiah married Dorothy Hildreth on January 13, 1757. After her death, he then married Elizabeth Hartwell on October 15, 1782. Pelatiah was a farmer.

In the 1771 Tax Inventory, Pelatiah Fletcher is one of the few listed as a "servant owner" having a "servant for life."

FLETCHER, PELATIAH Town of Westford, Middlesex County			
Farm Animals/Livestock			
Horses 01	Oxen 03	Cows 7	Goats and Sheep 11
Owns Goats or Sheep Y	Swine 04		
Buildings and Boats			
Dwelling Houses and Shops Adjoining 1	Shops Adjoining 0	Tanhouses -- etc. 0	Stillhouses 0
Warehouses 0	Superficial Feet of Wharf 00000	Gristmills -- etc. 0	Ironworks -- etc. 1
Tons of Vessels			
General Population Characteristics and Assessed Worth			
Servants for Life 1	Servant Owner Y	Annual worth of the Whole Real Estate (£) 015	Value of Trading Stock (£) 00000
Value of Factorage or Commissions (£) 0000	Value of Money Lent at Interest (£) 00000		
Land and Agriculture			
Acres of Pasture 15	Number of Cows the Pasture will Keep 12	Acres of Tillage 15	Bushels of Grain Produced per Year 160
Barrels of Cider Produced per Year 024	Acres of Salt Marsh 0	Tons of Salt Marsh Hay per Year 0	Acres of English and Upland Mowing Land 8
Tons of English and Upland Hay Per Year 8	Acres of Fresh Meadow 6	Tons of Fresh Meadow Hay Per Year 6	

He was assessed for a slave 1770, 1771, 1773, 1775. By 1774, Pelatiah was ranked second among Westford's taxpayers in 1774. He signed the Solemn League and Covenant. He worked on the committee to raise a new meetinghouse frame after the first meetinghouse burned. In January of 1775, Fletcher

184 Prescott, *Patriots and Taxpayers,* A-38.

was one of seven men who made up the first "Committee of Inspection," who saw that the Resolves of the American and Provincial Congresses be "faithfully observed and complied with." Fletcher was commissioned and appointed Captain of one of the two Westford companies in the 6th Militia Regiment. Captain Fletcher used his wealth to assist other families in town while their family members were off fighting in the Revolution.

His house still stands at 54 Lowell Road. No other records could be found at this time.

Once Known (enslaved by William Read)

There is a William Read born April 2, 1715 who was the son of John Read and Jane Chamberlin. William Read was ordered in 1732 to repair a road. In present day road names, this is essentially West Prescott Street from the Groton line to Forge Village Road to Main Street to the Chelmsford Line.[185] William Read had a place similar to Nathaniel Boynton as Prescott places him 1200 feet west of the beginning of Flagg Road and Main Street. Hodgman notes that William Read, "said to be a sea captain" had twelve acres of land on the east side of Boutwell's Brook and Benjamin Butterfield had a few acres adjoining him. This description still places him on what became the Oren Coolidge property and is visible on the 1730 map of Westford.[186]

He married Thankful Spaulding on December 9, 1741.[187] They had three sons, Thaddeus born May 15, 1742 (who served in the Revolution), William born in 1753,[188] and Oliver, born in 1756. Oliver Read died in 1791 in his 35th year according to records.

William Read was first assessed for a slave in 1763, then again from 1768-1771.

---

185 Hodgman, 34.

186 Hodgman, , 10.

187 Hodgman, 471.

188 Hodgman lists his birth as 1743, however Westford Vital Records lists 1753. Hodgman, 471.

legacy.sites.fas.harvard.edu/~hsb41/masstax/masstax.cgi?state=person&person=03490106

READ, WILLIAM Town of Westford, Middlesex County			
Farm Animals/Livestock			
Horses 00	Oxen 00	Cows 2	Goats and Sheep 0
Owns Goats or Sheep N	Swine 00		
Buildings and Boats			
Dwelling Houses and Shops Adjoining 1	Shops Adjoining 0	Tanhouses -- etc. 0	Stillhouses 0
Warehouses 0	Superficial Feet of Wharf 00000	Gristmills -- etc. 0	Ironworks -- etc. 0
Tons of Vessels			
Land and Agriculture			
Acres of Pasture 6	Number of Cows the Pasture will Keep 2	Acres of Tillage 2	Bushels of Grain Produced per Year 018
Barrels of Cider Produced per Year 007	Acres of Salt Marsh 0	Tons of Salt Marsh Hay per Year 0	Acres of English and Upland Mowing Land 1
Tons of English and Upland Hay Per Year 1	Acres of Fresh Meadow 0	Tons of Fresh Meadow Hay Per Year 0	
General Population Characteristics and Assessed Worth			
Servants for Life 1	Servant Owner Y	Annual worth of the Whole Real Estate (£) 002	Value of Trading Stock (£) 00000
Value of Factorage or Commissions (£) 0000	Value of Money Lent at Interest (£) 00000		

On the 1771 tax list as being a servant owner for life, 1 servant. As there were nine years between the last tax listing and slavery being abolished in Massachusetts in 1780, one can hope that the person was emancipated in some form. The tax form doesn't reveal much of a farm or cider produced or hay. Perhaps this servant was in the house as opposed to a farmer. Then, it would have typically been a female.

William Read, Senior died in or before 1791.[189] There is no *official* record of his death or burial. There is no probate available. Thankful Read is on the 1790 census and is not noted as living with any males, only 2 free white females. It is unclear who these women could be. Thankful died in January 1805.[190]

There is one William Read on the 1790 Census for Westford. He is listed: 1 male over 16, 1 under 16, and 2 free white females. William, born 1753, would have been too young to be included on the 1771 tax inventory as an enslaver. So the record above is for the father. No other records could be found at this time.

---

189 Hodgman, 135.

190 Hodgman, 418.

Once Known Woman (enslaved by Moses Burge)

Born in Westford October 19, 1728, Moses was the son of Josiah and Susanna (Jacquith) Burge. Moses was apparently the second son, but no records have yet been found of his older brother Samuel (b. 1726). Assuming Samuel died and it is not recorded, Moses must have inherited his father's property as the oldest son. Moses had other siblings, including a sister, Elizabeth.

On October 2, 1749, Moses's brother John died. On April 17, 1750, his mother Susanna died. On July 4, 1750, another brother, Josiah died.[191] According to Hodgman, at some point, his father Josiah Burge moved to Townsend.[192] Hodgman places Josiah Burge's land as "west of the railroad at Westford Depot…whose house stood near the residence of Asia Nutting. He gave his name to Burge's Pond nearby."[193]

In 1757, Moses appeared as a Private on a Muster Roll for Samuel Bancroft's Company on the Service to Springfield. They marched from Westford to Springfield on alarm to Fort William Henry for August 15, 1757. General Montcalm took Fort William Henry on August 9, 1757. In Springfield, upon hearing of its surrender to Montcalm, the group turned around but they were compensated for their time.[194]

In 1762, Moses paid £1 4s into the Town Treasury for a new bell. In 1768 Moses served as a town selectman.

There are no records of a marriage or for births or baptisms of children, however there is an adopted child, Samuel Hayward (son of Josiah Hayward), on February 11, 1787.[195] Born in Braintree, Josiah Hayward (1765-1845) was the son of Jonathan (1740-1771) and Elizabeth Burge Hayward (1743-1772). Josiah would be Moses's nephew, and the adopted Samuel was Moses's grand- nephew.

---

191 Hodgman, 414-415.

192 Hodgman, 171.

193 Hodgman, 10-11.

194 Hodgman, 62.

195 *Westford Vital Records*, 18.

Samuel was baptized on February 11, 1787, just 11 months after his parents' marriage intentions were filed. Samuel was obviously born prior to February and you have to wonder how much earlier he was born?! On the 1790 Federal Census, Moses is listed as over 16 and living with one male under 16 years old.[196] This is, presumably, Samuel Howard.

The practice of primogeniture was popular at the time. This is where a man, in order to maintain the family legacy without children of his own, would adopt a relative's child and raise the child in order to have an heir. Moses was also without a wife to help raise the child he brought to his home. Whereas Josiah was born in 1765, the author believes that Moses brought Josiah to live with him and an enslaved woman helped to raise him. According to the 1764/5 census, there were seven females enslaved in town. For these census numbers to be accurate, Moses had to enslave someone in 1764/5 (earlier than the tax record indicates) *and* that person had to be a woman.[197]

When Josiah married and had children of his own, Moses then adopted Samuel to continue the practice of primogeniture. In 1769, Moses Burge was assessed for a slave 7 shilling, 4 pence equal to 3.67 horses.[198]

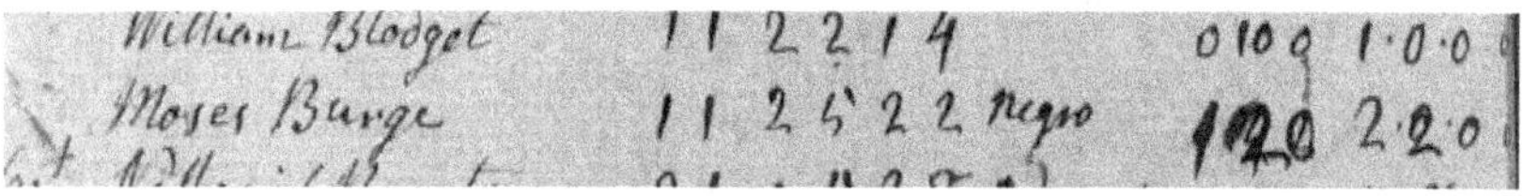
William Blodget 1 1 2 2 1 4 0 10 9 1.0.0
Moses Burge 1 1 2 5 2 2 negro 1.2.0 2.2.0

Upon Ephraim Coming Jr.'s death, the children were under the care of Moses Burge (two small children named Wilson and Patty). He was compensated for this (see above, Noble Comings, pages 40-45). Could these children have been under the care of Moses's enslaved woman as well? This means she was likely still enslaved in 1777 when Ephraim died.

Slavery was abolished in 1780 and it is unclear what may have happened to her.

196 1790 Federal Census for Westford.

197 Howard, "Enslaved Persons in Westford."

198 Town of Westford Tax Records, Volume 1, 276.

Moses died on 22 December 1796 at 68 years old. He named his "beloved" friend Lt. Josiah Hayward [Howard] his executor and sole heir. As Samuel was not of age upon Moses's death in 1796, Moses' estate went to Josiah. Moses asked for a decent Christian burial. No other records could be found at this time.

Once Known (enslaved by Jonathan Keyes)

Jonathan Keyes was born on January 21, 1721 to Jonathan and Elizabeth Keyes. In 1745, he married Elisabeth Fletcher. They had five children together. After Elisabeth's death in 1761, he married Elizabeth "Betty" Hartwell (b. Feb 17, 1731) in 1762. They had four children. Their daughter, Lydia, married Isaac Patten.

Jonathan Keyes lived in a house that still stands on Frances Hill Road. There are parts of it that may have once been part of the Solomon Keyes house, long thought to be the oldest house in what is now Westford.

The 1771 Tax Inventory does not list Keyes as a servant owner. In 1773, Keyes was taxed for a slave.[199]

Jon.ⁿ Keyes 1 1 0 4 3 6 Negro 0 16 3 2 18 0

He may have enslaved a man, due to the enormity of land he owned in town, and all the farming acres. However, because of all the land, he also could have enslaved a woman to help in the house *and* the farm. To make the numbers for the 1764/5 Census accurate, Keyes would have had to enslave a woman.[200]

Jonathan died on June 20, 1781, at 60 years old. According to his probate, he also had land near "Flushing" and Long Sought For, including 85 acres of "mowing, pasturing, and orcharding" land on the northerly side of Long Sought For with a barn and dwelling house (land and house worth £305), as well as Farm on Frances Hill with a house, barn, cider mill, and corn

---

[199] Town of Westford Tax Records, Volume 1, 369.

[200] Howard, "Enslaved Persons in Westford."

house. He also owned land on Flushing Pond, Hill Pasture, Butterfield Lot, Gideon's Pasture, Wheat Pine, and 12 acres on the north side of Nabemist [sic] Pond, and a pew in the meetinghouse (£10), among other land holdings, all totaling £797. [201] His land bordered Ephraim Chandler's land. There is no mention of a slave in the probate, of course, slavery was abolished by then. Although enslaved people were not always emancipated after that.

Upon Jonathan's death, Elizabeth married Pelatiah Fletcher. They lived in the house at 54 Lowell Road. According to the 1790 Census, there were two white males over 16, two white males under 16, and four free white females. After Pelatiah's death in 1807, she moved back to the Keyes house on Frances Hill. No other records could be found at this time.

Once Known (enslaved by John Robins)

John Robins was born October 15, 1727.[202] When John Robins was born in Chelmsford, his father, Benjamin Robbins, was 43 and his mother, Hannah Hildreth, was 43. Hannah died December 9, 1731 and Benjamin remarried Annis Chandler, herself a widow.[203]

John Robins married Sarah Davis of Acton, their intentions were filed May 5, 1750. John was 23 years old. They were the parents of at least 3 daughters and 9 sons, including one named John.

John Robins, Sr. was a Private in the French and Indian War in 1757 in Captain Samuel Bancroft's company. He was paid for an alarm for the relief of Fort William Henry on August 15, 1757. They answered the call before learning of the Fort's surrender. After hearing that, they apparently returned home.[204]

---

201 "Jonathan Keyes (1722-1781)" Wiki Tree. Accessed 5 May 2024. https://www.wikitree.com/wiki/Keyes-71

202 Hodgman, 475.

203 Van Essen, John S. "Robbins Genealogical Collection" 29 February 2012. Accessed 2 February 2024. https://sites.rootsweb.com/~johniel/robbgenc.html

204 Hodgman, 63.

It appears John, Sr. returned home and settled into life in Westford. His father, Benjamin, resided near Nashoba Hill (Robbins Road). John Robins is listed on the South Tax List for 1757. Based on records, John also owned a large area of Dunstable. There is a Robbins Farm Road in Dunstable, on the border with Nashua, New Hampshire.

On the 1771 Tax List, John Robins appears as an enslaver and is tied for 55th wealthiest man in Westford in 1774.[205] On his land in Westford in 1771, he had a house and an ironworks on about 23 acres of land. He owned 2 horses, 2 oxen, 4 cows, 9 goats and sheep, and 3 swine.

legacy.sites.fas.harvard.edu/~hsb41/masstax/masstax.cgi?state=person&person=03490213

ROBINS, JOHN Town of Westford, Middlesex County			
Buildings and Boats			
Dwelling Houses and Shops Adjoining 1	Shops Adjoining 0	Tanhouses -- etc. 0	Stillhouses 0
Warehouses 0	Superficial Feet of Wharf 00000	Gristmills -- etc. 0	Ironworks -- etc. 1
Tons of Vessels			
Land and Agriculture			
Acres of Pasture 3	Number of Cows the Pasture will Keep 3	Acres of Tillage 8	Bushels of Grain Produced per Year 080
Barrels of Cider Produced per Year 008	Acres of Salt Marsh 0	Tons of Salt Marsh Hay per Year 0	Acres of English and Upland Mowing Land 0
Tons of English and Upland Hay Per Year 0	Acres of Fresh Meadow 12	Tons of Fresh Meadow Hay Per Year 14	
Farm Animals/Livestock			
Horses 02	Oxen 02	Cows 4	Goats and Sheep 9
Owns Goats or Sheep Y	Swine 03		
General Population Characteristics and Assessed Worth			
Servants for Life 1	Servant Owner Y	Annual worth of the Whole Real Estate (£) 009	Value of Trading Stock (£) 00000
Value of Factorage or Commissions (£) 0000	Value of Money Lent at Interest (£) 00000		

John and his family removed to Dunstable, New Hampshire with their extended family around 1775-1777.[206] It

205 https://legacy.sites.fas.harvard.edu/~hsb41/masstax/masstax.cgi?state=person&person=03490213

206 Van Essen, John S. "Robbins Genealogical Collection" 29 February 2012. Accessed 4/26/2024. https://sites.rootsweb.com/~johniel/robbjohn.html

seems John, Sr. was rewarded for his grandfather's probable role in Lovewell's War (1725) fighting Chief Paugus and the Abenaki near Lake Winnipesaukee and was given land in the area east of the Merrimack River (present day Tyngsboro).[207]

John is listed on the 1790 Census for Dunstable, New Hampshire with five sons and a daughter. However, there is an additional female listed. From a genealogical website, it has this table[208]:

The 1790 Federal Census for New Hampshire shows this:

State: New Hampshire
County: Various
Town: Various

	Males 16+	Males 0-15	Fem All	County	Town	
Robins, John	6	-	3	Hillsborough	Dunstable	b. 1727
Robins, Joseph	2	1	5	Hillsborough	Dunstable	unrelated
Robens, John	4	3	1	Cheshire	Westmoreland	not Jr.

<u>COMMENT</u>: John in Dunstable is John, b. 1727. Unmarried sons Ezekiel, Timothy, Benjamin, Abel, Willard and daughter Sarah living here? 3rd female unknown. Son Peter married in Dunstable in 1788.

207 Van Essen, "Robbins Genealogical Collection."
208 Van Essen, "Robbins Genealogical Collection."

However, the actual census looks like this:

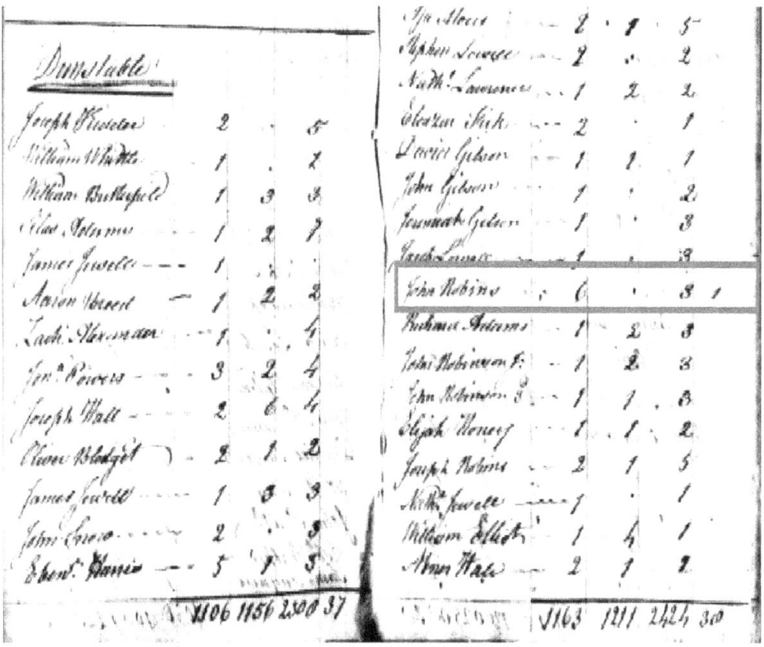

There are 6 men, 3 women, and 1 “all other free persons.” The three women would be John’s wife Sarah and their daughters Hannah and Sarah. This confirms that a non white person was living in the house with them in 1790.

The 1800 Census looks like this:

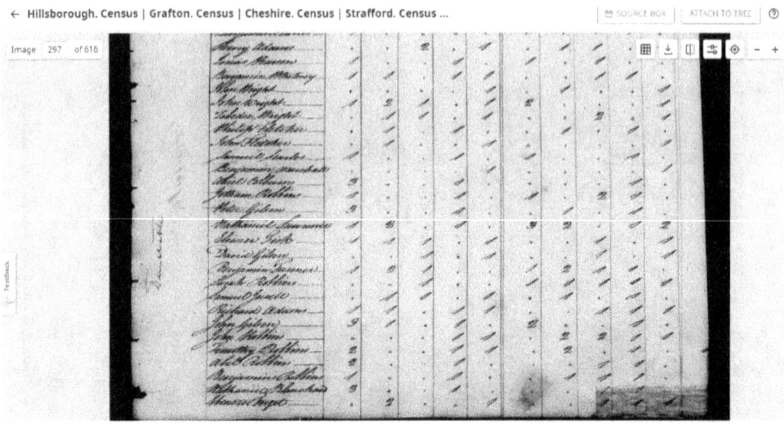

The genealogist suggests that the Sarah listed as a head of household is probably the wife of John, Jr. who was in Maine. The daughter Sarah would likely not be a head of household because she was declared non compos menti in 1801.[209] What this genealogist fails to note, is the "1" all other free persons listed in line with Timothy Robbins. This 3rd unknown female could possibly be their enslaved person. This supports the theory for the 1764 Census that Robins enslaved a woman. In New Hampshire, enslaved people were no longer taxed as property beginning in 1789, however slavery was never technically abolished until the passage of the 13th Amendment in 1865.[210] So this Once Known woman may have still been enslaved into the 19th Century. No other records could be found at this time.

---

209 Van Essen, "Robbins Genealogical Collection

210 "Slavery in New Hampshire." http://slavenorth.com/newhampshire.htm. Accessed 4/26/2024

Once Known (enslaved by Samuel Fitch and Francis Leighton)

Samuel was born February 14, 1699 in Bedford, Massachusetts. On April 24, 1732, he married Joanna (Keyes) Kidder. They settled in Westford and had a farm. According to the tax records, Samuel Fitch was assessed for a slave in 1757.[211]

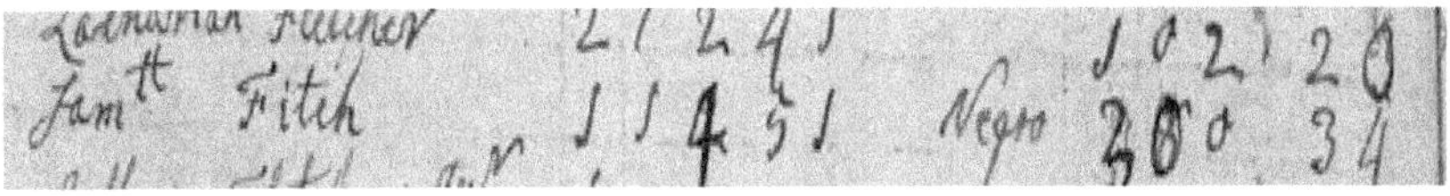

Fitch is not listed as a Servant Owner on the 1771 Tax Inventory. Fitch was assessed an extra poll tax in 1774. This can be surmised at being an extra person living in the house, perhaps the once enslaved individual.

Samuel Fitch died on January 9, 1775. His will is dated June 6, 1772 and probate dated February 21, 1775.[212] His land was left to his two daughters, Joanna and Lydia. Samuel and Joanna had a son, Samuel, but he died when he was young. Lydia was born in what was the Samuel Fitch Bed and Breakfast on Powers Road.

---

211 Town of Westford Tax Records, Volume 1, 42.

212 His probate could not be located.

Lydia married Francis Leighton on October 20, 1760. Francis was born in Ipswich, Massachusetts on July 22, 1734 to Captain John Leighton and his wife Hannah. Weary of seafaring life, John and his family removed to Littleton in 1748. In 1755, Francis fought in the French and Indian Wars in Captain Daniel Fletcher's company under the command of Colonel John Cummings. Francis and Lydia lived at the Fitch Farm.

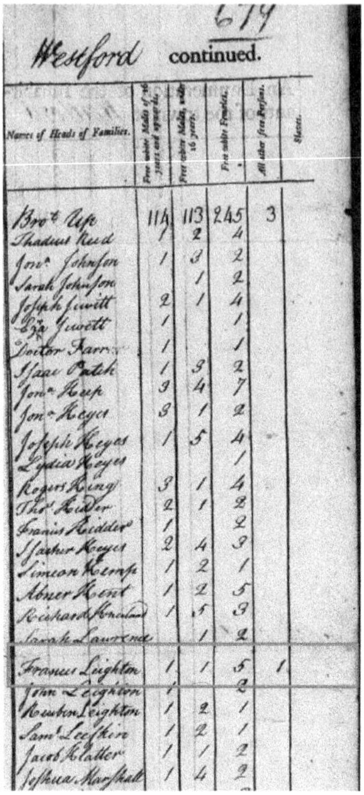
679

Westford continued.

Names of Heads of Families.	Free white Males of 16 years and upward	Free white Males under 16 years.	Free white Females.	All other free Persons.	Slaves.
Brot Up	114	113	245	3	
Thadeus Reed	1	2	4		
Jona Johnson	1	3	2		
Sarah Johnson		1	2		
Joseph Jewett	2	1	4		
Eza Jewett	1		1		
Doctor Farr	1		1		
Isaac Patch	1	3	2		
Jona Keep	3	4	7		
Jona Keyes	3	1	2		
Joseph Keyes	1	5	4		
Lydia Keyes			1		
Rogers King	3	1	4		
Thos Kidder	2	1	3		
Francis Kidder	1		2		
Issacher Keyes	2	4	3		
Simeon Kemp	1	2	1		
Abner Kent	1	2	5		
Richard Rowland	1	5	3		
Sarah Lawrence		1	2		
Francis Leighton	1	1	5	1	
John Leighton	1		2		
Reuben Leighton	1	2	1		
Saml Leeshin	1	2	1		
Jacob Latter	1	1	2		
Joshua Marshall	1	4	2		

Francis Leighton is on the list of enslavers in Westford because on the 1790 Federal Census, he is listed as having 1 "all free other persons" in his household.

The lack of a son, the timing of Samuel's death, and Francis inheriting his property and the Federal Census lends itself to Samuel enslaving an individual and that individual remained on the property with Francis and Lydia. No other records could be found at this time.

Conclusion

The history of Westford is a microcosm of American History with its progression from agriculture to railroads to textile industry and ultimately to healthcare and technology. So, like the enslaved people of Mount Vernon and Monticello provided for George Washington and Thomas Jefferson and others to have the opportunity to create a country, the same can be true for the men creating the town of Westford. The names of Westford's enslavers are names of the "founding fathers" of Westford- Boynton, Hildreth, Prescott, Fletcher, Cummings- all of these Men held important positions in the town. It is difficult to think that these men were allowed to hold these positions because they were also enslavers, and that it was these enslaved men and women that provided them the opportunity to do this. We cannot forget them.

Appendix A

Taxation of Slave Owners in Colonial Westford

By Wm. B. Prescott

Preface by Leslie Howard

President, Westford Historical Society

Preface

I delved into researching slavery in Westford, Massachusetts in February 2023 and found William Prescott's research on the taxation of enslavers immediately helpful. He set up the background for much of my research. His other research proved helpful as well- *Patriots and Taxpayers of Colonial Westford, Massachusetts in 1774*.

While reading his research, I desperately wanted a searchable digital copy of this work. I knew I had to retype his original work. In doing so, I corrected spelling and minor grammatical mistakes. I created new tables in Excel. I have a true appreciation for his writing and creating the tables using a typewriter!

I have kept the words negro, slave, slave ownership, etc. as I wanted to preserve the original as much as possible. These are words that are no longer acceptable, instead, for instance, using enslaved and enslaver.

I have also added images of the tax documents. These were taken by me and the source is *Tax Lists Vol. 1 1745-1775.* These lists are on microfilm at the J.V. Fletcher Library and the originals are in Westford's Town Hall.

Leslie Howard

May 2024

Summary

The existing tax records for colonial Westford disclose eleven individuals who, in at least one of the years between 1752 and 1775, were assessed for the ownership of Negro slaves. The tax due to slave ownership did not exceed twenty five percent of their total taxes for any of these individuals. The total taxes due to slave ownership amounted to one percent or less of the total taxes raised in the town in the years for which such records are available. A special Massachusetts Bay Province valuation of all real and personal property in 1771 confirms the identity of three of the four Westford slave owners in that year.

Introduction

The subject of slaves or slave owners in colonial Westford is one on which there seems to be only sparse information. In my study of the Westford Town Book up through early February 1800 only one entry which may bear on this subject has come to my attention. On page 285 of Volume I of Westford Town Book there is recorded an order by the Selectmen of Westford (Jonas Prescott, Jabez Keep, John Abbot, William Fletcher, Jr. and Joseph Read) to the Town Treasurer (Ephraim Hildreth, Jr.) authorizing as follows:

> "Item, pay to Mr. Craft, for the sum of eight shillings and eight pence for corn he bought of Mr. Hall's Negro manservant"

This order was dated 12 February 1753. It does not indicate whether the man servant was a slave or a freedman. The Rev. George Downey has informed me that Mr. Hall's manservant was enrolled as a member of the church. This present study based on tax records, can shed no light on the status of the Reverend Hall's Negro manservant since Mr. Hall, as Minister of the Town of Westford, appears not to have been required to pay taxes. His name does not appear in any of the tax lists during the years of his ministry.

Mrs. Jean Downey in a recent discussion pointed out that the old church records contain references to individuals as "Negro" or "Mulatto" but they throw no light on the status (slave or free) of these individuals.

The published compilation entitled *Vital Records of Westford, Massachusetts*, like others in the series, contains Births, Marriages, and Deaths recorded through 1849. In each of the three sections of this volume the vital records which pertain to Negroes are segregated at the end of the respective section. Thus, we find in the "Births" section:

> Phillis, child belonging to
> Sam[uel] Lawrence
> Bp. June 2, 1745
>
> Prince, child belonging to John
> Read
> Bp. September 4, 1743
>
> TONY, Francis, d. Sarah, bp.
> November 24, 1751

The section on Negro marriages contains these two entries:

> Porter, Cato and Thomas Dugan
> of Concord at Concord
> December 21, 1791.
>
> Freeman, Olive, a. 23y. and Peter
> Hazard, Jr. of Littleton, a. 29 y.
> laborer b. Littleton, s. Peter and
> Susannah October 13, 1849.

While neither of the two marriage entries pertain to the colonial period, we can deduce that both of these young women were, at the time of their marriages, residents of Westford.

There are no Negro entries in the "Deaths" section of the above volume. Again, from the five entries cited above it is impossible to firmly ascertain the status of the five individuals named. In the case of the first two birth records, the wording, "child belonging to—" is suggestive that they were born in slavery.

The volume entitled Heads of Families at the First Census of the United States Taken in the Year 1790, Massachusetts indicates that there were no slaves in the Town of Westford in that year. In this census, in addition to the name of the head of the household, the number of individuals in the household falling into each of the following categories:

1. White males 16 years of age or older.
2. White males less than 16 years of age.
3. White females
4. All other free persons
5. Slaves

The tabulation of the 1790 Census date for Westford shows a total of four persons falling into Category 4,[1] which must be the category used for free Negroes. One of these persons is listed as being in the household of Francis Leighton. The other three are all in the household of Cato Grey, which household has no entries in the first three categories. We can conclude that the Cato Grey household was a small non-white, probably Negro, household.

I can find only one mention of slaves, slavery, slave owners, Negroes, etc. in the Rev. E. R. Hodgman's *History of the Town of Westford, Massachusetts.*[213] In discussing the participation of Westford militia-men in the "Bunker Hill Fight," Hodgman (page 113) notes that Cesar Bason, from Westford, and a member of the company of Capt. Abijah Wyman of Ashby, died at that battle on June 17, 1775. I also quote the following:

> In regard to Cesar Bason, this anecdote is told with good authority. In the battle he found his powder was nearly gone, and putting in his last charge, he exclaimed, 'Now, Cesar, give 'em one more.' He fired and was himself shot and fell back into the trench. Tradition intimates that Leonard Proctor went to Cambridge on the day before the battle and was on or near the ground. Mr. Tinker states that Jacob Bascom of Westford was killed. No such name occurs in our records, and there was probably a mistake in putting Bascom for Bason. Bason was a colored man and perhaps the servant of James Burns. There is some uncertainty as to his real name. In 1773 'Cesar Burn was paid four shillings for four crows killed in this town.'

The only entry under the "Bason" surname in Vital Records of Westford, Massachusetts is the marriage of Francis Bason to Philip Smith on December 1, 1776. At this point, we can only speculate concerning the relationship of Francis to Cesar.

---

213 There are actually two references. See reference to Caesar in Hodgman, *History of Westford*, 64.

We can also only speculate on the reasons for Hodgman's omission of any discussion of the matter of slavery. Less than two decades before his work it had been such an emotional factor in the War of the Rebellion. Or he may have been reluctant to address the topic in a book sponsored by a committee of prominent citizens who bore some of the same surnames as those individuals who had been slave owners a century and a quarter earlier. We know from an existing letter he wrote in reply to someone concerned about the absence of dates of death in his section on genealogy, that he was forces to limit the size of the volume. I prefer the most charitable explanation, namely, that he could not cover this topic and stay within his allotted page limitations.

I have been studying the microfilm copies of old Westford records in order to extract all entries which mention members of the Prescott family. In September 1987, I started on a reel (No. 902074) of microfilm containing Tax Records, Volume 1 and Volume 2. In the colonial era the records placed all Inhabitants on one of two lists, a "North List" covering the northern part of the town including present Graniteville, Forge Village, Nabnasset, and Westford Center, and a "South List" covering the southern part of the town, including Parkerville, Carlisle Depot, and residents near the Acton and Littleton boundaries. All the Prescotts lived in the vicinity of Forge Village and north of there, so I was mostly concerned with "North List" records, and did not examine "South List" records with the same detail, other than to record the page numbers in the record book on which they were found. I am much indebted to Ms. Tisa Jewell, then the new Reference Librarian of the J. V. Fletcher Library in Westford for her marked perceptiveness. I was explaining to her, in general terms, my research project involving Prescotts, but at that time had on the microfilm reader screen a "South List Single Rate" document. As she looked at it, she called my attention to a tiny "Negro" notation in the entries for two individuals.

Fortuitously, there had been no such entries on any of the "North List Single Rate" documents I had examined up to that point. This prompted me to go back to the beginning of the reel, closely examine all "Single Rate" documents, and with subsequent scrutiny of all later lists arrive at the basis for this present work.

We now have a small, but tantalizing, peek at the subject of slavery in Westford for several years prior to the Revolutionary War. As the references cited just above suggest, we know both John Read and James Burn were assessed for slaves. We have no confirmation of the suggestion that Samuel Lawrence was a slave owner. We know who were slave owners in each of the fourteen years between 1752 and 1775, have a rough ordering of the value of their slaves, but little information on how many each owner had, but absolutely no information on the names or gender of these slaves.

Availability of Records

It must be pointed out the *Westford Tax Book, Volume 1 & Volume 2* are incomplete. They do not contain any tax records for certain years and there are years in which only partial records are available. In Volume 2 the last "Single Rate" list that includes a breakdown of livestock and so permits a calculation of the valuation assessed for slaves, is in 1775. This same volume ends in 1783. *Westford Tax Book, Volume 3 & Volume 4* must have covered 1783-1800, but are not in the microfilm collection which continues with Volume 5 covering 1800 to 1806. Thus, the probability of further date of this sort seems very slight, and the information herein contained may be all that can be gleaned from the tax records on this subject.

The Valuation Process

The following is my synthesis of how the town officials in colonial Westford handled the valuation segment of the process of raising taxes.

At the town meeting in early March of each year, the Inhabitants of Westford elected, by written ballot, five Selectman. They also elected three Assessors, but more frequently they would vote to, "Chuse as Assessors the first three Selectmen," but there were years when this practice was not followed. At the same meeting they would elect a "North Constable" and a "South Constable." A major function of each of these Constables was to collect taxes. In fact, it appears that the elected Constables were personally liable to pay into the Town Treasurer the "rates" committed to them by Warrants and lists issued to them by the Assessors. If the Constable could not collect the sum of money set against each person's name on the list, he could be relieved of the responsibility for paying that amount of money to the Town Treasurer only if the Selectmen declared that for a specified person the "Rate is Not Gittable" and ordered the Town Treasurer to credit the Constable for that amount. Another mechanism of relief for the Constable was an Article in a Warrant for a subsequent Town Meeting, asking that the Inhabitants vote to Abate the particular rate for the specified individual. IT does not seem unusual for these Constables to still have small amounts of "Rates in Their Hands" unpaid to the Town Treasurer two or three years after their term as Constable had expired. The "Town Book" contains many items in Selectmen's Orders to the Town Treasurer to credit past Constables for "Rates Not Gittable." Votes at Town Meeting "to Abate rates" are much more infrequent, and sometimes "passed in the Negative."

The amount of money assessed against the town Inhabitants was determined by their vote at a Town Meeting, as is still the case even if the magnitude is much different. For example, at the March Town Meeting they might vote first "To mend Highways by a Rate." Then they would vote, "To Raise fifty pounds to mend Highways." Separate Rates would be voted on at either May or September Town Meetings for various other purposes such as:

Minister Rate—to pay Minister's salary
Provincial Rate—to pay Provincial Taxes
Town Rate—to pay town debts and charges
County Rate—to pay County taxes
Other Rates—voted for some special non-recurring purpose such as purchasing land and building a pound or two build a new meeting house

In some of the years under consideration the town voted to combine into oner ate the amounts for town debts and charges (including school costs), for Minister's salary, and for the County taxes. Usually, the vote to raise money would also specify how and when it was to be paid into the Town Treasury, for example one half in a term of a few weeks and the remainder in a term of a few or several months.

As is still the case, the allocation of the proper proportion of each Rate to each of the Inhabitants was done by the Assessors. The total amount of each Rate was raised by four separate mechanisms, the head or poll tax, the tax on personal property, the tax on real property, and the tax on "Faculty & Money." The first step in this process each year was the compilation of the "Single Rate," somewhat comparable to the "Valuation" of later years. The process of compiling the "Single Rate" is referred to in the Town Book as "Taking the Invoices & Making the Single Rate," and the Assessors were reimbursed for each hour they spent at this task. If one Assessor provided subsistence for the others while they were all so engaged, he would also be reimbursed for this. Alternatively, the Assessors might use the facilities of one of the taverns and the tavern owners would be reimbursed "for supporting the Assessors." I have concluded that the "Invoices" from each Inhabitant, each male, twenty-one years of age or older, and widowed females, listed the following:

1. The number of males, 16 years through 20 years of age in the household. This figure was the number

of "heads" or "polls" the individual would be assessed.

2. The Personal estate of the individual which included the number of horses, oxen, cows, swine, and sheep. This category also must have included something about slaves owned by the individual, since the total personal estate valuation for slave owners is greater than the livestock can account for.
3. The real estate located within the Town of Westford that was owned by the individual. Non-resident owners of land located in Westford are included in the "Single Rate" lists, but with entries only in the "Real" column.
4. Any money the individual had, particularly that loaned out at interest.
5. Certain individuals who derived income from other than the produce of their land were also assessed for "Faculty." Few persons were so taxed. Those that were other references suggest were tavern-keepers, store-keepers, carpenters, & cabinet makers. It appears that doctors and lawyers were not so taxed. Some later "Single Rates" lists show persons taxed in this category for "trading stock" or inventory for a business.

All the existing copies of "Single Rate" lists are about the same with a name column followed by six narrow columns for polls, Horses, oxen, cows, swine, and sheep. The order of the remaining columns seems to vary, but usually the next was a column for the valuation of the Personal Estate, followed by a wide column headed "Money" with the amount of money in pounds within parentheses followed by the amount assessed. The "Faculty" column usually followed with only the amount of assessment for the few cases to which it applied. The final column was the "Real Estate" column and contained only the assessment figure.

I have made no attempt to deduce how the assessment figure for "Real Estate" was arrived at. For some members of the Prescott family, this figure remained constant over several years (Not included in this work). From a careful study of "Single Rate" list for a given year I have deduced how the "Personal Estate" assessment was arrived at. For those who did not own slaves it is the sum of the products of a fixed value for each type of livestock and the number of that type owned by an individual. For some unknown reason, the assigned fixed value for each type of animal was changed starting in 1759.

The table below lists the values for each animal in the two time periods:

	Assigned Value	
	Through 1758 **£=s=p=f**	**After 1758** **£=s=p=f**
1 Horse	0=0=2=0	0=2=0=0
1 Ox	0=0=2=0	0=2=0=0
1 Cow	0=0=1=2	0=1=6=0
1 Swine	0=0=0=2	0=0=5=0
1 Sheep	0=0=0=1/2	0=0=1=3

When an inhabitant was assessed for slaves that he owned, his line entry for the number of each type of livestock was followed by the notation "Negro" and the "Personal Estate" entry was larger than that predicted from the values of the livestock entries. I have concluded that this difference was his assessment for slaves he owned.

The "Single Rate" lists do not have a final column to list the sum for the assessments for the line entry for each Inhabitant. Some lists have at the bottom of the list a statement of the Total assessment for that List and a statement of the number of "heads" or polls. I have concluded that this "Single Rate" mechanism was used solely as a "Valuation" mechanism for ascertaining the proportion of each subsequent "Rate" (for example a "Town Rate") that each individual was expected to pay. This conclusion is bolstered, in my judgement [sic], by the fact that the line entries in "Single Rate" list are not summed for each individual, and the fact that all other "Rate" lists always (some Highway Rate lists are an exception) broken down to show how much each individual was assessed for that Rate because of Polls, Personal Estate, Real Estate, and "Money + Faculty" and the total sum.

Who Owned Slaves in Colonial Westford?

From the "Single Rate" list in *Westford Tax Book Volume 1*, it was possible to identify eleven individuals who during one or more of the years between 1752 and 1775, were recorded as owning slaves. Such records were available for only fourteen years of the twenty-three-year period, yielding thirty-five "Single Rate" entries over the years.

In Table I, I have collated the thirty-five entries, first alphabetically by surname, then chronologically. Each line entry includes only the date bearing on the "Personal Estate." Data on "Real Estate" or "Money" or "Faculty" have not been included. Included is my calculation of the amount attributable to livestock and my calculated amount of the "Personal Estate" due to slave ownership (Personal Estate minus the Amount due to Livestock), and the amount due to slaves expressed as a percentage of the "Personal Estate" entry. Since, as mentioned above, two different valuation systems were used during this period, I have also tried to put a slave valuation on a common basis by converting it to "Equivalent Horses" by dividing the amount due to slaves by the valuation of one horse for that year. It must be pointed out that in this and all subsequent tables, money amounts have all been recorded in a common format (Pounds, Shillings, Pence, Farthings) even though the same entries in the original list may have omitted Pounds or Farthings in some lists.

In order to illustrate the variability in slave ownership from year to year, the entries in Table I for valuation expressed as "Equivalent Horses" have been sorted by year to give the chronological form to Table II. This table suggests that for the years that data are available, there were more slaves in Westford in 1757-1758, followed by a decline to a low point in 1768, and then followed by another high point in 1773.

Table I

Individual Assessments for Slaves in Westford 1752-1775

									Personal Assessment				
											Due To Slaves		
									Total	Due to Animals	Amount	% of Total	Horse Equivalent #
Year	Individual	Polls	Horses	Oxen	Cows	Swine	Sheep		£=s=p=f	£=s=p=f	£=s=p=f		
1769	Moses Burge	1	1	2	5	3	2	Negro	1=2=0=0	0=14=8=0	0=7=4=0	33.32	5.67
1752	James Buss	1	1	2	5	1	0	Neg. (5)	0=14=3=0	0=9=6=0	0=4=9=0	33	2.5
1768	James Buss	1	1	2	3	2	0	Negro	0=13=4=0	0=11=4=0	0=2=0=0	15	1
1771	Ephraim Cummings	1	1	2	4	3	9	Negro	0=18=6=0	0=14=7=0	0=3=11=0	21.17	1.96
1773	Ephraim Cummings	1	1	2	3	1	6	Negro	0=19=11=0	0=11=10=0	0=8=1=0	40.56	4.05
1757	Samuel Fitch	1	1	4	5	1	9	Negro	0=3=0=0	0=1=6=0	0=1=6=0	50	9
1757	Gershom Fletcher	2	1	4	5	1	0	Negro	0=3=0=2	0=1=7=0	0=1=5=2	47.95	8.75
1758	Gershom Fletcher	2	1	4	1	2	0	Negro	0=2=2=0	0=1=3=2	0=0=10=2	40.36	5.25
1759	Gershom Fletcher	1	1	4	5	3	9	Negro	1=8=9=0	0=18=9=0	0=10=0=0	34.78	5
1760	Gershom Fletcher	1	1	4	5	3	9	Negro	1=8=9=0	0=18=9=0	0=10=0=0	34.78	5
1761	Gershom Fletcher	1	1	2	9	3	9	Negro	1=8=1=0	1=0=9=0	0=7=11=0	27.61	3.98
1762	Gershom Fletcher	1	1	2	9	3	9	Negro	1=6=5=0	1=0=9=0	0=5=8=0	22.2	2.96
1763	Gershom Fletcher	1	1	2	2	2	0	Negro	0=15=10=0	0=9=10=0	0=6=0=0	37.9	3
1770	Pelatiah Fletcher	2	1	2	7	1	10	Negro	1=10=0=0	0=19=3=0	0=10=9=0	33.61	5.04
1771	Pelatiah Fletcher	1	1	3	8	4	11	Negro	1=13=3=0	1=3=3=0	0=10=0=0	30.08	5
1773	Pelatiah Fletcher	1	1	2	7	2	12	Negro	1=11=4=0	0=19=1=0	0=12=3=0	39.1	6.13
1775	Pelatiah Fletcher	1	2	2	7	1	13	Negro	1=17=8=0	1=1=8=0	0=16=0=0	42.7	8
1752	Joseph Hildreth, Jr	1	2	4	6	4	15	Neg (10)	0=1=11=1	0=1=1=3	0=0=10=0	42.11	5
1757	Joseph Hildreth, Jr	2	2	4	6	2	0	Negro	0=3=3=0	0=1=10=0	0=1=5=3	43.4	8.75
1758	Joseph Hildreth, Jr	1	1	4	6	1	0	Negro	0=3=5=0	0=1=8=2	0=1=8=2	50	10.25
1759	Joseph Hildreth, Jr	1	1	4	8	3	10	Negro	2=0=0=0	1=1=9=0	0=18=3=0	45.63	9.13
1760	Joseph Hildreth, Jr	1	2	2	5	4	10	Negro	1=15=0=0	0=18=5=0	0=16=7=0	47.38	8.29
1761	Joseph Hildreth, Jr	2	2	2	6	2	10	Negro	1=16=0=0	0=19=1=0	0=16=11=0	46.99	8.46
1762	Joseph Hildreth, Jr	2	2	2	7	2	12	Negro	1=17=6=0	1=1=1=0	0=16=5=0	43.79	8.21
1763	Joseph Hildreth, Jr	1	2	2	7	2	12	Negro	1=15=0=0	1=1=1=0	0=13=11=0	39.76	6.96
1773	Jonathan Keyes	1	1	0	4	1	6	Negro	0=16=5=0	0=10=2=0	0=6=1=0	37.43	3.05
1757	John Read	1	1	2	4	1	0	Negro	0=1=8=0	0=1=0=2	0=0=7=2	37.5	3.75
1758	John Read	1	1	0	5	0	0	Negro	0=1=9=2	0=0=9=2	0=1=0=0	55.81	6
1763	William Read	1	1	2	1	0	0	Negro	0=15=6=0	0=7=6=0	0=8=0=0	48.38	4
1768	William Read	1	1	2	1	1	0	Negro	1=0=0=0	0=7=11=0	0=12=1=0	60.4	6.04
1769	William Read	1	1	2	1	1	0	Negro	1=0=0=0	0=7=11=0	0=12=1=0	60.4	6.04
1770	William Read	1	1	2	1	1	6	Negro	0=13=11=0	0=7=11=0	0=6=0=0	43.1	3
1771	William Read	1	1	2	1	2	0	Negro	0=13=10=0	0=8=4=0	0=5=6=0	39.77	2.75
1773	Abner Wilkins	1	1	2	1	1	0	Negro	0=13=11=0	0=7=11=0	0=6=0=0	43.1	3
1775	Abner Wilkins	1	1	0	2	0	0	Negro	0=13=0=0	0=5=0=0	0=8=0=0	62.5	4

Table II

Chronological Listing of Assessment for Slaves (Expressed as Equivalent Horses) In Westford 1752 to 1775

Year	Individual	For Individual	Total for Year	Change for Year
		Assessment expressed as Horses		
1752	James Burn	2.5	7.5	
	Joseph Hildreth, Jr.	5		
1757	Samuel Fitch	9		
	Gershom Fletcher	8.75		
	Joseph Hildreth, Jr.	8.75		
	John Read	3.75	30.25	22.75
1758	Gershom Fletcher	5.25		
	Joseph Hildreth, Jr.	10.25		
	John Read	6	21.5	(8.75)
1759	Gershom Fletcher	5		
	Joseph Hildreth, Jr.	9.13	14.13	(7.37)
1760	Gershom Fletcher	5		
	Joseph Hildreth, Jr.	8.29	13.29	(0.84)
1761	Gershom Fletcher	3.96		
	Joseph Hildreth, Jr.	8.46	12.42	(0.87)
1762	Gershom Fletcher	2.96		
	Joseph Hildreth, Jr.	8.21	11.17	(1.25)
1763	Gershom Fletcher	3		
	Joseph Hildreth, Jr.	6.96		
	William Read	4	13.96	2.79
1768	James Burn	1		
	William Read	6.04	7.04	(6.92)
1769	William Read	6.04		
	Moses Burge	3.67	9.71	2.67
1770	William Read	3		
	Pelatiah Fletcher	5.04	8.04	(1.67)
1771	William Read	2.75		
	Ephraim Comings	1.96		
	Pelatiah Flethcer	5	9.71	1.67
1773	Ephraim Comings	4.04		
	Pelatiah Flethcer	6.13		
	Jonathan Keyes	3.04		
	Abner Wilkins	3	16.21	6.5
1775	Pelatiah Fletcher	8		
	Abner Wilkins	4	12	(4.21)

The Monetary Value of the Slaves in Colonial Westford

With respect to the "Single Rate" compilation made each year, I am convinced that it was intended completely internally consistent as to the relative value of the various species of livestock, slaves, money at loan, but is not to be considered as a list of the absolute value of each of these categories. For example, it is not reasonable to state that a pair of oxen had an absolute value of four shillings in 1759, when in answering the Highway Rate for that year and Inhabitant who worked on mending highways for one day and provided the use of a pair of oxen and a cart, was credited a total of three shillings, six pence, two shillings six pence for his labor and one shillings for the use of the oxen and cart.[2] However, in the 1759 "Single Rate North List" Captain Jonas Prescott was assessed four shillings nine pence for eighty pounds money our at interest, or at a rate of one shilling for each sixteen pounds 13 shillings and four pence (£16=13=4). On this basis, the four shilling valuation for a pair of oxen would represent an actual value of £66=13=4, which does not seem unreasonable for a pair of oxen. On this same basis the various species of livestock would have had the following values in 1759:

	£=s=p=f
1 Horse	33=6=8=0
1 Ox	33=6=8=0
1 Cow	25=0=0=0
1 Swine	6=18=10=3
1 Sheep	2=8=7=1

Using this same basis, I generated from the data in Table II the data presented in Table III, wherein the slave valuation is based on the valuation placed on one hundred pounds of money, the valuation of a horse, each for the same year, and the “Equivalent Horses” data from Table II. It should be noted that the valuations included for 1775 may be only an aberration since in that year the assessment for money was tripled over the previous year with no concomitant increase of the same magnitude for all other categories of either real or personal estates. This may have been an attempt to tax “passive income,” to use modern terminology, at a higher rate than other items making up the taxes.

Table III

Chronological Listing of Estimated Value of Slaves In Westford 1752-1775

Year	Individual	Estimated Value of Slaves (£=s=p=f) For Individual	Total for Year	Change for Year
1752	James Burn	83=6=8		
	James Hildreth, Jr.	166=13=4	250=0=0	
1757	Samuel Fitch	300=0=0		
	Gershom Fletcher	291=13=4		
	James Hildreth, Jr.	291=13=4		
	John Read	200=0=0	1008=6=8	758=6=8
1758	Gershom Fletcher	175=0=0		
	James Hildreth, Jr.	341=13=4		
	John Read	200=0=0	717=13=4	(291=13=4)
1759	Gershom Fletcher	166=13=4		
	James Hildreth, Jr.	304=6=8	471=0=0	(245=6=8)
1760	Gershom Fletcher	166=13=4		
	James Hildreth, Jr.	276=6=8	443=0=0	(28=0=0)
1761	Gershom Fletcher	132=0=0		
	James Hildreth, Jr.	282=0=0	414=0=0	(29=0=0)
1762	Gershom Fletcher	98=13=4		
	James Hildreth, Jr	273=13=4	372=5=8	(41=13=4)
1763	Gershom Fletcher	100=0=0		
	James Hildreth, Jr.	232=0=0		
	William Read	133=6=8	465=6=8	93=0=0
1768	James Burn	33=6=8		
	William Read	201=6=8	234=13=4	(230=13=4)
1769	William Read	201=6=8		
	Moses Burge	122=6=8	323=13=4	89=0=0
1770	William Read	100=0=0		
	Pelatiah Fletcher	168=0=0	268=0=0	(55=13=4)
1771	William Read	91=13=4		
	Ephraim Comings	65=6=8		
	Pelatiah Fletcher	166=13=4	323=13=4	55=13=4
1773	Ephraim Comings	134=13=4		
	Pelatiah Fletcher	204=6=8		
	Jonathan Keyes	101=6=8		
	Abner Wilkins	100=0=0	540=6=8	216=13=14
1775	Pelatiah Fletcher	88=17=9=1		
	Abner Wilkins	44=8=10=3	133=6=8	(407=0=0)

The above figures are based on the following assessments made during the time period indicated for one hundred pounds of money:

1752 through 1758	£ 0=0-6-0
1759 through 1771	£0=6=0=0
1775	£0=18=0=0

<u>Increase in Actual Taxes Due to Ownership of Slaves</u>

The previous sections have dealt exclusively with the data extracted from the "Single Rate" documents. These, as noted above, were merely a valuation and proportioning tool in order for the Assessors to equitably proportion the "Rates" authorized at Town Meeting. A natural question is how much in additional taxes the slave owners were subjected to because of their slaves. In order to assist in answering this question I have made the following synthesis of how the Assessors proceeded from the "Single Rate" lists to the "Rate" lists given the Constables for collection.

I have concocted a hypothetical example to illustrate how, I believe, the Assessors went from the "Single Rate" list to the line entries in the money "Rate" lists. ASSUME----

	Polls	Sum of Real + Personal + Faculty, etc. £=s=p=f
North List Single Rate	90	90=0=0=0
South List Single Rate	60	60=0=0=0
Total for Town	150	150=0=0=0

ASSUME SINGLE RATE ENTRY FOR Inhabitant A:
Polls: 2
Real Estate: £1=0=0=0
Personal Estate: 0=10=0=0
Faculty, etc.: 0=0=0=0

ASSUME SINGLE RATE ENTRY FOR Inhabitant B:
Polls: 1
Real Estate: £0=10=0=0
Personal Estate: 1=0=0=0
Faculty, etc.: 0=0=0=0

ASSUME THE TOWN HAS VOTED TO RAISE £50=0=0=0 to pay town Debts.

The Assessor first had to decide what proportion of the Rate would be raised from the "Polls" and what proportion from the "Estates." I have found no clue as to how this decision was made. It could have been based on their own judgement [sic], or on a directive from the Provincial government. The 1730 Tax Lists, the first after the incorporation of the Town, raised about sixty percent of the rates from the "Heads." However, the proportion due to poll taxes in these years now under consideration seems to be less than that. In this procedural vacuum, for our example:

ASSUME THAT 40% IS TO BE RAISED BY POLLS AND 60% FROM THE ESTATES

Thus, £20=0=0=0 will be raised by polls. Since there are 150 polls in town, each poll will be assessed:

£20=0=0=0/150 or £0=2=8=0

So Inhabitant A with 2 polls is assessed £ 0=5=4=0, and Inhabitant B with 1 poll is assessed £0=2=8=0.

Since £20=0=0=0 was to be raised by polls, this leaves only £30=0=0=0 to be raised by "Estates." Since we assumed that the Sum of Personal plus Real plus Money and Faculty on the Single Rate would be £150=0=0=0, and one this Single Rate we assumed Inhabitant A had a Real Estate Valuation of £1=0=0=0, his assessment on the Town Rate for Real Estate is:

$$\frac{(1 = 0 = 0 = 0) \times (30 = 0 = 0 = 0)}{(150 = 0 = 0 = 0)} = £0 = 4 = 0 = 0$$

While the amount for his Personal Estate is:

$$\frac{(0 = 10 = 0 = 0) \times (30 = 0 = 0 = 0)}{(150 = 0 = 0 = 0)} = £0 = 2 = 0 = 0$$

For Inhabitant B, the similar calculations are:
For Real Estate:

$$\frac{(0 = 10 = 0 = 0) \times (30 = 0 = 0 = 0)}{(150 = 0 = 0 = 0)} = £0 = 2 = 0 = 0$$

For Personal Estate:

$$\frac{(1 = 0 = 0 = 0) \times (30 = 0 = 0 = 0)}{(150 = 0 = 0 = 0)} = £0 = 4 = 0 = 0$$

Therefore, the Town Rate list committed with a Warrant to the Constable to collect, would read, in part:

	Polls S=p	Money +Faculty £=s=p=f	Personal £=s=p=f	Real £=s=p=f	Sum Total £=s=p=f
Inhabitant A	5=4	0=0=0=0	0=2=0=0	0=4=0=0	0=11=4=0
Inhabitant B	2=8	0=0=0=0	0=4=0=0	0=2=0=0	0=8=8=0

By using this technique, the Assessors provided lists for each Rate, collectible by the Constables that detailed the amount assessed in each of the categories as well as the total amount due. If at Town Meeting, the voters agreed to raise £100=0=0=0 for some other purpose, the list given the Constable for the new rate would have had amounts exactly double those in the above example.

In order to estimate how much slave ownership contributed to the taxes that the individual slave owners were assessed, all separate Rate lists for the years in which "Single Rate" lists were available were scanned. The Personal Estate portion of the assessment and the total assessment were extracted for those individuals which the "Single Rate" lists identified as slave owners. The amount lists as "personal" for a given individual was multiplied by the fraction of the "Personal Estate" due to slaves as calculated from the appropriate "Single Rate" and included in Table I to give the amount of the specific Rate entry due to slave ownership. This product, then multiplied by 100 and divided by the Sum Total assessment for a given individual for a specific Rate gave the percentage of the "Sum Total" which that individual had to pay because of his ownership of slaves. There are a total of fifty-six such individual-year-rate entries included in Table IV. Twenty-one (38%) of these entries show that slave ownership contributed less than ten percent to the tax assessed. Thirty (54%) of the entries show that slave ownership contributed between ten percent and twenty percent of the tax assessed, and only five (9%) of the entries show that between twenty percent and twenty-five percent of the taxes assessed are due to slave ownership. Of these five entries, three are for rates against William Read in 1769 and two are against Abner Wilkins in 1773 and 1775. We can conclude from the data in Table IV that slave ownership did not contribute excessively to the tax burden of most slave owners during the period covered by this data.

A corollary question to be addressed is how much the assessment for slaves relieved the total tax burden on the town. To make this estimate, the total of the Personal Assessments due to slaves for a given Rate was ratioed against the total amount of the Rate (sum of North and South lists) and the ratio expressed as a percentage. These data are included in Table V.

Table IX

Amount of Tax and Percentage of Total Taxes Paid Due to Ownership of Slaves

Year	Rate	Individual	Total Personal (£-s-d)	Due to Slaves: Fraction of Personal	Due to Slaves: Amount (£-s-d)	Due to Slaves: % of Rate Total
[illegible]	Province	Samuel Finch	[illegible]	.5	[illegible]	15.22
	Province	Gershom Fletcher	[illegible]	[illegible]	[illegible]	[illegible]
	Province	Joseph Hildreth, Jr	[illegible]	[illegible]	[illegible]	[illegible]
	Province	John Reed	[illegible]	[illegible]	[illegible]	[illegible]
[illegible]	Highway	Samuel Finch	[illegible]	.5	[illegible]	15
	Highway	Gershom Fletcher	[illegible]	[illegible]	[illegible]	[illegible]
	Highway	Joseph Hildreth, Jr	[illegible]	[illegible]	[illegible]	[illegible]
	Highway	John Reed	[illegible]	[illegible]	[illegible]	[illegible]
	Minister	Gershom Fletcher	[illegible]	[illegible]	[illegible]	[illegible]
	Minister	Joseph Hildreth, Jr	[illegible]	.5	[illegible]	[illegible]
	Minister	John Reed	[illegible]	[illegible]	[illegible]	[illegible]
	Town	Gershom Fletcher	[illegible]	[illegible]	[illegible]	4.22
	Town	Joseph Hildreth, Jr	[illegible]	.5	[illegible]	[illegible]
	Town	John Reed	[illegible]	[illegible]	[illegible]	[illegible]
	Province	Gershom Fletcher	[illegible]	[illegible]	[illegible]	[illegible]
	Province	Joseph Hildreth, Jr	[illegible]	.5	[illegible]	[illegible]
	Province	John Reed	[illegible]	[illegible]	[illegible]	[illegible]
[illegible]	Minister	Gershom Fletcher	[illegible]	[illegible]	[illegible]	[illegible]
	Minister	Joseph Hildreth, Jr	[illegible]	[illegible]	[illegible]	[illegible]
	Town	Gershom Fletcher	[illegible]	[illegible]	[illegible]	[illegible]
	Town	Joseph Hildreth, Jr	[illegible]	[illegible]	[illegible]	[illegible]
	Province	Gershom Fletcher	[illegible]	[illegible]	[illegible]	[illegible]
	Province	Joseph Hildreth, Jr	[illegible]	[illegible]	[illegible]	[illegible]
[illegible]	Minister	Gershom Fletcher	[illegible]	[illegible]	[illegible]	5
	Minister	Joseph Hildreth, Jr	[illegible]	[illegible]	[illegible]	[illegible]
	Town	Gershom Fletcher	[illegible]	[illegible]	[illegible]	8
	Town	Joseph Hildreth, Jr	[illegible]	[illegible]	[illegible]	[illegible]
	Province	Gershom Fletcher	[illegible]	[illegible]	[illegible]	[illegible]
	Province	Joseph Hildreth, Jr	[illegible]	[illegible]	[illegible]	[illegible]
[illegible]	Town + Minister + County	Gershom Fletcher	[illegible]	[illegible]	[illegible]	[illegible]
	Town + Minister + County	Joseph Hildreth, Jr	[illegible]	[illegible]	[illegible]	[illegible]
	Province	Gershom Fletcher	[illegible]	[illegible]	[illegible]	[illegible]
	Province	Joseph Hildreth, Jr	[illegible]	[illegible]	[illegible]	[illegible]
[illegible]	New Meeting House	Moses Barge	[illegible]	[illegible]	[illegible]	[illegible]
	New Meeting House	William Reed	[illegible]	[illegible]	[illegible]	[illegible]
	Town	William Reed	[illegible]	[illegible]	[illegible]	25
	Province	Moses Barge	[illegible]	[illegible]	[illegible]	[illegible]
	Province	William Reed	[illegible]	[illegible]	[illegible]	[illegible]
[illegible]	Town + Minister + County	Pelatiah Fletcher	[illegible]	[illegible]	[illegible]	[illegible]
	Town + Minister + County	William Reed	[illegible]	[illegible]	[illegible]	[illegible]
	New Meeting House	Pelatiah Fletcher	[illegible]	[illegible]	[illegible]	[illegible]
	New Meeting House	William Reed	[illegible]	[illegible]	[illegible]	[illegible]
[illegible]	Minister	Ephraim Coverage	[illegible]	[illegible]	[illegible]	[illegible]
	Minister	Pelatiah Fletcher	[illegible]	[illegible]	[illegible]	[illegible]
	Minister	Jonathan Keyes	[illegible]	[illegible]	[illegible]	[illegible]
	Minister	Abner Wilkins	[illegible]	[illegible]	[illegible]	[illegible]
	Town	Ephraim Coverage	[illegible]	[illegible]	[illegible]	[illegible]
	Town	Pelatiah Fletcher	[illegible]	[illegible]	[illegible]	[illegible]
	Town	Jonathan Keyes	[illegible]	[illegible]	[illegible]	[illegible]
	Town	Abner Wilkins	[illegible]	[illegible]	[illegible]	[illegible]
	Province	Ephraim Coverage	[illegible]	[illegible]	[illegible]	[illegible]
	Province	Pelatiah Fletcher	[illegible]	[illegible]	[illegible]	[illegible]
	Province	Jonathan Keyes	[illegible]	[illegible]	[illegible]	[illegible]
	Province	Abner Wilkins	[illegible]	[illegible]	[illegible]	[illegible]
[illegible]	Province	Pelatiah Fletcher	[illegible]	[illegible]	[illegible]	[illegible]

Table V

Chronological Listing of Percentage of Taxes Due to Slave Ownership

Year	Rate	Total Rate £=s=p=f	*Due to Slaves* Amount £=s=p=f	% of Total Rate
1757	Province	259=8=0=0	1=2=8=1	0.435
1758	Highway	30=0=0=0	0=2=5=2	0.409
	Minister	65=0=0=0	0=3=3=0	0.25
	Town	105=0=0=0	0=5=0=2	0.24
	Province	218=14=0=0	0=12=7=1	0.284
1760	Minister	70=0=0=0	0=3=0=0	0.214
	Town	60=0=0=0	0=1=11=1	0.161
	Province	286=18=3=0	0=10=1=1	0.176
1761	Minister	80=0=0=0	0=4=1=2	0.258
	Town	60=0=0=0	0=3=1=1	0.257
	Province	246=8=9=0	0=11=10=1	0.239
1762	Town + Minister +County	129=19=10=0	0=6=1=1	0.235
	Province	305=15=9=0	0=19=3=1	0.371
1769	New Meeting House	120=0=0=0	0=4=4=0	0.181
	Province	145=12=6=0	0=5=4=3	0.185
1770	Town + Minister +County	120=0=0=0	0=3=2=3	0.135
	New Meeting House	100=0=0=0	0=2=4=2	0.148
1773	Minister	45=0=0=0	0=2=8=2	0.361
	Town	140=0=0=0	0=9=1=1	0.325
	Province	127=17=2=0	0=8=3=0	0.33
1775	Province	39=1=0=0	0=8=5=0	1.078

From Table V, it is clear that the effect of taxes on slaves paid by slave owners on the taxes paid by the other Inhabitants was small, barely exceeding one per cent of the total in 1775, and in all other years not exceeding one half percent. Thus the ownership of slaves by a few individuals in colonial Westford did little to reduce the taxes of the other residents, and, as shown in Table IV did not impose a great tax burden on the slave owners.

The 1771 Massachusetts Tax List

One additional bit of evidence has been found which confirms in part the ownership of slaves by Inhabitants of Westford in the colonial era. In 1771 the provincial government required that a special valuation be made of all Inhabitants and the personal and real property of each individual. This covered many categories of property. Two folio pages were required to accommodate the many columns for the entry desired for each individual. One of these columns is headed "Servants for Life" which the enabling legislation defined as follows: "All Indian, Negro, or Mulatto servants for life from fourteen to forty-five years of age…"

All the records from the various towns have been converted to computer compatible format and a computer derived printout published in 1978.[3] The Westford entries show that the following individuals each had one "Servant for Life" as defined above:

Ephraim Comings
Pelatiah Fletcher
William Read
John Robins

The first three are listed in the "Single Rate" for 1771 as owning slaves, but John Robins is not. I should note that we do not know whether the criteria with those used for assessment as a slave in the "Single Rate."

In the Mormon microfilms of Westford Records there is a single frame on one reel that suggests that a similar valuation was carried out in 1792. Only one sheet is found in the microfilm, and in this version while many columns have identical headings to those used in 1772, THERE IS NO COLUMN HEADED "SERVANTS FOR LIFE." In this connection, we recall that the first Federal Census made in 1790 showed no entries in the column headed "Slaves," but entries in the column, "Other Free Persons," which is interpreted to include all persons who were not white.

We know from Table II that in 1771, the following valuations of slaves (expressed as Equivalent Horses) were made:

	Equivalent Horses
William Read	2.75
Ephraim Comings	1.96
Pelatiah Fletcher	5

The Massachusetts Tax List indicated that each of the above individuals owns only one "Servant for Life," it is difficult to accept that each of the above valuations represents only one slave unless the one owned by Pelatiah Fletcher was the only adult male with artisan skills and the ones owned by Ephraim Comings and William Read were immature males or females.

<u>Conclusion</u>

This has provided, as stated in the Introduction, a brief and dim glimpse into a subject that seems not to have been much researched in the past. It is my hope that this short scrutiny may be a catalyst for research in greater depth by others who may follow.

William B. Prescott

Bound Brook, NJ December 31, 1987

---

[1] See Appendix C for Westford's 1790 Census

[2] Rates voted at the March 5, 1759 Town Meeting, see page 370 of Town Book, Volume 1.

[3] The Massachusetts Tax List of 1771. Betty Hobbs Pruitt, Editor. G. K. Hall & Co. 70 Lincoln Street Boston, MA. 1978.

Note: Since then, Harvard University has digitized this inventory and it is available online here: https://legacy.sites.fas.harvard.edu/~hsb41/masstax/masstax.cgi

Appendix B: Westford's Early Tax Records

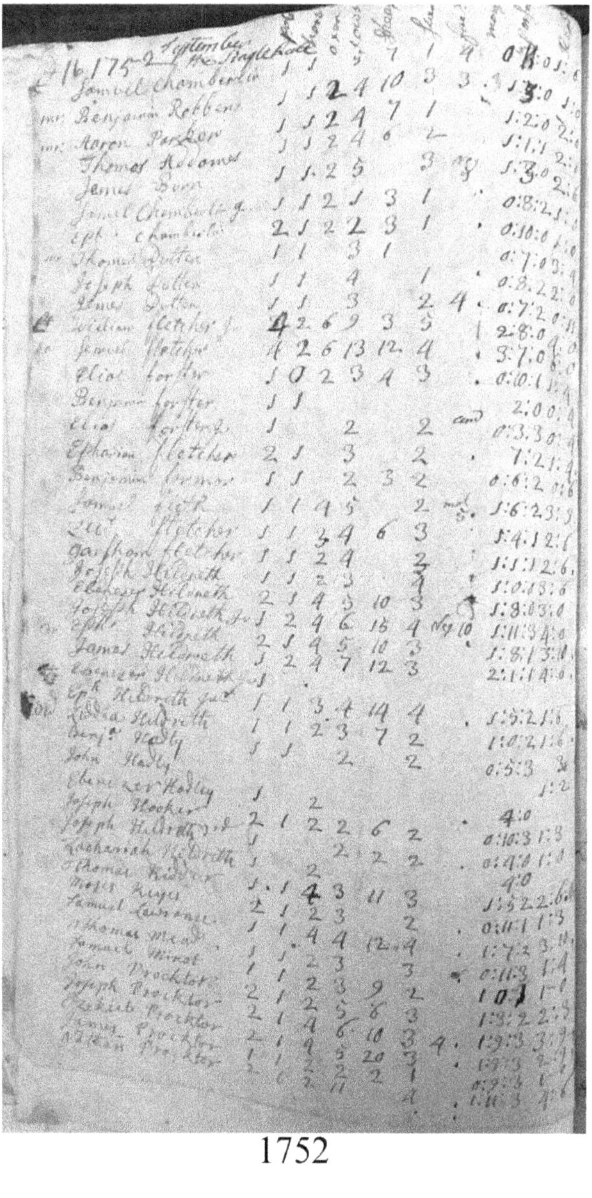

1752

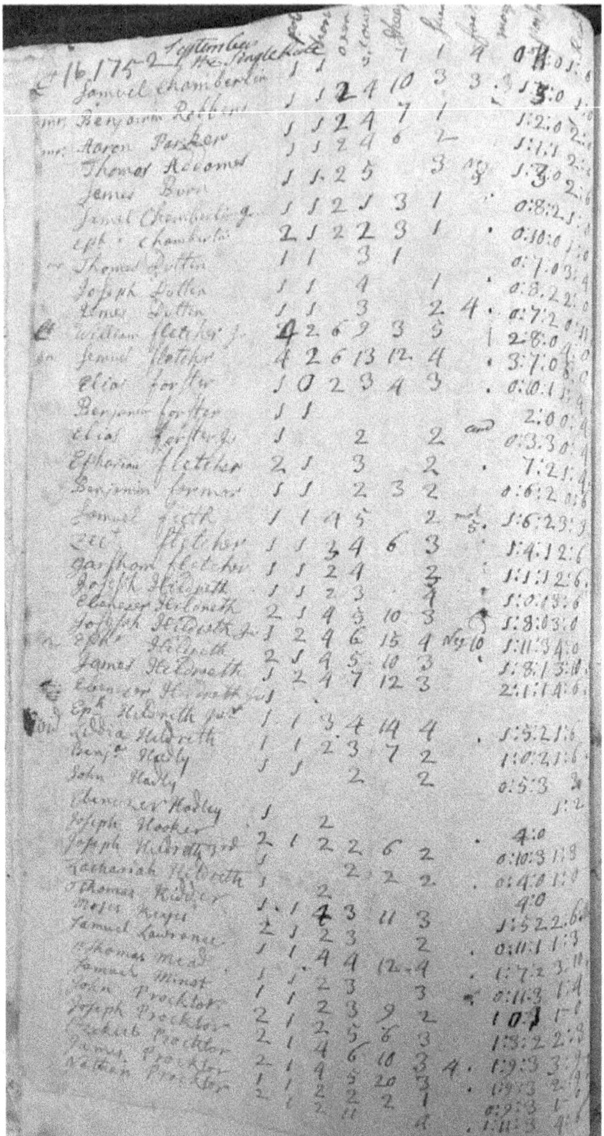

16 1757 September the Single Rate	1	1			7	1	4	0:11:0
Samuel Chamberlin	1	1	2	4	10	3	3	1:5:0
mr Benjamin Robbins	1	1	2	4	7	1		1:2:0
mr Aaron Parker	1	1	2	4	6	2		1:1:1
Thomas Adams	1	1	2	5		3		1:3:0
James Burn								
Samuel Chamberlin jr	1	1	2	1	3	1		0:8:2
Ephraim Chamberlin	2	1	2	2	3	1		0:10:0
Thomas Dutton	1	1		3	1			0:7:0
Joseph Dutton	1	1		4		1		0:8:2
James Dutton	1	1		3		2	4	0:7:2
William Fletcher jr	4	2	6	9	3	3		2:8:0
Samuel Fletcher	4	2	6	13	12	4		3:7:0
Elias Forster	1	0	2	3	4	3		0:10:1
Benjamin Forster	1	1						2:0:0
Elias Forster jr	1			2		2		0:3:3
Ephraim Fletcher	2	1		3		2		7:2
Benjamin Freeman	1	1		2	3	2		0:6:2
Samuel Frith	1	1	4	5		2		1:6:2
Zec^t Fletcher	1	1	3	4	6	3		1:4:1
Garshom Fletcher	1	1	2	4		2		1:1:1
Joseph Hildreth	1	1	2	3		1		1:0:1
Ebenezer Hildreth	2	1	4	3	10	3		1:8:0
Joseph Hildreth jr	1	2	4	6	15	4		1:8:0
Ephr Hildreth	2	1	4	5	10	3		1:11:3
James Hildreth	1	2	4	7	12	3		1:8:1
Ebenezer Hildreth jr	1							2:1:1
Eph Hildreth jr								
Zidra Hildreth	1	1	3	4	14	4		1:5:2
Benja Hadly	1	1	2	3	7	2		1:0:2
John Hadly	1	1		2		2		0:5:3
Ebenezer Hadley								
Joseph Hooker	1		2					
Joseph Hildreth 3d	2	1	2	2	6	2		4:0
Zachariah Hildreth	1			2	2	2		0:10:3
Thomas Kidder	1		2					0:4:0
Moses Keyes	1	1	4	3	11	3		4:0
Samuel Lawrence	2	1	2	3		2		1:5:2
Thomas Mead	1	1	4	4	12	4		0:11:1
Samuel Minot	1	1	2	3		3		1:7:2
John Procktor	1	1	2	3	9	2		0:11:3
Joseph Procktor	2	1	2	5	6	3		1 0
Ezekiel Procktor	2	1	4	6	10	3	4	1:8:2
James Procktor	2	1	4	5	20	3		1:9:3
Nathan Procktor	1	1	2	2	2	1		1:9:3
	2	1	2	11		2		0:9:3
								1:11:3

1757

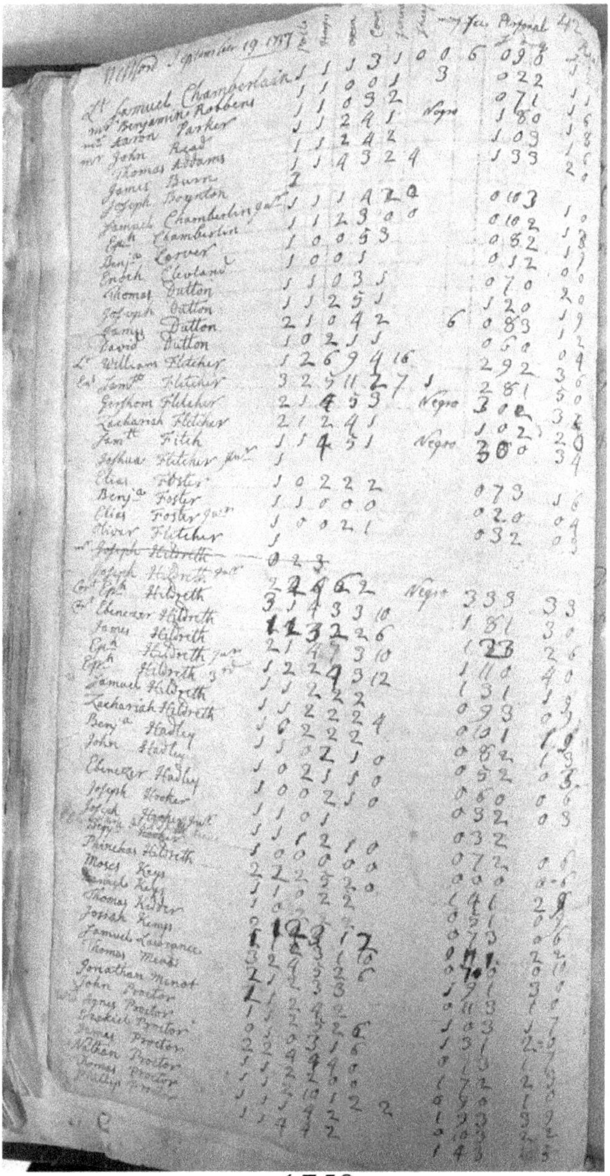
Wilton September 19 1757

Lt Samuel Chamberlain
mr Benjamin Robbens
mr Aaron Parker
mr John Read
Thomas Addams
James Burn
Joseph Boynton
Samuel Chamberlin jur
Eph Chamberlin
Benja Carver
Enoch Cleveland
Thomas Dutton
Joseph Dutton
James Dutton
David Dutton
Lt William Fletcher
Ens Tim° Fletcher
Gershom Fletcher
Zachariah Fletcher
Timth Fitch
Joshua Fletcher jur
Elias Foster
Benja Foster
Elias Foster jur
Oliver Fletcher
~~Joseph Hildreth~~
Joseph Hildreth jur
Cort Eph Hildreth
Ens Ebenezer Hildreth
James Hildreth
Eph Hildreth jur
Eph Hildreth 3rd
Samuel Hildreth
Zachariah Hildreth
Benja Hadley
John Hadley
Ebenezer Hadley
Joseph Hooker
Joseph Hooker jur
Phinehas Hildreth
Moses Keys
Joseph Keys
Thomas Kidder
Josiah Kemp
Samuel Lawrance
Thomas Meads
Jonathan Minot
John Proctor
Agnes Proctor
Ezekiel Proctor
James Proctor
Nathan Proctor
Thomas Proctor
Phillip Proctor

1758

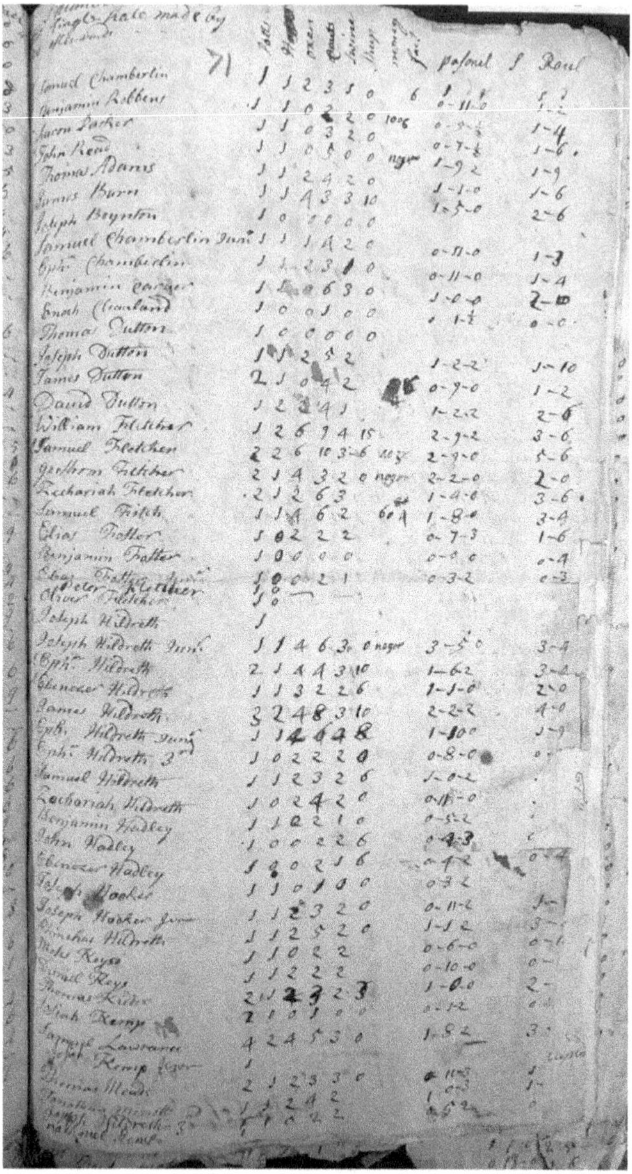

[illegible] Single Rate made by [illegible]

71

	Polls	Horses	Oxen	Cows	Swine	Sheep	[illegible]	Personal	Real
Samuel Chamberlin	1	1	2	3	1	0	6	1-1-[illegible]	5-[illegible]
Benjamin Robbens	1	1	0	2				0-11-0	[illegible]
Aaron Parker	1	1	0	[illegible]	2	0	100£	0-9-[illegible]	1-4
Ephm Reed	1	1	0	1	0	0	negro	0-7-½	1-6
Thomas Adams	1	1	2	4	2	0		1-9-2	1-9
James Burn	1	1	4	3	3	10		1-1-0	1-6
Joseph Boynton	1	0	1	0	0	0		1-5-0	2-6
Samuel Chamberlin Junr	1	1	1	4	2	0			
Ephm Chamberlin	1	1	2	3	1	0		0-11-0	1-3
Benjamin Parker	1	[illegible]	0	6	3	0		0-11-0	1-4
Enoch Cleaveland	1	0	0	1	0	0		1-0-0	2-10
Thomas Dutton	1	0	0	0	0	0		0-1-½	0-0
Joseph Dutton	1	1	2	5	2			1-2-2	1-10
James Dutton	2	1	0	4	2			0-9-0	1-2
David Dutton	1	2	2	4	1			1-2-2	2-6
William Fletcher	1	2	6	9	4	15		2-9-2	3-6
Samuel Fletcher	2	2	6	10	3	6	neg[illegible]	2-9-0	5-6
Jethro Fletcher	2	1	4	3	2	0	negro	2-2-0	2-0
Zechariah Fletcher	2	1	2	6	3			1-4-6	3-6
Samuel Fitch	1	1	4	6	2		60 A	1-8-[illegible]	3-4
Elias Foster	1	0	2	2	2			0-7-3	1-6
Benjamin Foster	1	0	0	0	0			0-0-0	0-4
Elias Foster Junr	1	0	0	2	1			0-3-2	0-3
Peter Fletcher	1	0							
Oliver Fletcher	1	0							
Joseph Hildreth	1								
Joseph Hildreth Junr	1	1	4	6	3	0	negro	3-5-0	3-4
Ephm Hildreth	2	1	4	4	3	10		1-6-2	3-[illegible]
Ebenezer Hildreth	1	1	3	2	2	6		1-1-0	2-0
James Hildreth	3	2	4	8	3	10		2-2-2	4-0
Ephm Hildreth Junr	1	1	4	6	4	8		1-10-0	1-9
Ephm Hildreth 3rd	1	0	2	2	2	0		0-8-0	0-[illegible]
Samuel Hildreth	1	1	2	3	2	6		1-0-2	[illegible]
Zachariah Hildreth	1	0	2	4	2	0		0-11-0	[illegible]
Benjamin Hadley	1	1	0	2	1	0		0-5-2	[illegible]
John Hadley	1	0	0	2	2	6		0-4-3	[illegible]
Ebenezer Hadley	1	0	0	2	1	6		0-4-2	0-4
Joseph Hooker	1	1	0	1	0	0		0-3-2	
Joseph Hooker Jun	1	1	2	3	2	0		0-11-2	1-[illegible]
Phinehas Hildreth	1	1	2	5	2	0		1-1-2	3-[illegible]
Moses Keyes	1	1	0	2	2			0-6-0	0-[illegible]
Israel Keyes	1	1	2	2	2			0-10-0	0-[illegible]
Thomas Kidder	2	1	2	3	2	3		1-0-0	2-[illegible]
Josiah Kemp	2	1	0	1	0	0		0-1-2	0-[illegible]
Samuel Lawrance	4	2	4	5	3	0		1-5-2	3-[illegible]
Joseph Kemp Esqr	1							0-11-3	1-[illegible]
Thomas Meads	2	1	2	3	3	0		1-0-3	1-[illegible]
Jonathan Meads	1	1	2	4	2			0-6-2	0-[illegible]
Joseph Hildreth 3rd	1	1	0	2	2				
Nathaniel Kemp	1								

1758

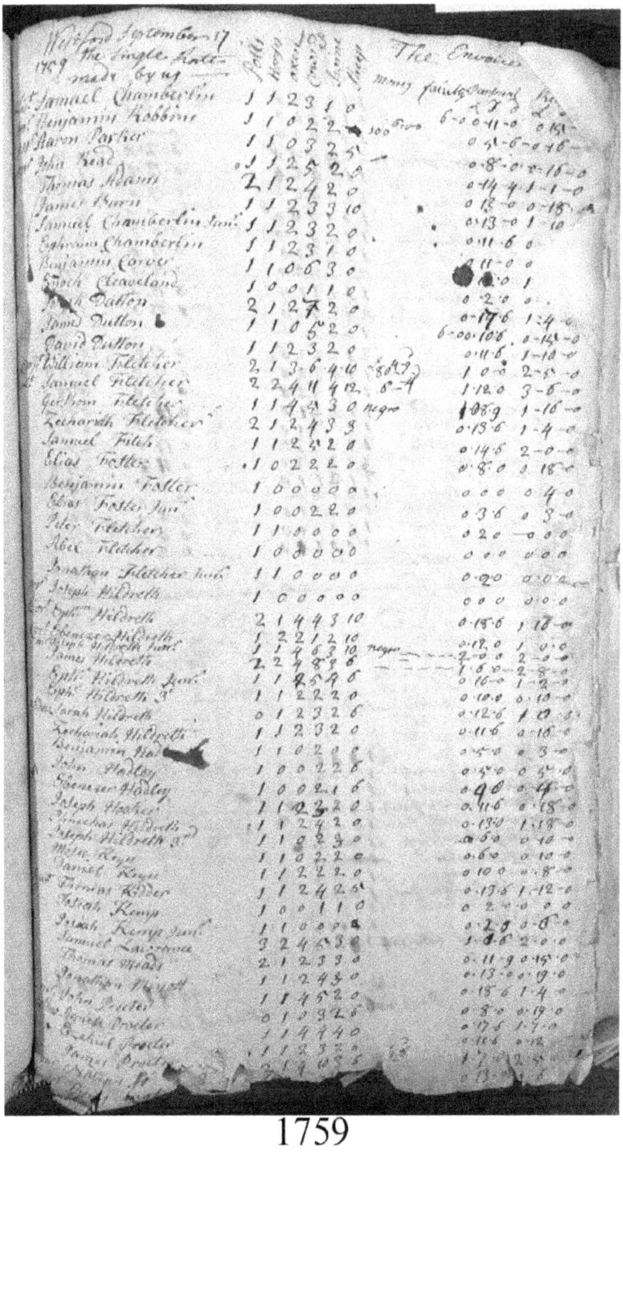

Westford September 17 1759 the Single Rate made by us

Name	Polls	Horses	Oxen	Cows	Swine	Sheep		Real	Personal
Samuel Chamberlin	1	1	2	3	1	0			
Benjamin Robbins	1	1	0	2	2		100	6-0-0-11-0	0-15
Aaron Parker	1	1	0	3	2	5		0-5-6	0-16
John Read	1	1	2	5	2	0		0-8-0	0-16-0
Thomas Adams	2	1	2	4	2	0		0-14-4	1-1-0
James Burn	1	1	2	3	3	10		0-15-0	0-15
Samuel Chamberlin Jun	1	1	2	3	2	0		0-13-0	1-10
Ephraim Chamberlin	1	1	2	3	1	0		0-11-6	0
Benjamin Carver	1	1	0	6	3	0		0-11-0	0
Enoch Cleaveland	1	0	0	1	1	0		[illegible]-0	1
[illegible] Dutton	2	1	2	7	2	0		0-2-0	0
James Dutton	1	1	0	5	2	0		0-17-6	1-4-0
David Dutton	1	1	2	3	2	0		6-00-10-6	0-14-0
William Fletcher	2	1	3	6	4	10	80-19	0-11-6	1-10-0
Samuel Fletcher	2	2	4	11	4	12	6-4	1-0-0	2-5-0
Gershom Fletcher	1	1	4	4	3	0	negro	1-12-0	3-6-0
Zechariah Fletcher	2	1	2	4	3	3		1-08-9	1-16-0
Samuel Fitch	1	1	2	4	2	0		0-13-6	1-4-0
Elias Foster	1	0	2	2	2	0		0-14-6	2-0-0
Benjamin Foster	1	0	0	0	0	0		0-8-0	0-18
Elias Foster Jun	1	0	0	2	2	0		0-0-0	0-4-0
Peter Fletcher	1	1	0	0	0	0		0-3-6	0-3-0
Abel Fletcher	1	0	0	0	0	0		0-2-0	0-0-0
Jonathan Fletcher Jun	1	1	0	0	0	0		0-0-0	0-0-0
Joseph Hildreth	1	0	0	0	0	0		0-2-0	0-0-0
Ephm Hildreth	2	1	4	4	3	10		0-0-0	0-0-0
Ebenezer Hildreth	1	2	2	1	2	10		0-18-6	1-18-0
Joseph Hildreth Jun	1	1	4	6	3	10	negro	0-12-0	1-0-0
James Hildreth	2	2	4	8	4	6		2-0-0	2-0-0
Ephm Hildreth Jun	1	1	4	5	4	6		1-6-0	2-8-0
Ephm Hildreth 3d	1	1	2	2	2	0		0-16-0	1-2-0
Sarah Hildreth	0	1	2	3	2	6		0-10-0	0-10-0
Zechariah Hildreth	1	1	2	3	2	0		0-12-6	1-0-0
Benjamin Hal[illegible]	1	1	0	2	0	0		0-11-6	0-16-0
John Hadley	1	0	0	2	2	6		0-5-0	0-3-0
Ebenezer Hadley	1	0	0	2	1	6		0-5-0	0-5-0
Joseph Hooker	1	1	0	3	2	0		0-9-0	0-4-0
[illegible] Hildreth	1	1	2	4	2	0		0-11-6	0-15-0
Joseph Hildreth 3d	1	1	0	2	3	0		0-13-0	1-18-0
[illegible] Keyes	1	1	0	2	2	0		0-6-0	0-10-0
Samuel Keyes	1	1	2	2	2	0		0-6-0	0-10-0
Thomas Kidder	1	1	2	4	2	5		0-10-0	0-8-0
Josiah Kemp	1	0	0	1	1	0		0-17-6	1-12-0
Josiah Kemp Jun	1	1	0	0	0	0		0-2-0	0-0
Samuel Lawrence	3	2	4	6	3	0		0-2-0	0-6-0
Thomas Mead	2	1	2	3	3	0		1-6-6	2-0-0
Jonathan Minot	1	1	2	4	3	0		0-11-9	0-15-0
John Procter	1	1	4	5	2	0		0-13-0	0-19-0
[illegible] Procter	0	1	0	3	2	6		0-15-6	1-4-0
Ezekiel Procter	1	1	4	4	4	0		0-8-0	0-19-0
James Procter	1	1	2	3	2	0		0-17-6	1-7-0
[illegible]	2	1	4	10	5	5		0-15-6	0-12
[illegible]	[illegible]							1-7-0	2-5
[illegible]								0-13-0	[illegible]

1759

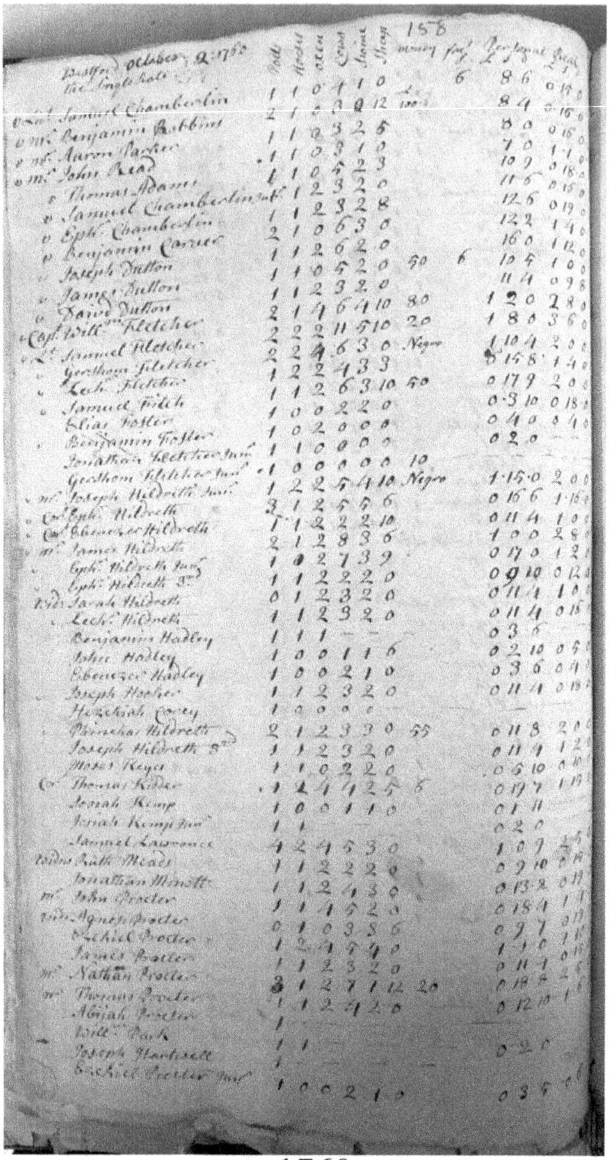

158

Bedford October 2 1760
the single rate

Name	Poll	Horses	Oxen	Cows	Swine	Sheep	Money	Fac.	Personal £ s d	Real £ s d
Lt. Samuel Chamberlin	1	1	0	4	1	0		6	8 6	0 15 0
Mr. Benjamin Robbins	2	1	0	3	0	12	£ 100		8 4	0 16 0
Mr. Aaron Parker	1	1	0	3	2	5			8 0	0 16 0
Mr. John Read	1	1	0	3	1	0			7 0	1 1 0
Thomas Adams	1	1	0	5	2	3			10 9	0 18 0
Samuel Chamberlin Jun.	1	1	2	3	2	0			11 6	0 15 0
Eph. Chamberlin	1	1	2	3	2	8			12 6	0 19 0
Benjamin Carter	2	1	0	6	3	0			12 2	1 4 0
Joseph Dutton	1	1	2	6	2	0			16 0	1 12 0
James Dutton	1	1	0	5	2	0	50	6	10 5	1 0 0
David Dutton	1	1	2	3	2	0			11 4	0 9 8
Capt. Willm. Fletcher	2	1	4	6	4	10	80		1 2 0	2 8 0
Lt. Samuel Fletcher	2	2	2	11	5	10	20		1 8 0	3 6 0
Gersham Fletcher	2	2	4	6	3	0	Negro		1 10 4	2 0 0
Zech. Fletcher	1	2	2	4	3	3			0 15 8	1 4 0
Samuel Fitch	1	1	2	6	3	10	50		0 17 9	2 0 0
Elias Foster	1	0	0	2	2	0			0 3 10	0 18 0
Benjamin Foster	1	0	2	0	0	0			0 4 0	0 4 0
Jonathan Fletcher Jun.	1	1	0	0	0	0			0 2 0	—
Gersham Fletcher Jun.	1	0	0	0	0	0	10			
Mr. Joseph Hildreth Jun.	1	2	2	5	4	10	Negro		1 15 0	2 0 0
Col. Eph. Hildreth	3	1	2	5	5	6			0 16 6	1 16 0
Col. Ebenezer Hildreth	1	1	2	2	2	10			0 11 4	1 0 0
Mr. James Hildreth	2	1	2	8	3	6			1 0 0	2 8 0
Eph. Hildreth Jun.	1	0	2	7	3	9			0 17 0	1 2 0
Eph. Hildreth 3d	1	1	2	2	2	0			0 9 10	0 12 0
Wid. Sarah Hildreth	0	1	2	3	2	0			0 11 4	1 0 [illegible]
Zech. Hildreth	1	1	2	3	2	0			0 11 4	0 15 [illegible]
Benjamin Hadley	1	1	1	—	—				0 3 6	
John Hadley	1	0	0	1	1	6			0 2 10	0 5 [illegible]
Ebenezer Hadley	1	0	0	2	1	0			0 3 6	0 4 [illegible]
Joseph Hooker	1	1	2	3	2	0			0 11 4	0 13 [illegible]
Hezekiah Corey	1	0	0	0	0				—	
Phinehas Hildreth	2	1	2	3	3	0	55		0 11 8	2 0 [illegible]
Joseph Hildreth 3d	1	1	2	3	2	0			0 11 4	1 2 [illegible]
Moses Keyes	1	1	0	2	2	0			0 5 10	0 10 [illegible]
Col. Thomas Kidder	1	2	4	4	2	5	6		0 17 7	1 13 [illegible]
Josiah Kemp	1	0	0	1	1	0			0 1 11	
Josiah Kemp Jun.	1	1							0 2 0	
Samuel Lawrence	4	2	4	5	3	0			1 0 7	2 5 [illegible]
Widow Ruth Meads	1	1	2	2	2	0			0 7 10	0 14 [illegible]
Jonathan Minott	1	1	2	4	3	0			0 13 2	0 11 [illegible]
Mr. John Procter	1	1	4	5	2	0			0 18 4	1 1 [illegible]
Wid. Agnes Procter	0	1	0	3	8	6			0 9 7	0 11 [illegible]
Ezekiel Procter	1	2	4	5	4	0			1 1 0	1 1 [illegible]
James Procter	1	1	2	3	2	0			0 11 1	0 1 [illegible]
Mr. Nathan Procter	3	1	2	7	1	12	20		0 18 7	2 [illegible]
Mr. Thomas Procter	1	1	2	4	2	0			0 12 10	1 [illegible]
Abijah Procter	1									
Willm. Park	1	1							0 2 0	
Joseph Hartwell	1									
Ezekiel Procter Jun.	1	0	0	2	1	0			0 3 5	0 [illegible]

1760

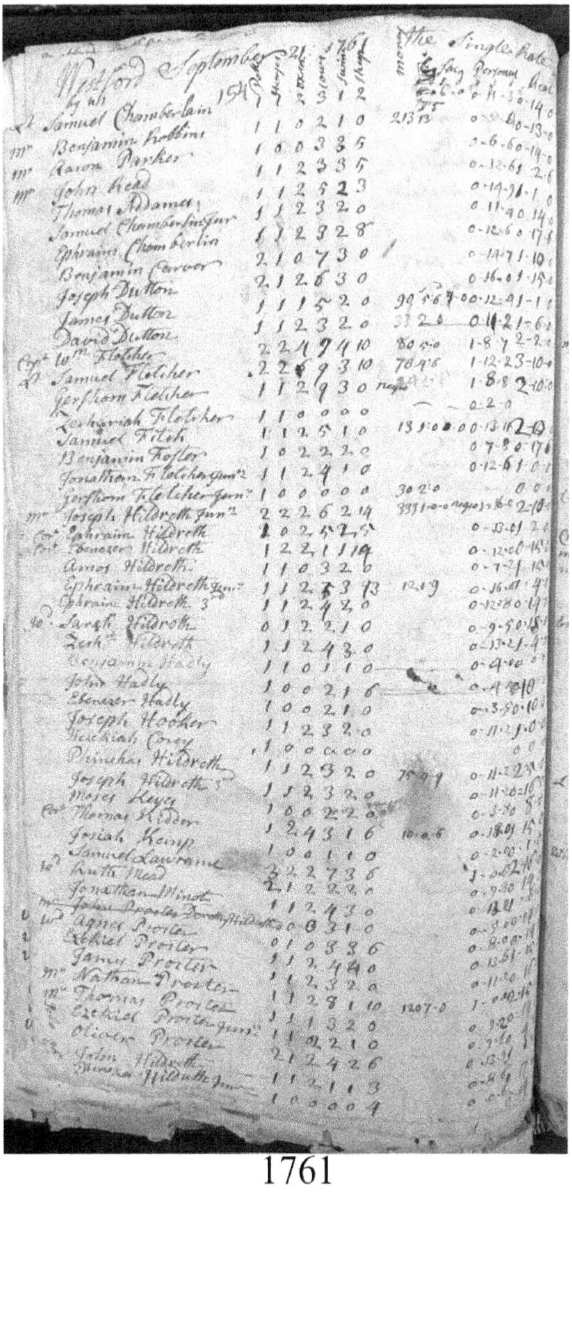

Westford September 21 1761 by us

	Name	Polls	Horses	Oxen	Cows	Swine	Sheep	Money	The Single Rate (Personal / Real)
	154	1	[illegible]	[illegible]	3	1	2	[illegible]	0-11-3 0-14-0
Lt	Samuel Chamberlain	1	1	0	2	1	0	213 13	0-[illegible] 0-13-0
Mr	Benjamin Robbins	1	0	0	3	3	5		0-6-6 0-14-0
Mr	Aaron Parker	1	1	2	3	3	5		0-12-6 1-2-6
Mr	John Read	1	1	2	5	2	3		0-14-9 1-1-0
	Thomas Adams	1	1	2	3	2	0		0-11-4 0-14-0
	Samuel Chamberlin Junr	1	1	2	3	2	8		0-12-6 0-17-6
	Ephraim Chamberlin	2	1	0	7	3	0		0-14-7 1-10-0
	Benjamin Carver	2	1	2	6	3	0		0-16-0 1-15-0
	Joseph Dutton	1	1	1	5	2	0	90 5 6	0-12-4 1-1-0
	James Dutton	1	1	2	3	2	0	33 2 0	0-11-2 1-6-0
	David Dutton	2	2	4	7	4	10	80 0 0	1-8-7 2-2-0
Capt	Wm Fletcher	2	2	6	9	3	10	78 4 6	1-12-2 3-10-0
Lt	Samuel Fletcher	1	1	2	9	3	0	negro	1-8-8 2-10-0
	Gershom Fletcher								0-2-0
	Zechariah Fletcher	1	1	0	0	0	0		
	Samuel Fitch	1	1	2	5	1	0	13 1 0	0-13-1 2-0
	Benjamin Foster	1	0	2	2	2	0		0-7-3 0-17-0
	Jonathan Fletcher Junr	1	1	2	4	1	0		0-12-6 1-0-0
	Gershom Fletcher Junr	1	0	0	0	0	0	30 2 0	0 0
Mr	Joseph Hildreth Junr	2	2	2	6	2	14	337 0 0 negro	2-10-0
Cor	Ephraim Hildreth	1	0	2	5	2	5		0-13-0 2-0
Ens	Ebenezer Hildreth	1	2	2	1	1	14		0-12-0 1-15
	Amos Hildreth	1	1	0	3	2	6		0-7-2 1-15
	Ephraim Hildreth Junr	1	1	2	5	3	13	12 1 9	0-16-0 1-4
	Ephraim Hildreth 3d	1	1	2	4	2	0		0-12-8 0-1[illegible]
Wd	Sarah Hildreth	0	1	2	2	1	0		0-9-5 0-15
	Zech. Hildreth	1	1	2	4	3	0		0-13-2 1-4
	Benjamin Hadly	1	1	0	1	1	0		0-4-0
	John Hadly	1	0	0	2	1	6		0-4 0-10
	Ebenezer Hadly	1	0	0	2	1	0		0-3-5 0-10
	Joseph Hooker	1	1	2	3	2	0		0-11-2 1-0
	Hezekiah Corey	1	0	0	0	0	0		0 0
	Phinehas Hildreth	1	1	2	3	2	0	75 0 9	0-11-2 2
	Joseph Hildreth 3d	1	1	2	3	2	0		0-11-2 0-1[illegible]
	Moses Keyes	1	0	0	2	2	0		0-3-8 0-8
Cor	Thomas Kidder	1	2	4	3	1	6	10 0 6	0-18-0 1-15
	Josiah Kemp	1	0	0	1	1	0		0-2-0 1
	Samuel Lawrance	3	2	2	7	3	6		1-0 2-1[illegible]
Wd	Ruth Mead	2	1	2	2	2	0		0-9-3 0-19
	Jonathan Minot	1	1	2	4	3	0		0-13
Mr	~~John Procter~~ Dorothy Hildreth	0	0	3	3	1	0		0-5-0 0-1[illegible]
Wd	Agnes Procter	0	1	0	3	3	6		0-8-0 0-1[illegible]
	Ezekiel Procter	1	1	2	4	4	0		0-13-6 1-1[illegible]
	James Procter	1	1	2	3	2	0		0-11-2 0-1[illegible]
Mr	Nathan Procter	1	1	2	8	1	10	1207-0	1-0 2-1[illegible]
Mr	Thomas Procter	1	1	1	3	2	0		0-9-2
	Ezekiel Procter Junr	1	1	0	2	1	0		0-7-1
	Oliver Procter	2	1	2	4	2	6		0-13-[illegible]
	John Hildreth	1	1	2	1	1	3		0-8-[illegible]
	Timothy Hildreth Junr	1	0	0	0	0	4		0-6-[illegible]

1761

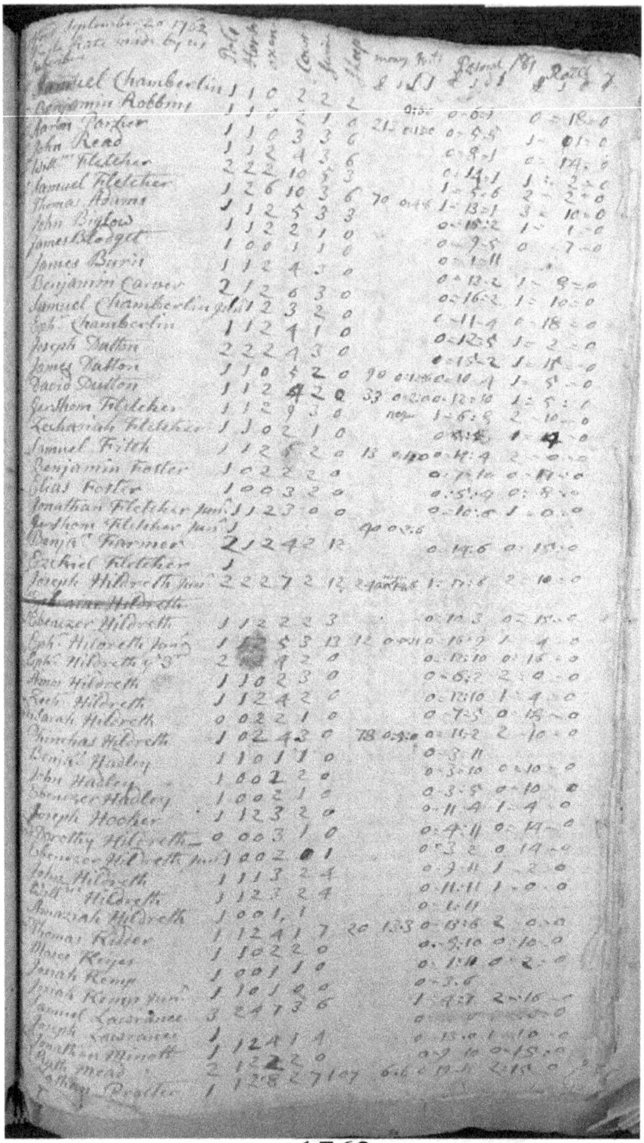

September 20 1762 Rate made by us

Name	Poll	Horse	Oxen	Cows	Swine	Sheep	Money at int.		Real Est.	Rate
							£	s d	£ s d	£ s d
Samuel Chamberlin	1	1	0	2	2	2		0:1:0	0-6-1	0-18-0
Benjamin Robbins	1	1	[illegible]	2	1	0	21	0:1:0	0-5-5	1-01-0
Aaron Parker	1	1	0	3	3	6			0-8-1	0-14-6
John Read	1	1	2	4	3	6			0-14-1	1-2-0
Willm Fletcher	2	2	2	10	5	3			1-5-6	2-2-0
Samuel Fletcher	1	2	6	10	3	6	70	0:4:6	1-13-1	3-10-0
Thomas Adams	1	1	2	5	3	3			0-15-2	1-1-0
John Bigelow	1	1	2	2	1	0			0-9-5	0-7-0
James Blodget	1	0	0	1	1	0			0-1-11	
James Burns	1	1	2	4	3	0			0-12-2	1-9-0
Benjamin Carver	2	1	2	6	3	0			0-16-2	1-10-0
Samuel Chamberlin jun	1	1	2	3	2	0			0-11-4	0-18-0
Ephm Chamberlin	1	1	2	4	1	0			0-12-5	1-2-0
Joseph Dutton	2	2	2	4	3	0			0-15-2	1-15-0
James Dutton	1	1	0	5	2	0	90	0:13:6	0-10-4	1-5-0
David Dutton	1	1	2	4	2	0	33	0:2:0	0-12-10	1-5-1
Gershom Fletcher	1	1	2	9	3	0	nep		1-6-8	2-10-0
Zechariah Fletcher	1	1	0	2	1	0			0-8-[illegible]	1-4-0
Samuel Fitch	1	1	2	5	2	0	13	0:1:0	0-14-4	2-0-0
Benjamin Fuller	1	0	2	2	2	0			0-7-10	0-11-0
Elias Fuller	1	0	0	3	2	0			0-5-9	0-8-0
Jonathan Fletcher jun	1	1	2	3	0	0			0-10-8	1-0-0
Gershom Fletcher jun	1						90	0:3:6		
Benjn Farmer	2	1	2	4	2	12			0-14-6	0-15-0
Ezekiel Fletcher	1									
Joseph Hildreth jun	2	2	2	7	2	12	2 partial		1-17-6	2-10-0
~~[illegible] Hildreth~~										
Ebenezer Hildreth	1	1	2	2	2	3			0-10-3	0-15-0
Ephm Hildreth jun	1	[illegible]	[illegible]	5	3	13	12	0:4:10	0-16-9	1-4-0
Ephm Hildreth ye 3d	2	[illegible]	[illegible]	4	2	0			0-15-10	0-16-0
Amos Hildreth	1	1	0	2	3	0			0-6-2	2-0-0
Zech Hildreth	1	1	2	4	2	0			0-12-10	1-4-0
Sarah Hildreth	0	0	2	2	1	0			0-7-5	0-15-0
Phinehas Hildreth	1	0	2	4	3	0	78	0:5:0	0-16-2	2-10-0
Benjn Hadley	1	1	0	1	1	0			0-3-11	
John Hadley	1	0	0	2	2	0			0-3-10	0-10-0
Ebenezer Hadley	1	0	0	2	1	0			0-3-5	0-10-0
Joseph Hooker	1	1	2	3	2	0			0-11-4	1-4-0
Dorothy Hildreth	0	0	0	3	1	0			0-4-11	0-14-0
Ebenezer Hildreth jun	1	0	0	2	0	1			0-3-2	0-14-0
John Hildreth	1	1	1	3	2	4			0-7-11	1-2-0
Willm Hildreth	1	1	2	3	2	4			0-11-11	1-0-0
Amaziah Hildreth	1	0	0	1	1				0-1-11	
Thomas Rider	1	1	2	4	1	7	20	1:3:3	0-13-6	2-0-0
Moses Keyes	1	1	0	2	2	0			0-5-10	0-10-0
Josiah Kemp	1	0	0	1	1	0			0-1-10	0-2-0
Josiah Kemp jun	1	1	0	1	0	0			0-3-6	
Samuel Lawrance	3	2	4	7	3	6			1-4-7	2-16-0
Joseph Lawrance	1								[illegible]	[illegible]
Jonathan Minott	1	1	2	4	1	4			0-13-0	1-10-0
Jonth Mead	2	1	2	2	2	0			0-9-10	0-15-0
Nathan Reddler	1	1	2	8	2	7	107	6:6	0-19-4	2-15-0

1762

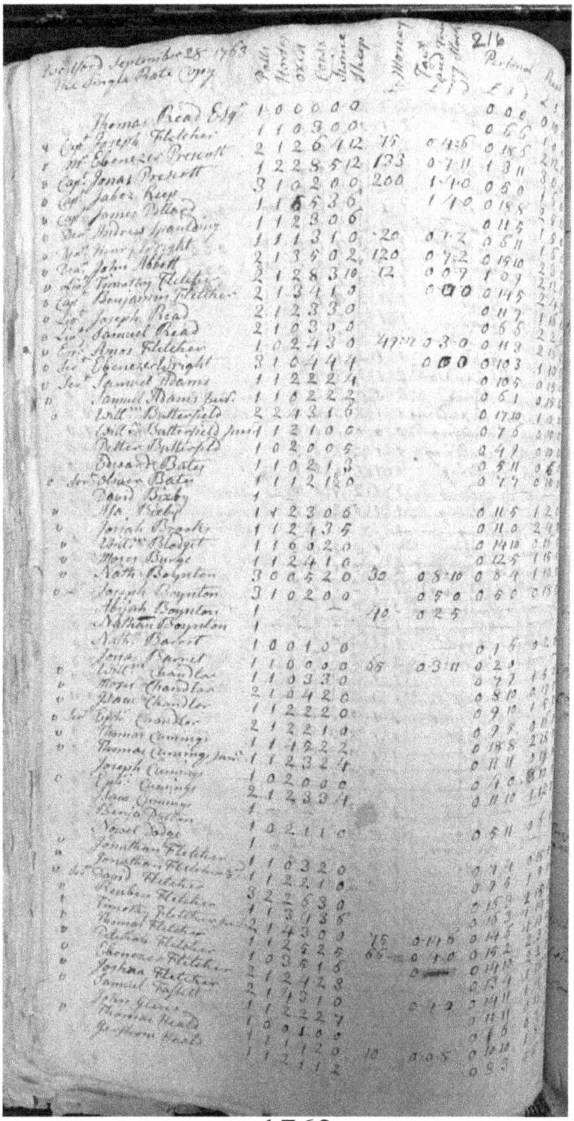

Westford September 28 1763
The Single Rate Copy

Name	Polls	Horses	Oxen	Cows	Swine	Sheep	Money	Tax	Personal £ s d
Thomas Read Esqr	1	0	0	0	0	0			0 0 0
Capt Joseph Fletcher	1	1	0	3	0	0			0 6 6
Mr Ebenezer Prescott	2	1	2	6	4	12	75	0 4 6	0 18 5
Capt Jonas Prescott	1	2	2	8	5	12	133	0 7 11	1 3 11
Capt Jabez Keep	3	1	0	2	0	0	200	1 4 0	0 6 0
Capt James Tellor	1	1	6	5	3	6		1 4 0	0 18 8
Dea^n Andrew Spaulding	1	1	2	3	0	6			0 11 5
Dea^n Henry Wright	1	1	1	3	1	0	20	0 1 2	0 6 11
Dea^n John Abbott	2	1	3	5	0	2	120	0 7 2	0 15 10
Lieu^t Timothy Fletcher	2	1	2	8	3	10	12	0 0 7	1 0 7
Capt Benjamin Fletcher	2	1	3	4	1	0		0 0 0	0 14 5
Lieu^t Joseph Read	2	1	2	3	3	0			0 11 7
Lieu^t Samuel Read	2	1	0	3	0	0			0 6 8
Ens^n Amos Fletcher	1	0	2	4	3	0	47	0 3 0	0 11 8
Serj^t Ebenezer Wright	3	1	0	4	4	4		0 0 0	0 10 3
Serj^t Samuel Adams	1	1	2	2	2	4			0 10 5
Samuel Adams Junr	1	1	0	2	2	2			0 6 1
Willm Butterfield	2	2	4	3	1	6			0 17 10
Willm Butterfield Junr	1	1	2	1	0	0			0 7 6
Petter Butterfield	1	0	2	0	0	5			0 4 7
Edward Bates	1	1	0	2	1	3			0 5 11
Serj^t Oliver Bates	1	1	1	2	1	0			0 7 7
David Bixby	1								
Asa Bixby	1	1	2	3	0	6			0 11 5
Josiah Brooks	1	1	2	4	3	5			0 11 0
Willm Blodget	1	1	6	0	2	0			0 14 10
Moses Burge	1	1	2	4	1	0			0 12 5
Nath Boynton	3	0	0	5	2	0	30	0 5 10	0 8 4
Joseph Boynton	3	1	0	2	0	0		0 5 0	0 6 0
Abijah Boynton	1						40	0 2 5	
Nathan Boynton	1								
Nathl Barret	1	0	0	1	0	0			0 1 5
Jonas Barret	1	1	0	0	0	0	65	0 3 11	0 2 0
Willm Chandler	1	1	0	3	3	0			0 7 7
Moses Chandler	2	1	0	4	2	0			0 8 10
Isaac Chandler	1	1	2	2	2	0			0 9 10
Serj^t Eph^m Chandler	2	1	2	2	1	0			0 7 8
Thomas Cummings	1	1	4	2	2	2			0 18 8
Thomas Cummings Junr	1	1	2	3	2	4			0 11 11
Joseph Cummings	1	0	2	0	0	0			0 4 0
Eph^m Cummings	2	1	2	3	3	4			0 11 10
Isaac Cummings	1								
Benj^a Dutton	1	0	2	1	1	0			0 5 11
Nowel Dodge	1								
Jonathan Fletcher	1	1	0	3	2	0			0 7 4
Jonathan Fletcher Junr	1	1	2	2	1	0			0 7 6
Serj^t David Fletcher	3	2	2	6	3	0			0 15 2
Reuben Fletcher	1	1	3	1	3	6			0 15 3
Timothy Fletcher Junr	2	1	4	3	0	0			0 14 8
Thomas Fletcher	1	1	2	5	2	5	75	0 11 5	0 19 2
Pelatiah Fletcher	1	0	3	5	1	5	65	0 4 0	0 14 10
Ebenezer Fletcher	2	1	2	4	2	8		0 —	0 13 4
Joshua Fletcher	2	1	1	3	1	0		0 1 3	0 14 11
Samuel Fassett	1	1	2	2	2	7			0 11 11
John Graves	1	0	0	1	0	0			0 1 6
Thomas Heald	1	1	1	1	2	0	10	0 0 8	0 10 11
Jotham Heald	1	1	2	1	1	2			0 8 5

1763

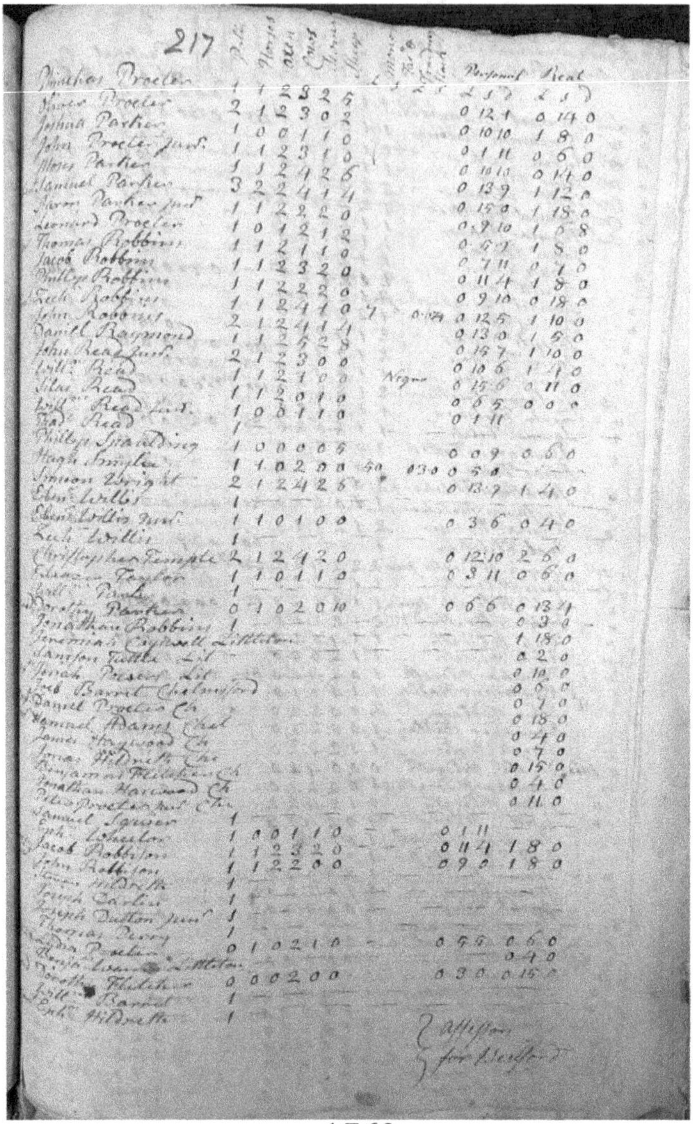

217

	Polls	Horses	Oxen	Cows	Swine	Sheep	Money	Stock in Trade	Faculty	Personal	Real
							£	s	d	£ s d	£ s d
Phinehas Procter	1	1	2	3	2	5					
James Procter	2	1	2	3	0	2				0 12 1	0 14 0
Joshua Parker	1	0	0	1	1	0				0 10 10	1 8 0
John Procter Junr	1	1	2	3	1	0				0 1 11	0 6 0
Moses Parker	1	1	2	4	2	6				0 10 10	0 14 0
Samuel Parker	3	2	2	4	1	4				0 13 9	1 12 0
Aaron Parker Junr	1	1	2	2	2	0				0 15 0	1 18 0
Leonard Procter	1	0	1	2	1	2				0 9 10	1 0 8
Thomas Robbins	1	1	2	1	1	0				0 5 7	1 8 0
Jacob Robbins	1	1	2	3	2	0				0 7 11	0 7 0
Phillip Robbins	1	1	2	2	2	0				0 11 4	1 8 0
Zech Robbins	1	1	2	4	1	0	7		0 0 4	0 9 10	0 18 0
John Robbins	2	1	2	4	1	4				0 12 5	1 10 0
Daniel Raymond	1	1	2	5	2	8				0 13 0	1 5 0
John Read Junr	2	1	2	3	0	0				0 15 7	1 10 0
Willm Read	1	1	2	1	0	0	Negro			0 10 6	1 4 0
Silas Read	1	1	2	0	1	0				0 15 6	0 11 0
Willm Read Junr	1	0	0	1	1	0				0 6 5	0 0 0
Thos Read	1									0 1 11	
Phillip Spaulding	1	0	0	0	0	5				0 0 9	0 6 0
Hugh Smyley	1	1	0	2	0	0	40		0 3 0	0 5 0	
Simeon Wright	2	1	2	4	2	5				0 13 7	1 4 0
Eben^r Willis	1										
Eben^r Willis Junr	1	1	0	1	0	0				0 3 6	0 4 0
Zech Willis	1										
Christopher Temple	2	1	2	4	2	0				0 12 10	2 6 0
Eleazer Taylor	1	1	0	1	1	0				0 3 11	0 6 0
Willm Parker	1										
Dorothy Parker	0	1	0	2	0	10				0 6 6	0 13 4
Jonathan Robbins	1										0 3 0
Jeremiah Cogswell Littleton											1 18 0
Samson Tuttle Lit											0 2 0
Jonah Pierce Lit											0 10 0
Joel Barret Chelmsford											0 6 0
Daniel Procter Ch											0 7 0
Samuel Adams Chel											0 18 0
James Haywood Ch											0 4 0
Jonas Hildreth Che											0 7 0
Benjamin Fletcher Ch											0 15 0
Jonathan Harwood Ch											0 4 0
Peter Procter Junr Che											0 11 0
Samuel Sawyer	1										
Eph. Wheeler	1	0	0	1	1	0				0 1 11	
Jacob Robbison	1	1	2	3	2	0				0 11 4	1 8 0
John Robbison	1	1	2	2	0	0				0 9 0	1 8 0
James Hildreth	1										
Josiah Parker	1										
Joseph Dutton Junr	1										
Thomas Perry	1										
Lydia Procter	0	1	0	2	1	0				0 5 5	0 6 0
Benja Lawrence Littleton											0 4 0
Dorothy Fletcher	0	0	0	2	0	0				0 3 0	0 15 0
Willm Barret	1										
Eph^m Hildreth	1										

} Assessors
} for Westford

1763

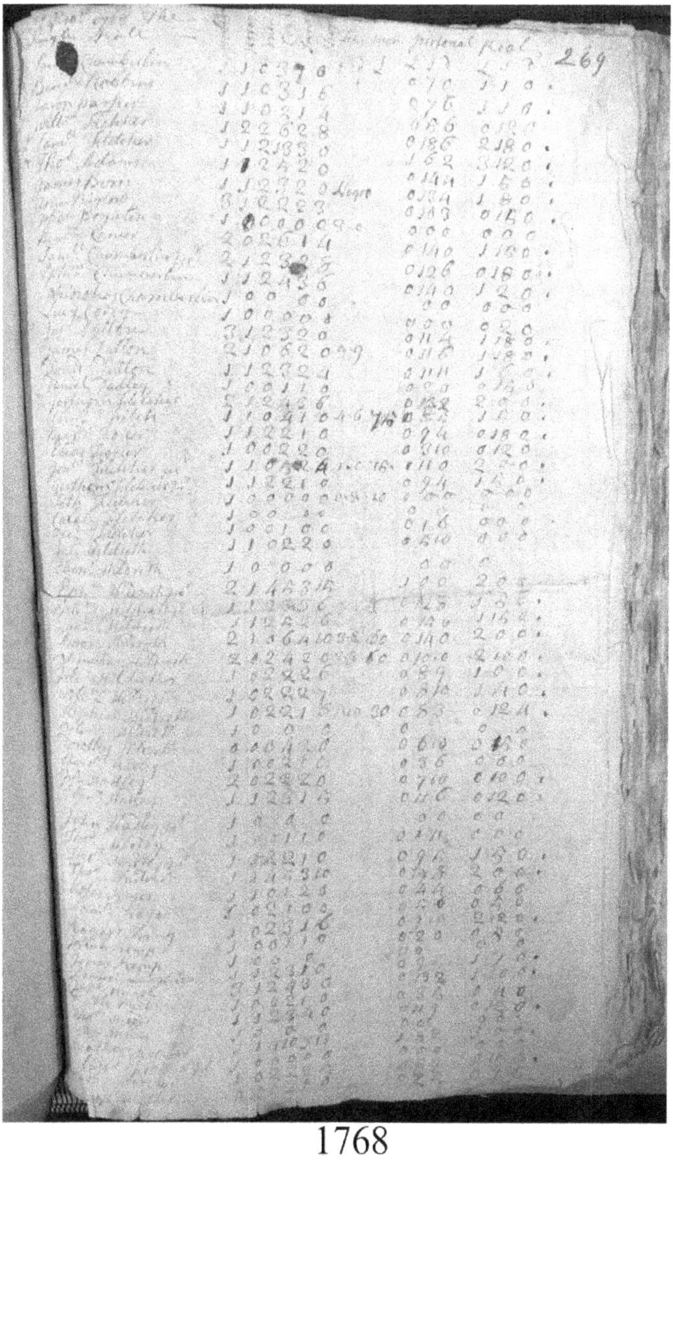

1768

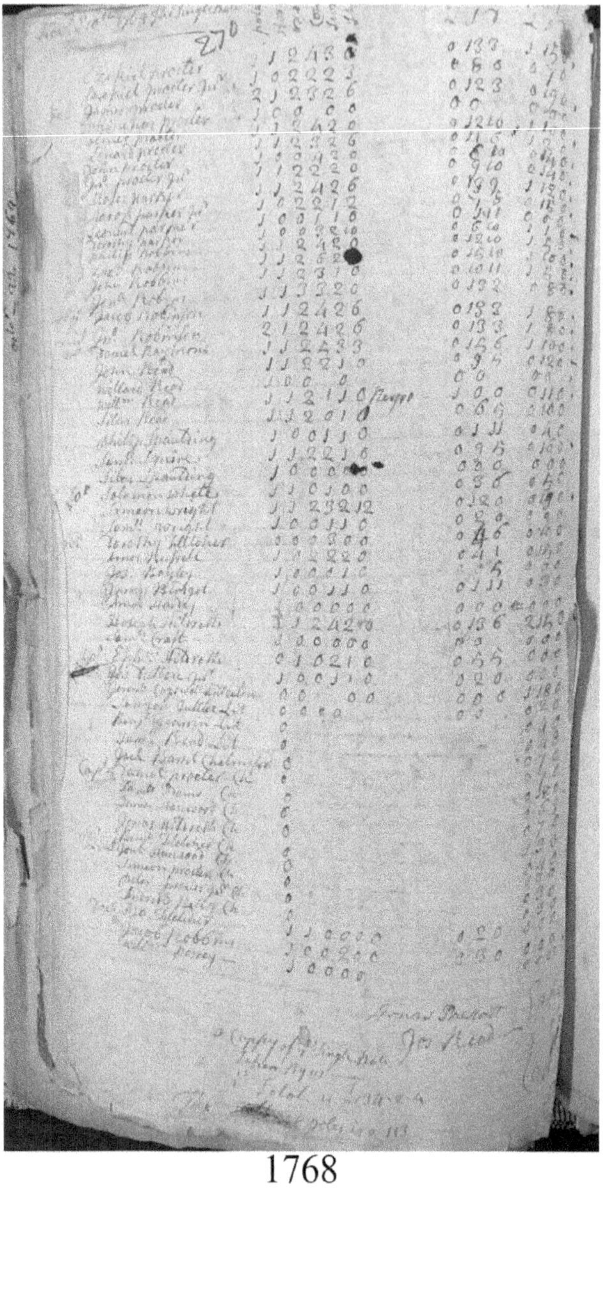

1768

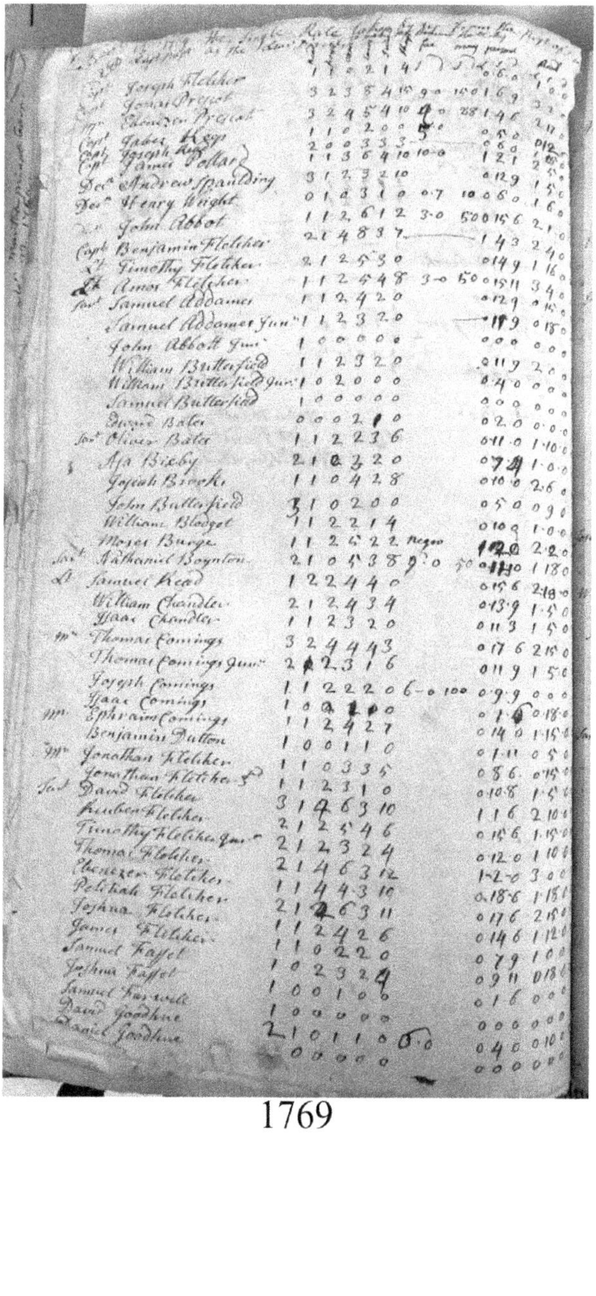

Capt Joseph Fletcher	1 1 0 2 1 4		0 6 0	1 0 0
Capt Jonas Prescot	3 2 3 5 4 15	9 0 150	1 6 9	1 0 0
Mr Ebenezer Prescot	3 2 4 5 4 10	4 0 28	1 4 6	2 2 0
Capt Jabez Keep	1 1 0 2 0 0	5 0		2 11 0
Capt Joseph Keep	2 0 0 3 3 3	5	0 5 0	0 12 0
Capt James Pollard	1 1 3 6 4 10	10 0	1 2 1	2 5 0
Decn Andrew Spaulding	3 1 2 3 2 10		0 12 9	1 5 0
Decn Henry Wright	0 1 4 3 1 0	0 7 10	0 8 0	1 6 0
Mr John Abbot	1 1 2 6 1 2	3 0 500	15 6	2 1 0
Capt Benjamin Fletcher	2 1 4 8 3 7		1 4 3	2 4 0
Lt Timothy Fletcher	2 1 2 5 3 0		0 14 9	1 16 0
Lt Amos Fletcher	1 1 2 5 4 8	3 0 50	0 15 11	3 4 0
Serjt Samuel Addames	1 1 2 4 2 0		0 12 9	0 15 0
Samuel Addames Junr	1 1 2 3 2 0		11 9	0 18 0
John Abbott Junr	1 0 0 0 0 0		0 0 0	0 0 0
William Butterfield	1 1 2 3 2 0		0 11 9	2 0 0
William Butterfield Junr	1 0 2 0 0 0		0 4 0	0 0 0
Samuel Butterfield	1 0 0 0 0 0		0 0 0	0 0 0
David Bates	0 0 0 2 1 0		0 2 0	0 0 0
Serjt Oliver Bates	1 1 2 2 3 6		0 11 0	1 10 0
Asa Bixby	2 1 0 2 2 0		0 7 4	1 0 0
Josiah Brooks	1 1 0 4 2 8		0 10 0	2 6 0
John Butterfield	3 1 0 2 0 0		0 5 0	0 9 0
William Blodget	1 1 2 2 1 4		0 10 9	1 0 0
Moses Burge	1 1 2 6 2 2	Negro	1 2 0	2 2 0
Serjt Nathaniel Boynton	2 1 0 5 3 8	9 0 50	0 17 0	1 18 0
Lt Samuel Read	1 2 2 4 4 0		0 15 6	2 18 0
William Chandler	2 1 2 4 3 4		0 13 9	1 5 0
Isaac Chandler	1 1 2 3 2 0		0 11 3	1 5 0
Mr Thomas Comings	3 2 4 4 4 3		0 17 6	2 15 0
Thomas Comings Junr	2 1 2 3 1 6		0 11 9	1 5 0
Joseph Comings	1 1 2 2 2 0	6 0 100	0 9 9	0 0 0
Isaac Comings	1 0 0 2 0 0		0 1 6	0 18 0
Mr Ephraim Comings	1 1 2 4 2 7		0 14 0	1 15 0
Benjamin Dutton	1 0 0 1 1 0		0 1 11	0 5 0
Mr Jonathan Fletcher	1 1 0 3 3 5		0 8 6	0 15 0
Jonathan Fletcher 3d	1 1 2 3 1 0		0 10 8	1 5 0
Serjt David Fletcher	3 1 4 6 3 10		1 1 6	2 10 0
Reuben Fletcher	2 1 2 5 4 6		0 15 6	1 15 0
Timothy Fletcher Junr	2 1 2 3 2 4		0 12 0	1 10 0
Thomas Fletcher	2 1 4 6 3 12		1 2 0	3 0 0
Ebenezer Fletcher	1 1 4 4 3 10		0 18 6	1 18 0
Pelatiah Fletcher	2 1 2 6 3 11		0 17 6	2 15 0
Joshua Fletcher	1 1 2 4 2 6		0 14 6	1 12 0
James Fletcher	1 1 0 2 2 0		0 7 9	1 0 0
Samuel Fassel	1 0 2 3 2 4		0 9 11	0 18 0
Joshua Fassel	1 0 0 1 0 0		0 1 6	0 0 0
Samuel Farwell	1 0 0 0 0 0		0 0 0	0 0 0
David Goodhue	2 1 0 1 1 0	6 0	0 4 0	0 10 0
Daniel Goodhue	0 0 0 0 0		0 0 0	0 0 0

1769

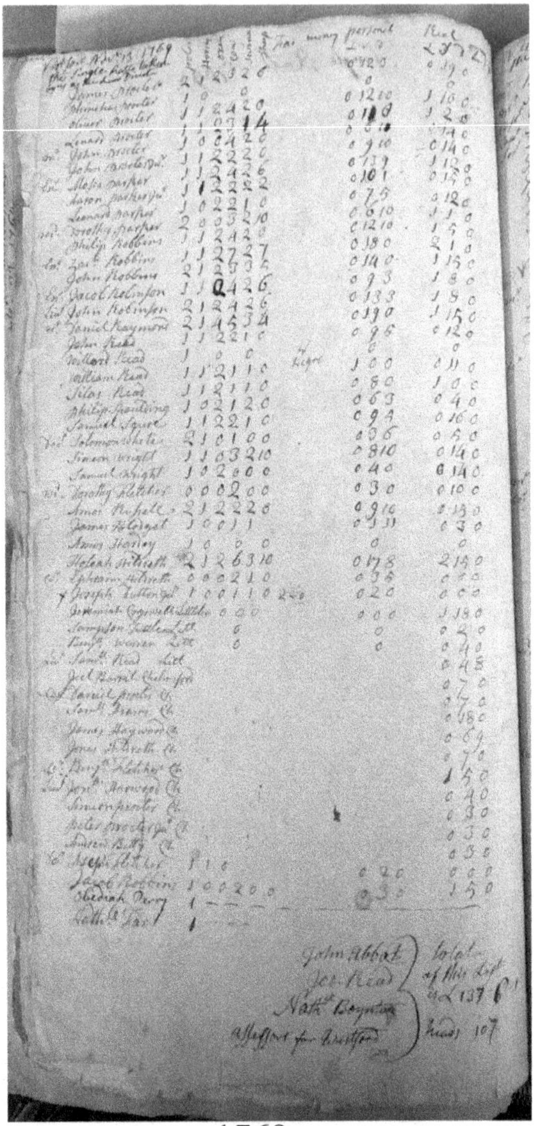

Name	Polls, Houses, etc.	Personal £ s d	Real £ s d
James Procter	2 1 2 3 2 6	0 12 0	0 19 0
Phinehas Procter	1 0 0	0	0
Oliver Procter	1 1 2 4 2 0	0 12 10	1 16 0
Lenard Procter	1 1 0 3 1 4	0 11 0	1 2 0
John Procter	1 0 0 4 2 0	0 9 10	0 14 0
John Procter Jur.	1 1 2 2 2 0	0 13 9	0 14 0
Moses Parker	1 1 2 4 2 6	0 10 1	1 12 0
Aaron Parker Jur.	1 1 2 2 2 2	0 7 5	0 15 0
Leonard Parker	1 0 2 2 1 0	0 6 10	0 12 0
Timothy Parker	2 0 0 3 2 10	0 12 10	1 1 0
Philip Robbins	1 1 2 4 2 0	0 18 0	1 5 0
Zach. Robbins	1 1 2 7 2 7	0 14 0	2 1 0
John Robbins	2 1 2 3 3 6	0 9 3	1 15 0
Jacob Robinson	1 1 2 4 2 6	0 13 3	1 8 0
John Robinson	2 1 2 4 2 6	0 19 0	1 8 0
Daniel Raymond	2 1 4 5 3 4	0 9 6	1 15 0
John Read	1 1 2 2 1 0	6	0 12 0
Willard Read	1 0 0	1 0 0	0
William Read	1 1 2 1 1 0	0 8 0	0 11 0
Silas Read	1 1 2 1 1 0	0 6 3	1 0 0
Philip Spaulding	1 0 2 1 2 0	0 9 4	0 4 0
Samuel Squire	1 1 2 2 1 0	0 0 6	0 16 0
Solomon White	2 1 0 1 0 0	0 8 10	0 5 0
Simeon Wright	1 1 0 3 2 10	0 4 0	0 14 0
Samuel Wright	1 0 2 0 0 0	0 3 0	0 14 0
Dorothy Fletcher	0 0 0 2 0 0	0 9 10	0 10 0
Amos Russell	2 1 2 2 2 0	0 3 3	0 13 0
James Holdgat	1 0 0 1 1	0	0 3 0
Amos Hartley	1 0 0 0	0 17 8	0
Josiah Hildreth	2 1 2 6 3 10	0 3 6	2 15 0
Ephraim Hildreth	0 0 0 2 1 0	0 2 0	0 0 0
Joseph Tuttle Jur.	1 0 0 1 1 0 2 0 0	0 0 0	0 0 0
Jeremiah Cogswell Littleton	0 0 0	0	1 18 0
Sampson Tuttle Lit.	0	0	0 2 0
Benj. Warren Lit.	0		0 4 0
Saml. Read Lit.			0 4 8
Joel Barret Chelmsford			0 7 0
Daniel Procter Ch.			0 7 0
Saml. Francis Ch.			0 18 0
James Haywood Ch.			0 6 9
Jonas Hildreth Ch.			0 7 0
Benj. Fletcher Ch.			1 5 0
Jona. Howard Ch.			0 4 0
Simeon Procter Ch.			0 3 0
Peter Procter Jur. Ch.			0 3 0
Andrew Betty Ch.			0 3 0
Joseph Fletcher	1 1 0	0 2 0	0 0 0
Jacob Robbins	1 0 0 2 0 0	0 3 0	1 5 0
Obediah Perry	1		
Nathl. Parr	1		

John Abbot
Jos. Read
Nathl. Boynton
Assessors for Westford

Total of this List is £137 6s 1d
Heads 107

1769

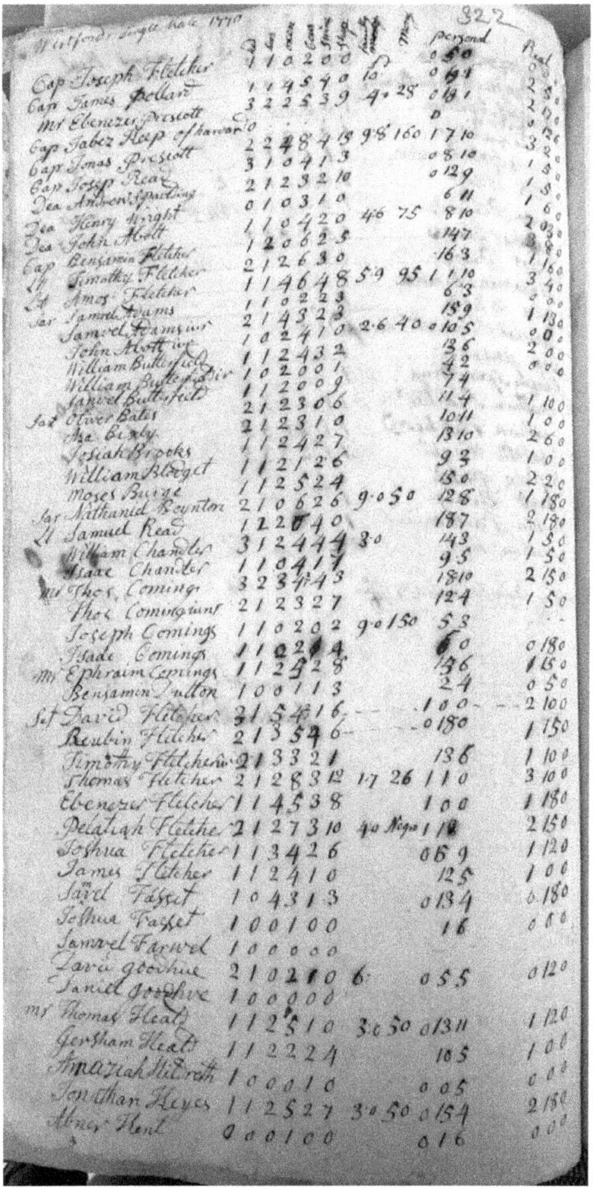

Westford Single Rate 1770 — 322

Name	[illegible]	[illegible]	[illegible]	[illegible]	[illegible]	[illegible]	£	[illegible]	Personal	Real
Cap Joseph Fletcher	1	1	0	2	0	0			0 5 0	0 0 0
Cap James Pollard	1	1	4	5	4	0	10		0 19 1	2 5 0
Mr Ebenezer Prescott	3	2	2	5	3	9	4·0	28	0 18 1	2 17 0
Cap Jabez Keep of Harvard	0								D	0 12 6
Cap Jonas Prescott	2	2	4	8	4	15	9·8	160	17 10	3 2 0
Cap Joseph Read	3	1	0	4	1	3			0 8 10	1 8 0
Dea Andrew Spalding	2	1	2	3	2	10			0 12 9	1 8 0
Dea Henry Wright	0	1	0	3	1	0			6 11	1 6 0
Dea John Abbott	1	1	0	4	2	0	46	75	8 10	2 03 0
Cap Benjamin Fletcher	1	2	0	6	2	5			14 7	3 8 0
Lt Timothy Fletcher	2	1	2	6	3	0			16 3	1 16 0
Lt Amos Fletcher	1	1	4	6	4	8	5·9	95	1 1 10	3 4 0
Ser Samuel Adams	1	1	0	2	2	3			6 3	0 0 0
Samuel Adams junr	2	1	4	3	2	3			15 9	1 13 0
John Abbott junr	1	0	2	4	1	0	2·6	40	0 10 5	0 0 0
William Butterfield	1	1	2	4	3	2			13 6	2 0 0
William Butterfield junr	1	0	2	0	0	1			4 2	0 0 0
Samuel Butterfield	1	1	2	0	0	9			7 4	
Sar Oliver Bates	2	1	2	3	0	6			11 4	1 10 0
Asa Bixby	2	1	2	3	1	0			10 11	1 0 0
Josiah Brooks	1	1	2	4	2	7			13 10	2 6 0
William Blodget	1	1	2	1	2	6			9 3	1 0 0
Moses Burge	1	1	2	5	2	4			15 0	2 2 0
Ser Nathaniel Boynton	2	1	0	6	2	6	9·0	50	12 8	1 18 0
Lt Samuel Read	1	2	2	[illegible]	4	0			18 7	2 18 0
William Chandler	3	1	2	4	4	4	3·0		14 3	1 5 0
Isaac Chandler	1	1	0	4	1	1			9 5	1 5 0
Mr Thos Coming	3	2	3	4	4	3			18 10	2 15 0
Thos Coming junr	2	1	2	3	2	7			12 4	1 5 0
Joseph Comings	1	1	0	2	0	2	9·0	150	5 3	
Isaac Comings	1	1	0	2	[illegible]	4			6 0	0 18 0
Mr Ephraim Comings	1	1	2	3	2	8			13 6	1 15 0
Benjamin Dutton	1	0	0	1	1	3			2 4	0 5 0
Sgt David Fletcher	2	1	5	4	1	6			1 0 0	2 10 0
Reubin Fletcher	2	1	3	5	4	6			0 18 0	1 15 0
Timothy Fletcher junr	2	1	3	3	2	1			13 6	1 10 0
Thomas Fletcher	2	1	2	8	3	12	1·7	26	1 1 0	3 10 0
Ebenezer Fletcher	1	1	4	5	3	8			1 0 0	1 18 0
Pelatiah Fletcher	2	1	2	7	3	10	40 Negro		1 1 [illegible]	2 15 0
Joshua Fletcher	1	1	3	4	2	6			0 6 9	1 12 0
James Fletcher	1	1	2	4	1	0			12 5	1 0 0
Saml Fasset	1	0	4	3	1	3			0 13 4	0 18 0
Joshua Fasset	1	0	0	1	0	0			1 6	0 0 0
Samuel Farwel	1	0	0	0	0	0				
David Goodhue	2	1	0	2	1	0	6		0 5 5	0 12 0
Daniel Goodhue	1	0	0	0	0	0				
mr Thomas Heald	1	1	2	5	1	0	3·0	50	0 13 11	1 12 0
Gersham Heald	1	1	2	2	2	4			10 5	1 0 0
Amaziah Hildreth	1	0	0	0	1	0			0 0 5	0 0 0
Jonathan Keyes	1	1	2	5	2	7	3·0	50	0 15 4	2 15 0
Abner Kent	0	0	0	1	0	0			0 1 6	0 0 0

1770

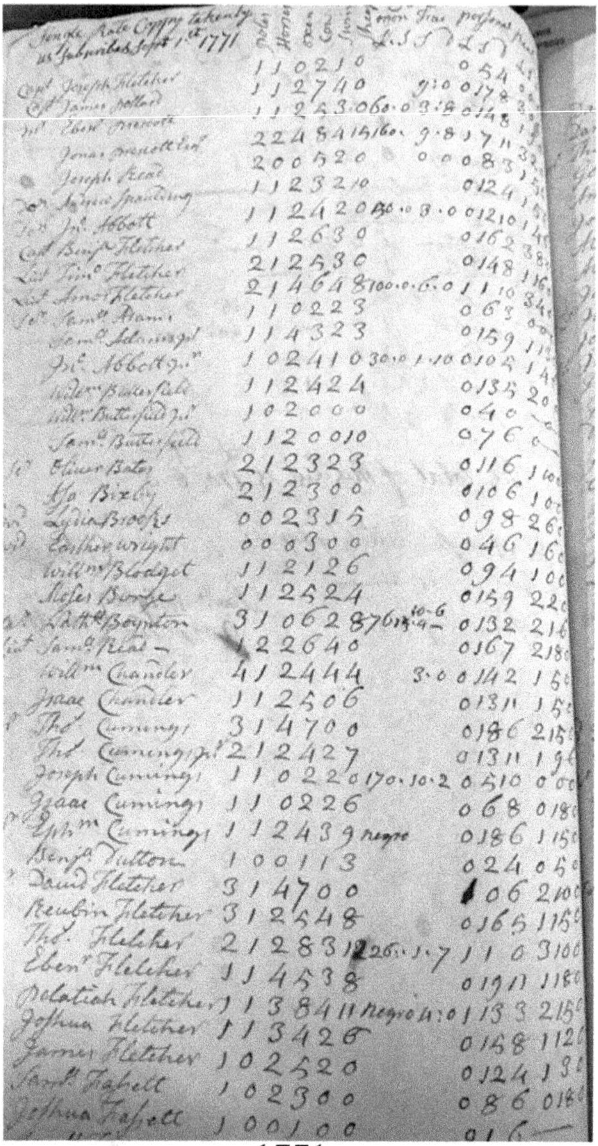

Single Rate Coppy taken by us subscribed Sept 1st 1771

	Polls, Horses, Oxen, Cows, Swine, Sheep	money Trade £ s	personal £ s d	
Capt Joseph Fletcher	1 1 0 2 1 0		0 5 4	
Capt James Pollard	1 1 2 7 4 0	9:0	0 17 8	
Mr Ebenr Prescott	1 1 2 4 5 3	060.0 3.8	0 14 8	
Jonas Prescott Esqr	2 2 4 8 4 15	160. 9.8	1 7 11	
Joseph Read	2 0 0 5 2 0	0 0	0 8 3	
Ensn Amos Spaulding	1 1 2 3 2 10		0 12 4	
Ensn Jno Abbott	1 1 2 4 2 0	30.0 3.0	0 12 10	
Capt Benja Fletcher	1 1 2 6 3 0		0 16 2	
Lieut Timo Fletcher	2 1 2 5 3 0		0 14 8	
Lieut Amos Fletcher	2 1 4 6 4 8	100.0 6.0	1 1 10	
Ensn Saml Adams	1 1 0 2 2 3		0 6 3	
Saml Adams jr	1 1 4 3 2 3		0 15 9	
Jno Abbott jr	1 0 2 4 1 0	30.0 1.10	0 10 5	
Willm Buttersfield	1 1 2 4 2 4		0 13 5	
Willm Butterfield jr	1 0 2 0 0 0		0 4 0	
Saml Butterfield	1 1 2 0 0 10		0 7 6	
Oliver Bates	2 1 2 3 2 3		0 11 6	
Asa Bixby	2 1 2 3 0 0		0 10 6	
Lydia Brooks	0 0 2 3 1 5		0 9 8	
Esther Wright	0 0 0 3 0 0		0 4 6	
Willm Blodget	1 1 2 1 2 6		0 9 4	
Moses Barron	1 1 2 5 2 4		0 15 9	
Zacheus Boynton	3 1 0 6 2 8	76 13.4 10.6	0 13 2	
Lieut Saml Read	1 2 2 6 4 0		0 16 7	
Willm Chandler	4 1 2 4 4 4	3.0	0 14 2	
Isaac Chandler	1 1 2 5 0 6		0 13 11	
Thos Cumings	3 1 4 7 0 0		0 18 6	
Thos Cumings jr	2 1 2 4 2 7		0 13 11	
Joseph Cumings	1 1 0 2 2 0	170.10.2	0 5 10	
Isaac Cumings	1 1 0 2 2 6		0 6 8	
Ephm Cumings	1 1 2 4 3 9	negro	0 18 6	
Benja Sutton	1 0 0 1 1 3		0 2 4	
David Fletcher	3 1 4 7 0 0		1 0 6	
Reubin Fletcher	3 1 2 5 4 8		0 16 5	
Thos Fletcher	2 1 2 8 3 12	26.1.7	1 1 0	
Ebenr Fletcher	1 1 4 5 3 8		0 19 11	
Pelatiah Fletcher	1 1 3 8 4 11	Negro 4:0	1 13 3	
Joshua Fletcher	1 1 3 4 2 6		0 15 8	
James Fletcher	1 0 2 5 2 0		0 12 4	
Saml Fassett	1 0 2 3 0 0		0 8 6	
Joshua Fassett	1 0 0 1 0 0		0 1 6	

1771

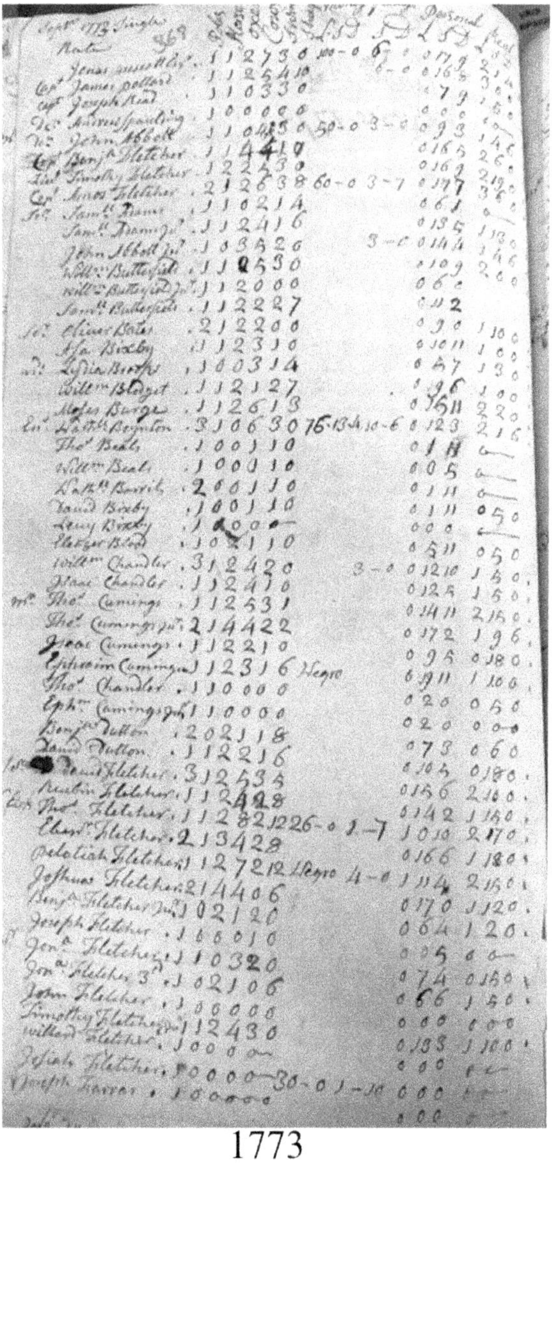
Sept 1773 Single Rate 368

Jonas Minott Esqr	1 1 2 7 3 0	100-0 6	0 17 9	2 1
Capt James Pollard	1 1 2 5 4 10	6-0	0 16 8	3
Capt Joseph Read	1 1 0 3 3 0		0 7 9	1 5 0
Dn Andrew Spaulding	1 0 0 0 0 0		0 0 0	
Dn John Abbott	1 1 0 4 2 5 0	50-0 3-0	0 9 3	1 4
Capt Benja Fletcher	1 1 4 4 1 0		0 16 5	2 6 0
Lieut Timothy Fletcher	1 2 2 4 3 0		0 16 2	2 10 0
Capt Amos Fletcher	2 1 2 6 3 8	60-0 3-7	0 17 7	3
Lt Saml Frame	1 1 0 2 1 4		0 6 1	
Saml Frame Jr	1 1 2 4 1 6		0 13 5	1 13 0
John Abbott Jr	1 0 3 4 2 0	3-0	0 14 4	1 4 6
Willm Butterfield	1 1 0 5 3 0		0 10 9	2 0 0
Willm Butterfield Jr	1 1 2 0 0 0		0 6 0	
Saml Butterfield	1 1 2 2 2 7		0 11 2	
Lt Oliver Bates	2 1 2 2 0 0		0 9 0	1 10 0
Asa Bixby	1 1 2 3 1 0		0 10 11	1 0 0
Josia Burge	1 0 0 3 1 4		0 4 7	1 3 0
Willm Blodget	1 1 2 1 2 7		1 9 6	1 0 0
Moses Burge	1 1 2 6 1 3		0 15 11	2 2 0
Ensn Nathl Boynton	3 1 0 6 3 0	76-13-4 10-6	0 12 3	2 1 6
Thos Beals	1 0 0 1 1 0		0 1 11	—
Willm Beals	1 0 0 1 1 0		0 0 5	—
Nathl Burris	2 0 0 1 1 0		0 1 11	—
David Bixby	1 0 0 1 1 0		0 1 11	0 5 0
Levy Bixby	1 0 0 0		0 0 0	—
Ebenezer Blood	1 0 2 1 1 0		0 5 11	0 5 0
Willm Chandler	3 1 2 4 2 0	3-0	0 12 10	1 5 0
Isaac Chandler	1 1 2 4 1 0		0 12 5	1 5 0
Mr Thos Cumings	1 1 2 5 3 1		0 14 11	2 15 0
Thos Cumings Jr	2 1 4 4 2 2		0 17 2	1 9 6
Isaac Cumings	1 1 2 2 1 0		0 9 5	0 18 0
Ephraim Cumings	1 2 3 1 6 Negro		0 19 11	1 10 0
Thos Chandler	1 1 0 0 0 0		0 2 0	0 5 0
Ephm Cumings Jr	1 1 0 0 0 0		0 2 0	0 0 0
Benja Dutton	2 0 2 1 1 8		0 2 0	0 0 0
David Dutton	1 1 2 2 1 6		0 7 3	0 6 0
Lt David Fletcher	3 1 2 5 3 3		0 10 5	0 18 0
Reubin Fletcher	1 1 2 4 2 8		0 15 6	2 10 0
Ens Thos Fletcher	1 1 2 8 2 12	26-0 1-7	0 14 2	1 15 0
Elnas Fletcher	2 1 3 4 2 8		1 0 10	2 17 0
Pelatiah Fletcher	1 1 2 7 2 12 Negro	4-0	1 11 4	1 18 0
Joshua Fletcher	2 1 4 4 0 6			2 15 0
Benja Fletcher Jr	1 0 2 1 2 0		0 17 0	1 12 0
Joseph Fletcher	1 0 0 0 1 0		0 6 4	1 2 0
Jona Fletcher	1 1 0 3 2 0		0 0 5	0 0
Jona Fletcher 3d	1 0 2 1 0 6		0 7 4	0 15 0
John Fletcher	1 0 0 0 0 0		0 6 6	1 5 0
Timothy Fletcher Jr	1 1 2 4 3 0		0 0 0	0 0 0
Willard Fletcher	1 0 0 0 0		0 13 3	1 10 0
Josiah Fletcher	1 0 0 0 0		0 0 0	
Joseph Farrar	1 0 0 0 0	30-0 1-10	0 0 0	

1773

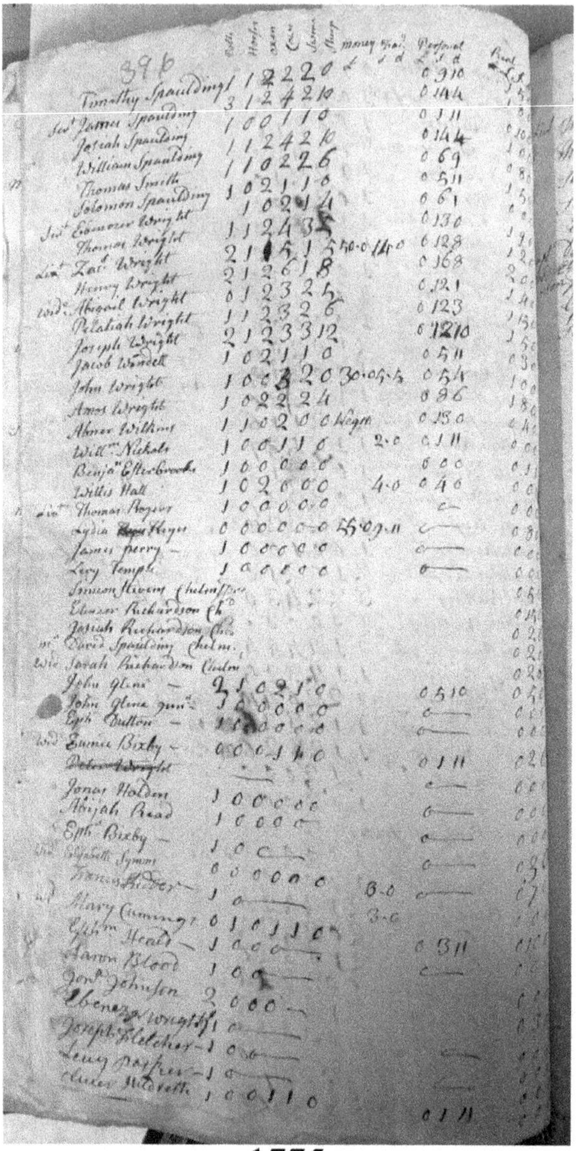

Name	Polls	Horses	Oxen	Cows	Swine	Sheep	Money £	Trade s d	Personal £ s d
Timothy Spaulding	1	1	2	2	2	0			0 9 10
	3	1	2	4	2	10			0 14 4
Sert. James Spaulding	1	0	0	1	1	0			0 1 11
Josiah Spaulding	1	1	2	4	2	10			0 14 4
William Spaulding	1	1	0	2	2	6			0 6 9
Thomas Smith	1	0	2	1	1	0			0 5 11
Solomon Spaulding		1	0	2	1	4			0 6 1
Sert. Ebenezer Wright	1	1	2	4	3	5			0 13 0
Thomas Wright	2	1	[illegible]	5	1	5	50.0	14.0	0 12 8
Lieut. Zacr. Wright	2	1	2	6	1	8			0 16 8
Henry Wright	0	1	2	3	2	4			0 12 1
Wid. Abigail Wright	1	1	2	3	2	6			0 12 3
Pelatiah Wright	2	1	2	3	3	12			0 12 10
Joseph Wright	1	0	2	1	1	0			0 5 11
Jacob Wendell	1	0	0	3	2	0	30.04.4		0 5 4
John Wright	1	0	2	2	2	4			0 8 6
Amos Wright	1	1	0	2	0	0	Wright		0 13 0
Abner Wilkins	1	0	0	1	1	0		2.0	0 1 11
Willm. Nichols	1	0	0	0	0	0			0 0 0
Benja. Esterbrooks	1	0	2	0	0	0		4.0	0 4 0
Willis Hall	1	0	0	0	0	0			0 —
Lieut. Thomas Rogers	0	0	0	0	0	0	55.07.11		0 —
Lydia ~~[illegible]~~ Heyes	1	0	0	0	0	0			0 —
James Perry	1	0	0	0	0	0			0 —
Levy Temple									
Simeon Havens Chelmsford									
Eleazer Richardson Ch.									
Josiah Richardson Ch.									
Wid. David Spaulding Chelm.									
Wid. Sarah Richardson Chelm.									
John Glenn	2	1	0	2	1	0			0 5 10
John Glenn junr.	1	0	0	0	0	0			0 —
Eph. Dutton	1	1	0	0	0	0			0 —
Wid. Eunice Bixby	0	0	0	1	4	0			0 1 11
~~Peter Wright~~									0 —
Jonas Holden	1	0	0	0	0	0			0 —
Abijah Read	1	0	0	0	0				0 —
Eph. Bixby	1	0	0						0 —
Wid. Elizabeth Symms	0	0	0	0	0	0			0 —
Francis Kidder	1	0						6.0	—
Wid. Mary Cummings	0	1	0	1	1	0		3.6	
Ephm. Heald	1	0	0	0					0 3 11
Aaron Blood	1	0	0						0 —
Jona. Johnson	2	0	0	0					
Ebenezer Wright	1	0							
Joseph Fletcher	1	0	0						—
Levy Parker	1	0							—
Oliver Hildreth	1	0	0	1	1	0			0 1 11

1775

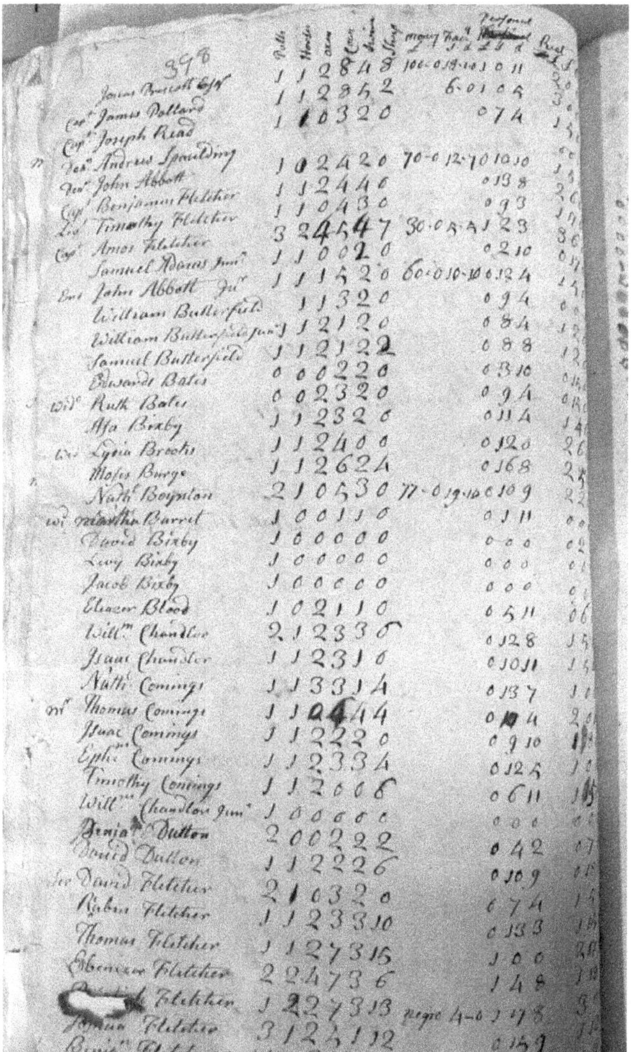

398

	Polls	Horses	Oxen	Cows	Swine	Sheep	Money / Trade £ s d	Personal £ s d
James Barrett Esqr	1	1	2	8	4	8	106-0-18-10	1 0 11
Capt. James Pollard	1	1	2	8	5	2	6-0	1 0 5
Capt. Joseph Read	1	1	0	3	2	0		0 7 4
Ser. Andrew Spaulding	1	0	2	4	2	0	70-0 12-7	0 10 10
Ser. John Abbott	1	1	2	4	4	0		0 13 8
Capt. Benjamin Fletcher	1	1	0	4	3	0		0 9 3
Lieut. Timothy Fletcher	3	2	4	5	4	7	30-0-5-4	1 2 3
Capt. Amos Fletcher	1	1	0	0	2	0		0 2 10
Samuel Adams Junr	1	1	1	5	2	0	60-0-10-10	0 13 4
Ens. John Abbott Jur								
William Butterfield		1	1	3	2	0		0 9 4
William Butterfield Junr	1	1	2	1	2	0		0 8 4
Samuel Butterfield	1	1	2	1	2	2		0 8 8
Edward Bates	0	0	0	2	2	0		0 3 10
Wid. Ruth Bates	0	0	2	3	2	0		0 9 4
Asa Bixby	1	1	2	3	2	0		0 11 4
Wid. Lydia Brooks	1	1	2	4	0	0		0 12 0
Moses Burge	1	1	2	6	2	4		0 16 8
Nathl Boynton	2	1	0	5	3	0	77-0-19-10	0 10 9
Wid. Martha Barret	1	0	0	1	1	0		0 1 11
David Bixby	1	0	0	0	0	0		0 0 0
Levy Bixby	1	0	0	0	0	0		0 0 0
Jacob Bixby	1	0	0	0	0	0		0 0 0
Eleazer Blood	1	0	2	1	1	0		0 5 11
Willm Chandler	2	1	2	3	3	0		0 12 8
Isaac Chandler	1	1	2	3	1	0		0 10 11
Nathl Comings	1	1	3	3	1	4		0 13 7
Wid. Thomas Comings	1	1	4	4	4	4		0 10 4
Isaac Comings	1	1	2	2	2	0		0 9 10
Ephm Comings	1	1	2	3	3	4		0 12 5
Timothy Comings	1	1	2	0	0	6		0 6 11
Willm Chandler Junr	1	0	0	0	0	0		0 0 0
Benjan Dutton	2	0	0	2	2	2		0 4 2
David Dutton	1	1	2	2	2	6		0 10 9
Ser. David Fletcher	2	1	0	3	2	0		0 7 4
Rubin Fletcher	1	1	2	3	3	10		0 13 3
Thomas Fletcher	1	1	2	7	3	15		1 0 0
Ebenezer Fletcher	2	2	4	7	3	6		1 4 8
[illegible] Fletcher	1	2	2	7	3	13	negro 4-0	1 7 8
Joshua Fletcher	3	1	2	4	1	12		0 14 9
Benjan Fletcher Junr	1	0	2	3	3	6		0 13 8

1775

Appendix C: Westford's 1790 Census

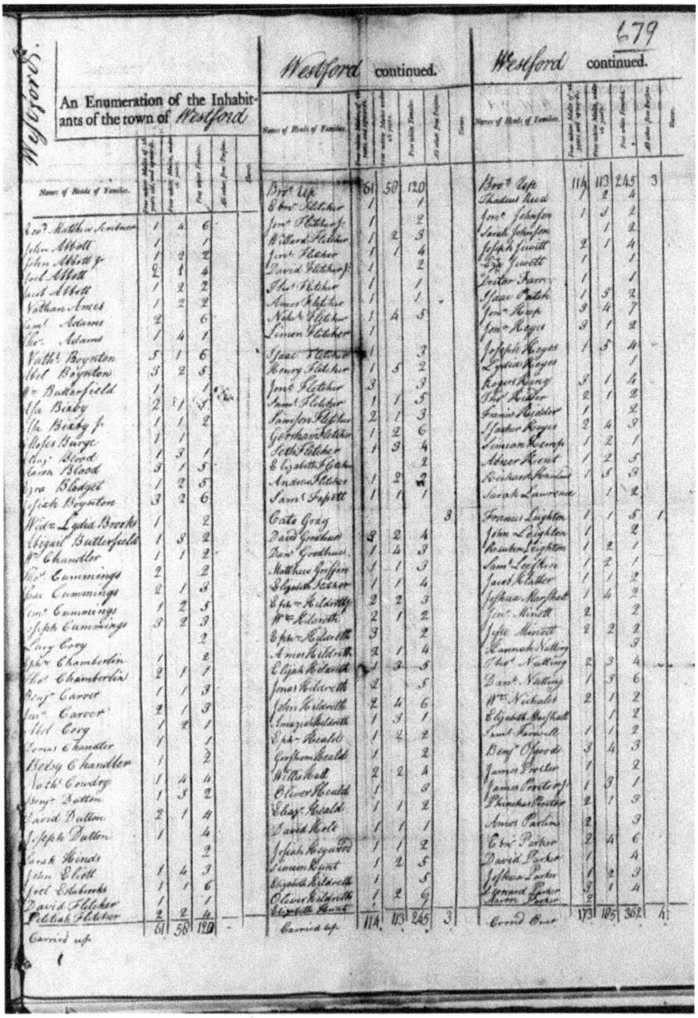

679

Westford

An Enumeration of the Inhabitants of the town of Westford

Names of Heads of Families.	Free white Males of 16 years and upwards	Free white Males under 16 years	Free white Females	All other free Persons	Slaves
Revd. Matthew Scribner	1	4	6		
John Abbott	1		1		
John Abbott Jr.	1	2	2		
Joel Abbott	2	1	4		
Jacob Abbott	1	2	2		
Nathan Ames	1	2	2		
Saml. Adams	2		6		
Thos. Adams	1	4	1		
Nathl. Boynton	5	1	6		
Abel Boynton	3	2	5		
Wm. Butterfield	1		1		
Asa Bixby	2	1	5		
Asa Bixby Jr.	1	1	2		
Moses Burge	1	1			
Eleazr. Blood	1	3	1		
Aaron Blood	3	1	5		
Ezra Bladget	1	2	5		
Josiah Boynton	3	2	6		
Widw. Lydia Brooks	1		2		
Abigail Butterfield	1	3	2		
Wm. Chandler	1	1	2		
Thos. Cummings	2		2		
Isaac Cummings	2	1	3		
Jona. Cummings	1	2	5		
Joseph Cummings	3	2	3		
Lucy Cory			2		
Ephm. Chamberlin	1		2		
Thos. Chamberlin	2	1	1		
Benjn. Carver	1	1	3		
Jona. Carver	2	1	3		
Abel Cory	1	2	1		
Lorias Chandler	1		1		
Betsy Chandler	1		2		
Nathl. Cowdry	1	4	4		
Benjn. Dutton	1	3	2		
David Dutton	2	1	4		
Joseph Dutton	1		4		
Sarah Hinds			2		
John Eliott	1	4	3		
Joel Estabrooks	1	1	6		
David Fletcher	1		1		
Pelatiah Fletcher	2	2	4		
Carried up	61	58	120		

Westford continued.

Names of Heads of Families.	Free white Males of 16 years and upwards	Free white Males under 16 years	Free white Females	All other free Persons	Slaves
Brot. up	61	58	120		
Ebenr. Fletcher	1		1		
Jona. Fletcher Jr.	1		2		
Willard Fletcher	1	2	3		
Jona. Fletcher	1	1	4		
David Fletcher Jr.	1		2		
Thos. Fletcher	1		1		
Amos Fletcher	1		1		
Nathl. Fletcher	1	4	5		
Simon Fletcher	1				
Isaac Fletcher	1		3		
Henry Fletcher	1	5	2		
Jona. Fletcher	3		3		
Saml. Fletcher	1	1	5		
Sampson Fletcher	2	1	3		
Gersham Fletcher	1	2	6		
Seth Fletcher	1	3	4		
Elizabeth Fletcher			2		
Andrew Fletcher	1	2	2		
Saml. Fassett	1	1	1		
Cato Gray				3	
David Goodhue	2	2	4		
Danl. Goodhue	1	4	3		
Matthew Griffin	1	1	3		
Elizabeth Fletcher	1	1	4		
Ephm. Hildreth	2	2	3		
Wm. Hildreth	2	1	2		
Ephm. Hildreth	3		2		
Amos Hildreth	2	1	4		
Elijah Hildreth	1	3	5		
Jonas Hildreth	2		5		
John Hildreth	2	4	6		
Amaziah Hildreth	1	3	1		
Ephm. Heald	1	4	2		
Gersham Heald	1		2		
Willis Hall	2	2	4		
Oliver Heald	1		3		
Eleazr. Heald	1	1	2		
David Holt	1	1	1		
Josiah Hayward	1	1	2		
Simeon Hunt	1	2	5		
Elizabeth Hildreth	1		5		
Oliver Hildreth	1	2	6		
Elizabeth Hunt					
Carried up	114	113	245	3	

Westford continued.

Names of Heads of Families.	Free white Males of 16 years and upwards	Free white Males under 16 years	Free white Females	All other free Persons	Slaves
Brot. up	114	113	245	3	
Thadeus Reed	1	2	4		
Jona. Johnson	1	3	2		
Sarah Johnson		1	2		
Joseph Jewett	2	1	4		
Ezra Jewett	1		1		
Dexter Farr	1		1		
Isaac Patch	1	3	2		
Jona. Keep	3	4	7		
Jona. Keyes	3	1	2		
Joseph Keyes	1	5	4		
Lydia Keyes			1		
Rogers Kemp	3	1	4		
Thos. Kidder	2	1	2		
Francis Kidder	1		2		
Issachar Keyes	2	4	3		
Simeon Kemp	1	2	1		
Abner Kent	1	2	5		
Richard [illegible]	1	5	3		
Sarah Lawrence		1	2		
Frances Leighton	1	1	5	1	
John Leighton	1		2		
Reuben Leighton	1	2	1		
Saml. Lufkin	1	2	1		
Jacob Kidder	1	1	2		
Joshua Marshall	1	4	2		
Jona. Minott	2		2		
Jesse Minott	2	2	2		
Hannah Nutting			3		
Thos. Nutting	2	3	4		
Danl. Nutting	1	3	6		
Wm. Nichols	2	1	2		
Elizabeth Marshall		1	2		
Saml. Farwell	1	1	2		
Benjn. Osgood	3	4	3		
James Proctor	1		2		
James Proctor Jr.	1	3	1		
Phinehas Proctor	2	1	3		
Amos Parlin	2		3		
Ebenr. Parker	2	4	6		
David Parker	1		4		
Joshua Parker	1	2	3		
Leonard Parker	3	1	4		
Aaron Parker	2				
Grand Amt.	173	105	362	4	

680

An Enumeration of the Inhabitants of the town of Westford

Continued

Names of Heads of Families.	Free white Males of 16 years old, and upwards.	Free white Males under 16 years.	Free white Females.	All other free Persons.	Slaves.
Brot. Over	173	105	362	4	
Moses Parker	1		3		
Jonas Prescott	4	1	4		
Ebnr. Prescott	2	3	4		
Joseph Prescott	1	4	3		
John Prescott	2	5	3		
Chas. Proctor	1	1	4		
Levi Parker	2	3	2		
Isaac Parker	1	2	2		
Danl. Pike	2		2		
Thos. Pike	1		1		
James Pike	1	4	4		
Andrew Pike	1	1	2		
Timo. Prescott	3	1	3		
Oliver Prescott	3	1	1		
Obadiah Perry	1	4	4		
Phebe Proctor	1		2		
Wm. Mears	1		3		
David Keyes	1		1		
Hannah Reed	1		3		
Peter Reed	1	1	1		
Joshua Reed	4	1	1		
Thos. Reed	2	1	3		
Saml. Richardson	3		2		
Abijah Richardson	2	3	4		
Daniel Raymond	1		2		
Danl. Raymond Jr.	2	1	4		
John Raymond	2		3		
Jacob Robins	1		1		
Jacob Robbins Jr.	1	1	3		
Abijah Reed	1	1	2		
Jere. Robbins	1	1	1		
Zach. Robbins	1		2		
Carried up	225	225	442	4	

Westford continued.

Names of Heads of Families.	Free white Males of 16 years and upwards.	Free white Males under 16 years.	Free white Females.	All other free Persons.	Slaves.
Brot. Up	225	225	442	4	
Benja. Robbins	1	2	3		
John Robinson	2	1	4		
Silas Reed	2	3	4		
Willard Reed	1	4	5		
Oliver Reed	1	1	4		
Wm. Reed	1	1	2		
Thos. Richardson	4	2	3		
Amos Russell	1		4		
Lydia Richardson			3		
Wiley Richardson	1	2	5		
Saml. Reed	1	2	6		
Timo. Spaulding	1				
Hannah Spaulding		1	5		
Thos. Scott	1	4	4		
Solomon Spaulding	1	3	2		
Caleb Symmes	1	1	3		
Thos. Symmes	1	2	1		
Benja. Swan	1	1	2		
Levi Spaulding	1				
Saml. Spaulding	4		1		
Thos. Smith	1	3	4		
Levi Snow	1	2	1		
Betty Reed			1		
Abraham Taylor	2	1	4		
John Tidd	2	3	3		
Thankful Reed			2		
Sibel Chamberlin			1		
Jere. Temple	1				
Benja. Foster	1		2		
Joanna Reed		1	2		
Peltiah Wright	1	1	3		
Joseph Wright	3	2	5		
Saml. Worcester	3	2	4		
John Wright	2	1	3		
Carried up	265	271	538	4	

Westford continued.

Names of Heads of Families.	Free white Males of 16 years and upwards.	Free white Males under 16 years.	Free white Females.	All other free Persons.	Slaves.
Brot. Up	265	271	530	4	
Asa Wright	1	1	5		
Ephm. Wright	1	1	3		
Nathan Wright	1	2	2		
Amos Wright	3	2	3		
Jonas Wright	1	2	3		
Jacob Wendell	1		3		
John Wilson	1		1		
Joseph Winn	1		4		
James Wright	1	1	4		
Saml. Wright	3	1	4		
Zach. Wright Jr.	2	1	2		
Mark White	3		2		
Ebnr. Barrett	1		1		
Wm. Blaisdell	1	2	2		
Jonas Kemp	1	3	3		
Abel Reed	1	2	3		
Dorcas Wright			2		
Peter Tower	1	4	3		
Molly Keyes			3		
Henry Richardson	1		1		
Olive Spaulding		1	2		
Henry Mair	1		1		
Christopher Shepherd	1		1		
Reuben Fletcher	1		1		
Thos. Fletcher Jr.	1	1	2		
Amos Fletcher Jr.	2	4	4		
Sarah Cummings			2		
Leonard Reed	1	3	4		
Benja. Estabrooks	1		4		
John Ingals	1		1		
Reuben Wright	1	1	1		
Jonas Blodgett	1	4	3		
Total -	301	306	610	4	

Aaron Brown. assistant to the Marshall of the district of Massachusetts

Once Known **Bibliography**

Books

—. Town of Westford Records, Volume I, 1726-1764.

—. Town of Westford Records, Volume II, 1764-1790.

—. *Vital Records of Westford, Massachusetts, to the end of the year 1849*. Salem: The Essex Institute, 1915.

Acts and Resolves of the Province of Massachusetts Bay: Volume 1 1692-1714. Boston: Wright and Potter, 1869.

Benton, Josiah H., *Early Census Making in Massachusetts 1655-1765*. Accessed 24 April 2023. https://archive.org/details/earlycensusmakin00bent/page/80/mode/2up.

—, *Warning Out in New England 1656-1817*, Boston: W.B. Clarke Company, 1911. https://shadowsofpineland.org/wp-content/uploads/2021/09/1656-1817-Warning-Out-in-New-England-Josiah-Henry-Benton-published-1911.pdf?utm_

Chandler, George, *The Chandler Family. The Descendents of William and Annis Chandler who settled in Roxbury, Mass 1637,* Worcester, MA: Press of C. Hamilton, 1883. Accessed 3 Mar 2024. https://archive.org/details/chandlerfamilyde00chan/page/72/mode/2up?q=ephraim

Curtin, Philip D., *The Atlantic Slave Trade: A Census*. Madison: The University of Wisconsin Press, 1969.

Colonel John Robinson Chapter of the Daughters of the American Revolution (DAR), *Old Houses of Westford*, 1957, compiled by Gertrude Fletcher and Julia Fletcher; revised by Marilyn Day and Ellen Harde with permission of the DAR, 2004.

Donnan, Elizabeth, *Documents Illustrative of the history of the slave trade to America Volume 3 New England and the Middle Colonies.* Washington, D.C.: Carnegie Institution of Washington, 1932.

Essex Institute. *Vital Records of Chelmsford, Massachusetts to the End of the Year 1849*. Salem, MA: Newcomb & Gauss, 1914.

Foster, F. Apthorp (ed.). *Vital Records of Billerica, Massachusetts, to the Year 1850*. Boston: New England Historic Genealogical Society, 1908.

Green, Samuel A. "The First Census of Massachusetts." *Publications of the American Statistical Association*, Vol. 2, No. 13 (Mar., 1891), pp. 182-185. https://www.jstor.org/stable/2276526

Greene, Lorenzo Johnston. *The Negro in Colonial New England.* New York: Atheneum, 1969.

Grimshaw, William H. *Official History of Freemasonry Among the Colored People in North America.* New York: Broadway Publishing Company, 1903. Accessed 9 February 2025. https://archive.org/details/officialhistoryo01grim/page/84/mode/2up

Gross, Robert. *The Transcendentalists and Their World.* New York: Farrar, Straus, and Giroux, 2021.

Grundset, Eric G., Editor. "Forgotten Patriots: African American and American Indian Patriots in the Revolutionary War." Washington, D.C: National Society Daughters of the American Revolution, 2008. Accessed June 2023. https://www.dar.org/sites/default/files/media/library/DARpublications/Forgotten_Patriots_ISBN-978-1-892237-10-1.pdf

Hall, Reverend Willard et al. *The Church Book Belonging to the Second Church in Chelmsford 1727*. Accessed 8 March 2023, https://www.digitalcommonwealth.org/book_viewer/commonwealth:76539x69n

Hardesty, Jared. *Black Lives, Native Lands, White World.* Amherst: Bright Leaf/University of Massachusetts, 2019.

Hodgman, Reverend Edwin R. *History of the Town of Westford in the County of Middlesex, Massachusetts, 1659-1883*. Lowell, MA: Morning Mail Company, 1883.

Lawrence, M.D., Robert M. *Historical Sketches of some members of the Lawrence Family. With An Appendix.* Boston: Rand Avery Company, 1888. https://ia800501.us.archive.org/17/items/historicalsketch1888lawr/historicalsketch1888lawr.pdf

Lemire, Elise. *Black Walden: Slavery and Its Aftermath in Concord, Massachusetts*. Philadelphia: University of Pennsylvania, 2009.

Moore, George H., *Notes on The History of Slavery in Massachusetts*, New York: D. Appleton and Co., 1866.

Nell, William Cooper. *The colored patriots of the American Revolution.* Boston: Robert F. Wallcut, 1855 https://www.google.com/books/edition/The_Colored_Patriots_of_the_American_Rev/Jy8OAAAAIAAJ?hl=en&gbpv=1

Oliphant, Robert W. *The Westford Gazetteer: A History of Westford, Massachusetts in its Place Names*. Westford, MA:by the author, 2010.

Prescott, William B. *Map of Westford in 1730.* Westford, MA: Privately Printed, Westford Historical Society files.

Prescott, William B. *Patriots and Taxpayers of Colonial Westford, Massachusetts in 1774.* Westford, MA: Privately Printed, Westford Historical Society files.

Prescott, William B. *Taxation of Slave Owners in Colonial Westford.* Westford, MA: Privately Printed, December 1987. Collection of the Westford Historical Society, W.2003.23

Proctor, Mr. and Mrs. William Lawrence. *Genealogy of Descendants of Robert Proctor of Concord and Chelmsford, Mass.* Ogdensburg, NY: Republican & Journal Print, 1898

Quintal, George Jr., *Patriots of Color: "A Peculiar Beauty and Merit": African Americans and Native Americans at Battle Road & Bunker Hill.* Boston: Division of Cultural Resources-Boston National Historic Park, 2004.

Articles

Desrochers, Robert E. "Slave-for-Sale Advertisements and Slavery in Massachusetts, 1704-1781," The William and Mary Quarterly 59, no. 3 (2002): 623-64. https://doi.org/10.2307/3491467.

Downey, Jean G., "Peggy, a Slave in 18th Century Westford 1732," Westford Museum files. 1989.

Green, Samuel A., "The First Census of Massachusetts," *Publications of the American Statistical Association*, Vol. 2, No. 13 (Mar., 1891), pp. 182-185 https://www.jstor.org/stable/2276526.

Miller, Yawu, "Black Masons Owe Lineage to 18th Century Pioneer Prince Hall," *Bay State Banner*, February 8, 2017. Accessed 10 May 2024. https://baystatebanner.com/2017/02/08/black-masons-owe-lineage-to-18th-century-boston-pioneer-prince-hall/

Sharples, Stephen, "Early Records of the First Church in Cambridge," in *The Genealogical Magazine* Vol. 1 No. 1, Eben Putnam: Boston. April 1905.

Weeden, William B., "The Early African Slave Trade in New England" American Antiquarian Society 1887 Issue 5, 111.

Websites

—, *A Memorial of the American Patriots who fell at the battle of Bunker Hill, June 17, 1775*, Boston City Council: Boston, 1896, accessed March 15, 2023, https://archive.org/details/memorialofameric00bost/mode/2up?q=bason.

—, "About." Samuel Fitch House Bed & Breakfast. Accessed July 2023. https://www.samuelfitchhouse.com/about

—. "Caesar Bason (U.S. National Park Service)" Accessed 25 February 2023. https://www.nps.gov/people/caesar-bason.htm

—. "Interactive Massachusetts Tax Inventory, 1771." accessed 2023. https://legacy.sites.fas.harvard.edu/~hsb41/masstax/masstax.cgi.

—. "James Pollard (abt. 1708-1781)." WikiTree. Accessed 9 February 2025. https://www.wikitree.com/wiki/Pollard-104#_note-residence

—. "Jonathan Keyes (1722-1781)" WikiTree. Accessed 5 May 2024. https://www.wikitree.com/wiki/Keyes-71

—, "Massachusetts Bodies of Liberty (1641)," accessed August 1, 2023, https://history.hanover.edu/texts/masslib.html

—. "Massachusetts Constitution and the Abolition of Slavery." Accessed 9 February 2025.

https://www.mass.gov/guides/massachusetts-constitution-and-the-abolition-of-slavery#-the-quock-walker-case-

—. *Massachusetts Soldiers and Sailors of the Revolutionary War*. Wright & Potter Printing Company: Boston, 1908.

—. "Samuel Lawrence Sr 1714- bef. 1789," accessed August 10, 2023. https://www.wikitree.com/wiki/Lawrence-4624

—. "Slavery, " Accessed 10 June 2023, http://www.54lowellroad.com/index_files/Page583.htm

—. icollector.com, "John Hancock Appointment Minuteman Abel Boynton," Accessed 5 May 2023, https://www.icollector.com/JOHN-HANCOCK-Appointment-Minuteman-ABEL-BOYNTON_i11029262.

—. "Abel Boynton 1755-1818," accessed 5 May 2023, https://www.wikitree.com/wiki/Boynton-1992.

—. PrimaryResearch.org, "1754 Slave Census," Accessed 24 April 2023, https://primaryresearch.org/1754slavecensus/64.jpg

Bell, J.L. "Boston's Population in 1765," Accessed 24 April 2023, https://boston1775.blogspot.com/2006/05/bostons-population-in-1765.html.

Bell, J.L. "Remembering Moses Parker." June 13, 2017. Accessed 24 April 2023. https://boston1775.blogspot.com/2017/06/remembering-moses-parker.html

Bell, J.L. "Moses Parker and his comrades in redoubt." June 12, 2017. Accessed 24 April 2023. https://boston1775.blogspot.com/2017/06/moses-parker-and-his-comrades-in-redoubt.html

Bell, J.L. "Moses Parker, The Most Prominent Military Character." June 11, 2017. Accessed 24 April 2023. https://boston1775.blogspot.com/2017/06/moses-parker-most-prominent-military.html

Lacroix, Daniel P. "Muster Rolls of the three Westford companies- 1775." Accessed 25 February 2023. https://www.westford.org/westford1775/muster_roll.htm

National Humanities Center Toolbox. "What About Slavery is Unchristian?" Accessed 9 February 2025. https://nationalhumanitiescenter.org/pds/becomingamer/ideas/text3/slaveryunchristian.pdf

Westford Historical Society. "Westford Women Dolls," Accessed 24 February 2023. https://museum.westford.org/westford-women-dolls/

Seaver, Randy. "Genea-Musings: 52 Ancestors- Week 211L #290 Jonas Prescott." Accessed 15 June 2023. https://www.geneamusings.com/2018/01/52-ancestors-week-211-290-jonas.html

Sewall, Samuel. "The Selling of Joseph." Accessed 20 July 2023. https://www.masshist.org/database/53?mode=transcript.

Van Essen, John S. "Robbins Genealogical Collection" 29 February 2012. Accessed 2 February 2024. https://sites.rootsweb.com/~johniel/robbgenc.html

Probate/Pension

Ephraim Chandler Probate 4248 *Middlesex County, MA: Probate File Papers, 1648-1871.*Online database. *AmericanAncestors.org.* New England Historic Genealogical Society, 2014. (From records supplied by the Massachusetts Supreme Judicial Court Archives. Digitized images provided by FamilySearch.org)

https://www.americanancestors.org/DB536/rd/14461/4248-co1/263806861

Ephraim Comings Probate 5418. *Middlesex County, MA: Probate File Papers, 1648-1871.* Online database. *AmericanAncestors.org.* New England Historic Genealogical Society, 2014. (From records supplied by the Massachusetts Supreme Judicial Court Archives. Digitized images provided by FamilySearch.org). Case number 5418. https://www.americanancestors.org/DB536/i/14461/5418-co4/38217691

Pension Number: S. 34270 . Case Files of Pension and Bounty-Land Warrant Applications Based on Revolutionary War Service, compiled ca. 1800 - ca. 1912, documenting the period ca. 1775 - ca. 1900. https://www.fold3.com/image/15213354/cummings-noble-page-8-us-revolutionary-war-pensions-1800-1900. Accessed 29 April 2024.

Gershom Fletcher Probate 7851, Middlesex County, MA: Probate File Papers, 1648-1871.Online database. AmericanAncestors.org. New England Historic Genealogical Society, 2014. (From records supplied by the Massachusetts Supreme Judicial Court Archives. Digitized images provided by FamilySearch.org) https://www.americanancestors.org/DB536/i/14471/7851-co9/38245145

Joshua Fletcher Probate 7875. *Middlesex County, MA: Probate File Papers, 1648-1871.*Online database. *AmericanAncestors.org.* New England Historic Genealogical Society, 2014. (From records supplied by the Massachusetts Supreme Judicial Court Archives. Digitized images provided by FamilySearch.org) https://www.americanancestors.org/DB536/i/14471/7875-co42/38245465

Peletiah Fletcher Probate 7903, Probate Records 1648-1924 (Middlesex County, Massachusetts), Probate docket FA-HA 7201-10800. Accessed 10 June 2023, https://www.familysearch.org/ark:/61903/3:1:3QS7-L9DL-DH58?cat=263304

York Hambleton Probate 10214, *Middlesex County, MA: Probate File Papers, 1648-1871.*Online database. *AmericanAncestors.org.* New England Historic Genealogical Society, 2014. (From records supplied by the Massachusetts Supreme Judicial Court Archives. Digitized images provided by FamilySearch.org) https://www.americanancestors.org/DB536/rd/14462/10214-co1/263877806

Joseph Hildreth Probate 11357*, Middlesex County, MA: Probate File Papers, 1648-1871.*Online database. *AmericanAncestors.org.* New England Historic Genealogical Society, 2014. (From records supplied by the Massachusetts Supreme Judicial Court Archives. Digitized images provided by FamilySearch.org) https://www.americanancestors.org/DB536/i/14462/11357-co1/263891952

Samuel Lawrence Probate 13788. Middlesex County, MA: Probate File Papers, 1648-1871.Online database. AmericanAncestors.org. New England Historic Genealogical Society, 2014. (From records supplied by the Massachusetts Supreme Judicial Court Archives. Digitized images provided by FamilySearch.org) https://www.americanancestors.org/DB536/i/14463/13788-co2/38315116

James Pollard Probate 17684 Middlesex County, MA: Probate File Papers, 1648-1871.Online database. AmericanAncestors.org. New England Historic Genealogical Society, 2014. (From records supplied by the Massachusetts Supreme Judicial Court Archives. Digitized images provided

by FamilySearch.org),
https://www.americanancestors.org/DB536/rd/14465/17684-col/263967881

Jonas Prescott Probate 18082 *Middlesex County, MA: Probate File Papers, 1648-1871.*Online database. *AmericanAncestors.org.* New England Historic Genealogical Society, 2014. (From records supplied by the Massachusetts Supreme Judicial Court Archives. Digitized images provided by FamilySearch.org)
https://www.americanancestors.org/DB536/i/14466/18082-col/0

John Proctor Probate Worcester County, MA: Probate File Papers, 1731-1881. Online database. AmericanAncestors.org. New England Historic Genealogical Society, 2015. (From records supplied by the Massachusetts Supreme Judicial Court Archives.)

John Read Probate 18533 Middlesex County, MA: Probate File Papers, 1648-1871.Online database. AmericanAncestors.org. New England Historic Genealogical Society, 2014. (From records supplied by the Massachusetts Supreme Judicial Court Archives. Digitized images provided by FamilySearch.org)
https://www.americanancestors.org/DB536/rd/14466/18533-col/263977635

<u>Muster Rolls</u>
Massachusetts State Archive Collection, colonial period, 1622-1788, v. 139 -- Revolutionary Miscellaneous (from p.297), 1776-1789 ; v. 140 -- Revolutionary Miscellaneous (to p.264), 1775-1788. Image 71.

Muster/payrolls, and various papers (1763-1808) of the Revolutionary War [Massachusetts and Rhode Island] on FamilySearch.org

Digital Sources: Podcasts, Videos, and Emails

Larsen, John. Email to Author. 22 July 2024.

Morgan, Jennifer, "Doing History: Jennifer Morgan, How Historians Research," Episode 70 February 23, 2016 in Ben Franklin's World, produced by Liz Covart and the Omohundro Institute of Early American History and Culture, 43:31, https://benfranklinsworld.com/episode-070-jennifer-l-morgan-how-historians-research/

Presti, Michael. Text message to Author. 20 July 2024.

Whiting, Gloria McCahon. "Belonging: An Intimate History of Slavery and Family in Early New England" YouTube video. Accessed 7 April 2025. https://youtu.be/5QmNMdFF-iw?si=WJnN37xwet-lgloz

Yap, Stacey. Email to Author. 3 November 2023.

Archives

Bills of lading for the ship Lydia, 1766. Small Manuscript Collection, Harvard Law School Library.

Boston, MA: Inhabitants and Estates of the Town of Boston, 1630-1822 (Thwing Collection). *Inhabitants and Estates of the Town of Boston, 1630–1800 and The Crooked and Narrow Streets of Boston, 1630–1822.* CD-ROM. Boston, Mass.: New England Historic Genealogical Society, 2001. (Online database. *AmericanAncestors.org*. New England Historic Genealogical Society, 2014.)

Boston, MA: Taking Records, 1800. (Original Online Database: *AmericanAncestors.org*, New England Historic Genealogical Society, 2014. (Transcribed by David Allen Lambert, NEHGS Chief Genealogist, from original volumes held by the Boston Public Library.)

Digital Archive of Massachusetts Anti-Slavery and Anti-Segregation Petitions., HOLLIS 013622572. Harry Elkins Widener Memorial Library, Harvard Library, Harvard University. https://id.lib.harvard.edu/ead/wid00004/catalog Accessed September 14, 2023.

Dolbeare family papers, Massachusetts Historical Society.

The Annotated Newspapers of Harbottle Dorr: The Boston Evening-Post, 6 May 1765. Massachusetts Historical Society Collection.
https://www.masshist.org/dorr/volume/1/sequence/83

Groton (Mass.) historical papers, Massachusetts Historical Society.

Hancock family. Hancock family papers, 1664-1854 (inclusive). Peter Faneuil papers, 1716-1739. Invoice book, 1725-1729. Mss:766 1712-1854 H234, Volume F-3, Baker Library Historical Collections, Harvard Business School.

Hancock family papers, 1664-1854 (inclusive). Volume F-1. Peter Faneuil ledger, 1725-1732. Mss:766 1712-1854 H234. Baker Library Historical Collections, Harvard Business School.

Hancock family. Hancock family papers, 1664-1854 (inclusive). Mss:766 1712-1854 H234 Volume F-2 Peter Faneuil daybook (accounts), 1731-1732. Baker Library Historical Collections, Harvard Business School.

Hancock family. Hancock family papers, 1664-1854 (inclusive). Peter Faneuil papers, 1716-1739. Letterbook (business), 1737-1739. Mss:766 1712-1854 H234, Volume F-4, Baker Library Historical Collections, Harvard Business School.

Hancock family. Hancock family papers, 1664-1854 (inclusive). Peter Faneuil papers, 1716-1739. Daybook (fragments, accounts), 1716. Mss:766 1712-1854 H234, Volume F-1a, Baker Library Historical Collections, Harvard Business School.

Hancock family papers, 1664-1854 (inclusive). Volume L-1. Ship Rebecca logbook, kept by James Scott, 1755-1757. Mss:766 1712-1854 H234. Baker Library Historical Collections, Harvard Business School.

Hancock family. Hancock family papers, 1664-1854 (inclusive). Ship Lydia logbook, 1766-1768. Mss:766 1712-1854 H234, Volume L-2, Baker Library Historical Collections, Harvard Business School.

Houghton Library Collection on the North American Slave Trade, 1803-1863 (MS Am 1278). Houghton Library, Harvard University. https://id.lib.harvard.edu/ead/hou02075/catalog Accessed September 14, 2023.

"Hugh Hall account book, 1728-1733," Hugh Hall papers, Massachusetts Historical Society, accessed May 2023, https://www.masshist.org/database/viewer.php?item_id=736&img_step=1&mode=large#page1

Jeffries Family Papers, Massachusetts Historical Society.

Massachusetts Commonwealth History - Vol. IV - Chap. XII - Villard - Slavery and Anti-Slavery (1820-1850) correspondence, [1929-1930]. Papers of Albert Bushnell Hart, HUG 4448, HUG 4448.6, Box: HUG 4448.6 Box 16, Folder: 20. Harvard University Archives. https://id.lib.harvard.edu/ead/c/hua29020c00881/catalog Accessed September 14, 2023.

"Massachusetts Deaths, 1841-1915, 1921-1924," images, *FamilySearch* (https://familysearch.org/ark:/61903/3:1:S3HY-XCZ7-SC2?cc=1463156&wc=MJZM-MNL%3A1043012301 :

13 December 2022), 0960216 (004221431) > State Archives, Boston.

"Massachusetts Deaths, 1841-1915, 1921-1924," images, FamilySearch (https://familysearch.org/ark:/61903/3:1:S3HY-DZCS-HF9?cc=1463156&wc=MJCG-PTL%3A1043009201 : 13 December 2022), 0960192 (004221408) > image 151 of 666; State Archives, Boston.

"Massachusetts, Town Clerk, Vital and Town Records, 1626-2001," *FamilySearch* (https://www.familysearch.org/ark:/61903/1:1:QG1K-6KTQ : Sat Mar 09 13:31:58 UTC 2024)

William Pepperrell papers, Massachusetts Historical Society.

Rowe, John. John Rowe letterbook, 1759-1762 (inclusive). Mss:766 1759-1762 R878, Baker Library Special Collections, Harvard Business School.

Ships' logs (records), 1752-1879. Low, Anthony. A journal of an intended voyage by God's promition in ye good snow Prince George, my self comander, bound from Rhode Island to Barbadoes on Prince George (Ship) : manuscript, 1752-1753 March 12 to October 11. MS Am 465.2. Houghton Library, Harvard University, Cambridge, Mass.

Wright, Ebenezer. Ebenezer Wright account book, 1710-1790 (inclusive), 1710-1732 (bulk). Mss:44 1710-1790 W948, Baker Library Special Collections, Harvard Business School.

Historical Newspapers at the American Antiquarian Society

Boston Gazette
New England Courant
Boston News Letter
New England Weekly Journal
Boston Evening Post

Census Records
1790 United States Federal Census
1800 United States Federal Census
1810 United States Federal Census
1820 United States Federal Census
1830 United States Federal Census
1840 United States Federal Census

www.ingramcontent.com/pod-product-compliance
Lightning Source LLC
Chambersburg PA
CBHW060525130626
46553CB00002B/658
9798218848019